Accents of English is about the way English is pronounced by different people in different places. Volume 1 provides a synthesizing introduction, which shows how accents vary not only geographically, but also with social class, formality, sex and age; and in volumes 2 and 3 the author examines in greater depth the various accents used by people who speak English as their mother tongue: the accents of the regions of England, Wales, Scotland and Ireland (volume 2), and of the USA, Canada, the West Indies, Australia, New Zealand, South Africa, India, Black Africa and the Far East (volume 3). Each volume can be read independently, and together they form a major scholarly survey of considerable originality, which not only includes descriptions of hitherto neglected accents, but also examines the implications for phonological theory.

Readers will find the answers to many questions: Who makes 'good' rhyme with 'mood'? Which accents have no voiced sibilants? How is a Canadian accent different from an American one, a New Zealand one from an Australian one, a Jamaican one from a Barbadian one? What are the historical reasons for British–American pronunciation differences? What sound changes are currently in progress in New York, in London, in Edinburgh? Dr Wells has written principally for students of linguistics, phonetics and English language, but the motivated general reader will also find the study both fascinating and rewarding.

An illustrative cassette accompanies volume 1.

The author is Reader in Phonetics, University College London

Cover design by Jan van de Watering

Accents of English 2

Accents of English 2

The British Isles

J. C. WELLS

CAMBRIDGE
UNIVERSITY PRESS

Published by the Press Syndicate of the University of Cambridge
The Pitt Building, Trumpington Street, Cambridge CB2 1RP
40 West 20th Street, New York, NY 10011–4211, USA
10 Stamford Road, Oakleigh, Victoria 3166, Australia

First published 1982
Reprinted 1984, 1989, 1992

Library of Congress catalogue card number: 81-10127

British Library cataloguing in publication data
Wells, J. C.
Accents of English.
2: The British Isles
1. English language – Pronunciation
I. Title
421.5'2 PE 1137

ISBN 0 521 22919 7 hardback Volume 1
ISBN 0 521 29719 2 paperback Volume 1
ISBN 0 521 24224 X hardback Volume 2
ISBN 0 521 28540 2 paperback Volume 2
ISBN 0 521 24225 8 hardback Volume 3
ISBN 0 521 28541 7 paperback Volume 3

Transferred to digital printing 2000

Contents

Volume 1: An Introduction

Contents

Contents

Volume 2: The British Isles

Contents

Volume 3: Beyond the British Isles

To the memory of my father,
Philip Wells (1909–1974),
who encouraged me

Preface

I believe that the three volumes of *Accents of English* represent the first attempt ever to offer a reasonably comprehensive account of the pronunciation of English in all its native-speaker varieties.

I have of course exploited my own familiarity with the various accents – such as it is, varying in depth in accordance with the varying exposure to them which life has happened to give me. These biases will no doubt be apparent. But I have also endeavoured to make appropriate use of all kinds of scholarly treatments of particular regional forms of speech, wherever they have been available to me and to whatever tradition they belong (philological, dialectological, structuralist, 'speech', generativist, sociolinguistic, variationist). My aim has been to bring together their principal findings within a unified and integrated framework.

My own descriptive standpoint, as will be seen, lies within the University College London 'phonetic' tradition of Daniel Jones, A. C. Gimson, and J. D. O'Connor. I am fortunate to have been their pupil. This standpoint could be said to involve an eclectic amalgam of what seems valuable from both older and newer theoretical approaches.

Where surveys based on substantial fieldwork exist, I have made use of their findings. Where they do not, I have had to rely partly on my own impressions. The reader must bear in mind that some of the statements I make are for this reason necessarily tentative.

Inevitably I may be laying myself open to the charge of rushing in where angels fear to tread. Many readers will know more about the socially sensitive pronunciation variables of their home areas than I can hope to. The Rotherham native will look here in vain for a discussion of the features which distinguish his speech from that of Sheffield a few miles away – features obvious to the native, but opaque to the outsider (vol. 1, 1.1.4). There is a great deal of descriptive work remaining to be done.

I see the original contribution of these volumes as lying princi-

Preface

pally in the following areas: (i) the description of certain neglected accents, including certain accents of the British Isles and the West Indies; (ii) the identification and naming of a number of phonological processes, both historical and synchronic; (iii) the bringing together into a single descriptive framework of accounts by scholars working in many different places and in many different traditions.

Many people have helped me through discussion or correspondence, and in some instances by reading parts of the manuscript. In this regard I would mention particularly D. Abercrombie, K. Albrow, C.-J. N. Bailey, A. Bliss, N. Copeland, R. Easton, A. C. Gimson, T. Hackman, J. Harris, S. Hutcheson, L. Lanham, R. Lass, F. MacEinrí, J. D. McClure, J. Milroy, J. D. O'Connor, H. Paddock, S. M. Ramsaran, H.-H. Speitel, P. Trudgill and J. Windsor Lewis. Our views do not always coincide, nor have I accepted all their suggestions; responsibility for the facts and opinions here presented remains mine. I am aware that these are far from the last word on the subject. For any shortcomings I beg indulgence on the grounds that something, however inadequate, is better than nothing.

I am also grateful to J. L. M. Trim for first suggesting that I write this work, and to G. F. Arnold and O. M. Tooley – not to mention Cambridge University Press – for enquiring so assiduously after its tardy progress.

London, January 1981   JOHN WELLS

Typographical conventions
and phonetic symbols

Examples of pronunciation are set in *italics* if in ordinary spelling, otherwise in / / or [ ]. Sometimes methods are combined, thus *disapp*[ɪə]*rance* (which draws attention to the quality of the diphthong corresponding to orthographic *ea* in this word).

/ / is used for **phonemic** transcriptions: for representations believed to be analogous to the way pronunciations are stored in the mental lexicon (= underlying phonological representations); for transcriptions in which only significant sound units (phonemes) are notated.

[ ] is used for **allophonic** transcriptions: for representations believed to include more phonetic detail than is stored mentally (= surface phonetic representations); for transcriptions involving the notation of certain non-significant phoneme variants (allophones); also for **general-phonetic** or **impressionistic** notation of unanalysed data.

Note that symbols enclosed in [ ] are only selectively 'narrowed'. Thus on occasion [r] is used to stand for the ordinary English voiced post-alveolar approximant, more precisely written as [ɹ]; similarly [i] or [iː] may sometimes stand for [ɪi], etc. But where the quality of /r/ or /i(ː)/ is the topic under discussion, then the precise symbols are employed.

Phonetic symbols are taken from the International Phonetic Alphabet (see chart, p. xx). The following additional symbols are employed:

ɝ   r-coloured ɜ
ɷ   unrounded ʊ
ʟ   voiced velar lateral
C˺   unreleased C
C˸   unaspirated C
C   any consonant

V   any vowel
→   goes to, becomes, is realized as
~   or
$ }
. }   syllable boundary (indicated only when relevant)
stem boundary, word boundary
‖   sentence boundary, end of utterance
Ø   zero
/   in the environment:
    X → Y / A — B   X becomes Y in the environment of a preceding A and a following B, i.e. AXB → AYB.

Words written in capitals

Throughout the work, use is made of the concept of **standard lexical sets**. These enable one to refer concisely to large groups of words which tend to share the same vowel, and to the vowel which they share. They are based on the vowel correspondences which apply between British Received Pronunciation and (a variety of) General American, and make use of **keywords** intended to be unmistakable no matter what accent one says them in. Thus 'the KIT words' refers to 'ship, bridge, milk . . .'; 'the KIT vowel' refers to the vowel these words have (in most accents, /ɪ/); both may just be referred to as KIT.

RP	GenAm		
ɪ	ɪ	1. KIT	ship, sick, bridge, milk, myth, busy . . .
e	ɛ	2. DRESS	step, neck, edge, shelf, friend, ready . . .
æ	æ	3. TRAP	tap, back, badge, scalp, hand, cancel . . .
ɒ	ɑ	4. LOT	stop, sock, dodge, romp, possible, quality . . .
ʌ	ʌ	5. STRUT	cup, suck, budge, pulse, trunk, blood . . .
ʊ	ʊ	6. FOOT	put, bush, full, good, look, wolf . . .
ɑː	æ	7. BATH	staff, brass, ask, dance, sample, calf . . .
ɒ	ɔ	8. CLOTH	cough, broth, cross, long, Boston . . .

ɜː	ɜr	9. NURSE	hurt, lurk, urge, burst, jerk, term ...
iː	i	10. FLEECE	creep, speak, leave, feel, key, people ...
eɪ	eɪ	11. FACE	tape, cake, raid, veil, steak, day ...
ɑː	ɑ	12. PALM	psalm, father, bra, spa, lager ...
ɔː	ɔ	13. THOUGHT	taught, sauce, hawk, jaw, broad ...
əʊ	o	14. GOAT	soap, joke, home, know, so, roll ...
uː	u	15. GOOSE	loop, shoot, tomb, mute, huge, view ...
aɪ	aɪ	16. PRICE	ripe, write, arrive, high, try, buy ...
ɔɪ	ɔɪ	17. CHOICE	adroit, noise, join, toy, royal ...
aʊ	aʊ	18. MOUTH	out, house, loud, count, crowd, cow ...
ɪə	ɪ(r	19. NEAR	beer, sincere, fear, beard, serum ...
ɛə	ɛ(r	20. SQUARE	care, fair, pear, where, scarce, vary ...
ɑː	ɑ(r	21. START	far, sharp, bark, carve, farm, heart ...
ɔː	ɔ(r	22. NORTH	for, war, short, scorch, born, warm ...
ɔː	o(r	23. FORCE	four, wore, sport, porch, borne, story ...
ʊə	ʊ(r	24. CURE	poor, tourist, pure, plural, jury ...

THE INTERNATIONAL PHONETIC ALPHABET

(Revised to 1979)

	Bilabial	Labiodental	Dental, Alveolar, or Post-alveolar	Retroflex	Palato-alveolar	Palatal	Velar	Uvular	Labial-Palatal	Labial-Velar	Pharyngeal	Glottal
Nasal	m	ɱ	n	ɳ		ɲ	ŋ	ɴ				
Plosive	p b		t d	ʈ ɖ		c ɟ	k g	q ɢ		k͡p g͡b		ʔ
(Median) Fricative	ɸ β	f v	θ ð s z	ʂ ʐ	ʃ ʒ	ç ʝ	x ɣ	χ ʁ	ɥ	ʍ w	ħ ʕ	h ɦ
(Median) Approximant		ʋ	ɹ	ɻ		j	(ɰ)			ɰ		
Lateral Fricative			ɬ ɮ									
Lateral (Approximant)			l	ɭ		ʎ						
Trill			r					ʀ				
Tap or Flap			ɾ	ɽ				ʀ				
Ejective	pʼ		tʼ				kʼ					
Implosive	ɓ		ɗ				ɠ					
(Median) Click	ʘ		ʇ									
Lateral Click			ʖ									

(pulmonic air-stream mechanism) — S I N V N O S
(non-pulmonic air-stream) — N O O

DIACRITICS

- ̥ Voiceless p̥ d̥
- ̬ Voiced ʂ̬ ţ
- ʰ Aspirated tʰ
- Breathy-voiced b̤ a̤
- ̪ Dental t̪
- ̣ Labialized ṭ
- ʲ Palatalized t̡
- ˠ Velarized or Pharyngealized ɫ, l̴
- ̩ Syllabic n̩ l̩
- ʼ or ‿ Simultaneous ʃ and x (but see also under the heading Affricates)

- ˈ or ̍ Raised e̍, e̤, ẹ̈, w
- ˌ or ̱ Lowered e̱, e, ɛ̱, ɹ
- ̠ or − Advanced u̟, ṭ
- − or ̱ Retracted i̱, i̱, ṭ
- ̈ Centralized ë
- ˜ Nasalized ã
- ˞ ̣ r-coloured a˞
- ː Long aː
- ˑ Half-long aˑ
- ̆ Non-syllabic ŭ
- ˔ More rounded ɔ̹
- ˓ Less rounded y̜

OTHER SYMBOLS

- ɕ, ʑ Alveolo-palatal fricatives
- ɟ, ʒ Palatalized ʃ, ʒ
- ɹ Alveolar fricative trill
- ɺ Alveolar lateral flap
- ʨ Simultaneous ʃ and x
- ɧ Variety of ʃ resembling s, etc.
- ɪ = ɩ
- ʊ = ɷ
- ɜ = Variety of ə
- ɚ = r-coloured ə

VOWELS

	Front		Back	Front	Back
Close	i y	ɨ ʉ	ɯ u		
Half-close	e ø		ɤ o		
Half-open	ɛ œ	ə	ʌ ɔ		
Open	a ɶ		ɑ ɒ		
	Unrounded			Rounded	

STRESS, TONE (PITCH)

- ˈ stress, placed at beginning of stressed syllable:
- ˌ secondary stress:
- ˉ high level pitch, high tone:
- ˍ low level:
- ˊ high rising:
- ˏ low rising:
- ˋ high falling:
- ˎ low falling:
- ˆ rise-fall:
- ˇ fall-rise.

AFFRICATES can be written as digraphs, as ligatures, or with slur marks; thus ts, tʃ, dʒ: t͡s t͡ʃ d͡ʒ; ʦ ʧ ʤ.
c, ɟ may occasionally be used for tʃ, dʒ.

4

England

4.1 RP revisited

4.1.1 Varieties of RP

In the first volume we took RP as something given, as something which – at least for British-oriented readers – is thoroughly familiar. RP is, after all, what anyone living in the United Kingdom hears constantly from radio and television announcers and newsreaders and from many other public figures. Everyone in Britain has a mental image of RP, even though they may not refer to it by that name and even though the image may not be very accurate. Many English people are also regularly exposed to RP in personal face-to-face contact. For a small minority, it is their own speech.

Yet no accent is a homogeneous invariant monolith – certainly not RP. So we must now proceed to consider the variability found within it. In doing so we are forced to be impressionistic: although RP is by far the most thoroughly described accent of English, there has been very little in the way of objective quantified investigation of its variability.

It is convenient to recognize first of all a central tendency which I shall call **mainstream RP**. We can define it negatively, by recognizing two other tendencies or types of RP, which are part of RP as a whole but distinct from mainstream RP. One is **U-RP** (4.1.2 below), the other **adoptive RP** (4.1.3 below). It is also convenient to recognize a rather vaguer entity, **Near-RP**, comprising accents which are not exactly RP though not very different from it. We shall consider each of these in turn.

A different set of distinctions within RP has been proposed by Gimson (1980): **conservative RP**, 'used by the older generation and, traditionally, by certain professions or social groups', **general RP**, 'most commonly in use and typified by the pronunciation adopted by the BBC', and **advanced RP** 'mainly used by young people of exclusive social groups – mostly of the upper classes, but also, for prestige value, in certain professional circles'. I am inclined to the view that the relationship between these varieties is not exactly a chronological one: although conservative and advanced RP are indeed chronologically related varieties, probably of U-RP, general RP corresponds to my term mainstream RP, and overlaps in time with both.

In recognizing these varieties or tendencies within RP, one must remember that they – like RP itself – are abstractions, not objectifiable entities. They represent areas within a multidimensional continuum. The frontiers we may attempt to set up between them may well correspond to our perceptions of social reality rather than to exclusively linguistic and phonetic considerations.

4.1.2 U-RP

The accent popularly associated with, say, a dowager duchess is not quite the same as mainstream RP. Even when we discount the special voice quality and manner of delivery there are other differences. The same applies to the speech of many upper-class army officers; to that of a Noel Coward sophisticate; to that of a Terry Thomas cad; to that of the popular image of an elderly Oxbridge don; and to that of a jolly-hockey-sticks schoolmistress at an expensive private girls' school. These all differ somewhat from one another as well as from the duchess. It is difficult in these matters to separate stereotype from reality, but it is reasonable to claim that these versions of RP are conspicuous in a way which makes it impossible to regard them as part of mainstream RP. Furthermore, they share one important social characteristic: they are, in the narrow sense, upper-class. They are not middle-class. In the terminology popularized by A. S. C. Ross (1954) and Nancy Mitford (1956), they are U, as opposed to non-U. We may refer to them collectively as **upper-crust RP**, or just U-RP, and so distinguish them from mainstream (upper-middle-class) RP. (The term **Oxford English**, sometimes encountered, is best avoided because of its vagueness: although it may refer to a form of RP 'in which certain tendencies are (sometimes affectedly) exaggerated' (*Chambers twentieth century dictionary* 1972) – i.e. perhaps to U-RP – it has also been used to refer both more narrowly to the don stereotype and more widely to RP in general.)

We must now examine the most salient phonetic characteristics of U-RP.

The TRAP vowel, /æ/, has an opening-diphthong realization [ɛæ], or even [eæ], thus *that man* ['ðɛæt 'mɛæn]. U-RP children, though, typically use a much opener quality, [a], which has also recently become very fashionable among younger actresses and others. It is not clear whether this latter variant should now count as U-RP, or whether it is more properly part of adoptive RP, exerting some influence on the rest of RP. But in any case it is certain that what would formerly have been considered a provincialism is now chic, while the once fashionable [ɛæ] type is outmoded.

The wide diphthongs of PRICE and MOUTH both have a relatively front starting-point, with that of /aɪ/ fronter than that of /aʊ/; the latter may have little or no lip rounding on the second element. Both the /ʌ/ of STRUT and the /ɑː/ of BATH–PALM–START are back; in attempting to imitate the U-RP /ʌ/ I find myself lowering my larynx and expanding my pharynx. The /uː/ of GOOSE, too, is fully back (though with a fronted allophone after /j/). The centring diphthongs of NEAR, SQUARE, and CURE, that is /ɪə, ɛə, ʊə/, have a very open second element when in free position, as *near* [nɪɑ̆], *where* [wɛɑ̆ ~ wæɑ̆] – at least in the duchess, officer, and don stereotypes. The NURSE vowel is very open: [nɐːs]. This too is where we find the GOAT vowel with a backish realization, lip-rounded throughout, [oʊ], and with a monophthongal allophone [o ~ ʊ] in many unstressed environments, thus *obey, November, poetic*, and even *follow* ['fɒlʊ]. Of the remaining reduction vowels, /ɪ/ is distinctly preferred over /ə/ in the cases which are variable within RP, as *wait*[ɪ]*d*, *hors*[ɪ]*s, poss*[ɪ]*bly, private* ['praɪvɪt], *carel*[ɪ]*ssn*[ɪ]*ss*. The *happy* vowel is strikingly open, even reaching [ë] in utterance-final position; thus *city* has the second vowel at least as open as the first, and usually opener – ['sɪtɪ ~ 'sɪtë]. Enclitic *me* always has this vowel, never /iː/, thus *tell me* ['tɛl mɪ]. Smoothing (vol. 1, 3.2.9) is very usual, as *do it* ['dʊ ɪt].

In old-fashioned U-RP (and often in old-fashioned RP in general), CLOTH words have /ɔː/ rather than the usual /ɒ/, thus *cross* /krɔːs/, *soft* /sɔːft/. Even in contemporary younger U-RP /ɔː/ is often found in a few CLOTH words, notably in *off* /ɔːf/ (mainstream RP

/ɒf/). Thus for example show-jumping commentators (an upper-crust type of television performer) have attracted some comment by their use of the pronunciation /ˈdʒʌmp ɔːf/ ('jump-orf') for *jump-off*.

U-RP voiceless plosives are never glottalled. They are usually not glottalized either. Consequently there is nasal release, with a transitional voiceless nasal, in words or phrases where /p, t, k/ are followed by a nasal, thus *cotton, chutney, department, Hockney, stop me* [ˈstɒpᵐ mɪ]. Preconsonantal /t/ is articulated in a way which accommodates to, or overlaps with, the following segment, thus *Le*[t̪] *them a*[tˡ] *least sta*[t]*e qui*[t]*e clearly wha*[t̪] *they intend*. This is distinct both from the [ʔ], replacing or reinforcing, of many other accents and from the separately exploded [t] of one travesty of RP (the elocuted quasi-RP of 4.1.3).

Initially in a stressed syllable, U-RP /p, t, k/ often have surprisingly little aspiration.

The tapped /r/, [ɾ], is typical of some varieties of U-RP. It is found intervocalically after a stressed vowel, as *very sorry* [ˈvɛɾɪ ˈsɒɾɪ], *far off* [ˈfɑːɾ ˈɔːf], and also sometimes in certain consonant clusters, as *three crates* [ˈθriː ˈkɾeɪts]. Since [ɾ] is rare in mainstream RP (except perhaps in the environment following a dental frica-tive), its frequent use can furnish a useful diagnostic. It is par-ticularly striking in accents like Noel Coward's, which is perhaps what has given many Americans the mistaken impression that [ɾ] is the usual realization of RP (or 'British') /r/.

Tapped /r/ may contribute to the crisp, clipped effect which many claim to detect in U-RP. Another stereotypical view of this accent, though, is that it is languid and effete. This alternative judgement might find support in another characteristically U-RP treatment of intervocalic /r/, namely its elision. This gives *very* the variant [ˈve.ɪ] (still, I think, disyllabic, and not a rhyme for *day*). Such elision of word-internal intervocalic /r/ is variable, and restricted to a small number of common words; another one is *terribly*. Compare mainstream RP [ˈvɛɪɪ, ˈtɛɪəblɪ]. Yet another pos-sibility for U-RP /r/ is the labiodental approximant, [ʋ]. Although this is often regarded as an upper-class affectation, I am not con-vinced that it is nowadays found more frequently among upper-class speakers than among those of other social classes. The same goes for the (extremely rare) use of [w] for /r/.

As mentioned in volume 1, one of the strange characteristics of
the *-ing* variable is that the [ɪn] variant, otherwise a relatively low-
status characteristic, is also found in some U-RP. (Mainstream
RP has only [ɪŋ].) The story is told of Edward VII coming upon
Frank Harris and noticing his inappropriately loud sports jacket.
'Mornin', Harris,' said the King, 'goin' rattin'?' Another otherwise
low-status characteristic of some U-RP is the frequent use of [mɪ]
or [mə] as a weak form of *my*; at Eton one addresses one's tutor as
[mə'tjuːtə], and in court opposing counsel is [mə 'lɜːnɪd 'frend]. But
mainstream RP *my* is virtually always [maɪ], with no weak form.

There are several prosodic phenomena characteristic of U-RP.
One is a trick of adding emphasis by prolonging the steady-state of
a consonant: usually, I think, a voiceless consonant following an
accented vowel, thus *frightfully sorry* ['fraɪːflɪ ˌsɒrɪ], *it was awfully
nice* [ɪt wəz 'ɔːfːlɪ ˌnaɪs]. Another is a particular rhythmic pattern
in words with penultimate stress, as *water, wider, places, reducing*.
This involves a shortening, greater than in mainstream RP, of the
duration of the stressed vowel and a compensatory lengthening of
the final unstressed vowel, without any change in quality. The
effect is most noticeable where the stressed vowel is one belonging
to the phonologically free ('long') category, as in the examples
quoted. The word *parking-meter* could serve as a shibboleth to
separate out the upper class from those who are not quite upper
class. In U-RP the [ɪŋ] of *parking* is considerably longer than the
[ɑː], and the [ə] of *meter* longer than the [iː] – in spite of what the
conventional use of length-marks suggests. When I put on a U-RP
accent for purposes of acting, demonstration, or caricature, I find
that this is one of the obvious changes I make in my ordinary
speech. The other obvious change I make involves voice quality:
U-RP demands a 'plumminess' achieved by lowering the larynx
and widening the oro-pharynx.

4.1.3 Adoptive RP

Adoptive RP is that variety of RP spoken by adults who did not
speak RP as children.

The usual reason for adopting RP – or at least attempting to do so
– is a change in the individual's social circumstances. Someone who
takes a job in which he is surrounded by RP-speaking colleagues, or

who acquires a circle of RP-speaking friends, may well experience a certain social pressure to conform to their norms, in speech just as in other areas of behaviour. If the individual concerned has a psychological make-up such that he or she readily responds to such pressure, and if the required ability in phonetic and other mimicry is at hand, then a new speaker of adoptive RP is recruited. There is also an occupational category which tends to demand ability in RP for professional reasons: the acting profession. Although the former insistence on RP for all rôles except comic/rural/domestic/ working-class ones has now largely disappeared, drama schools in Britain still insist on the student's mastering 'Standard English', by which is meant RP as the standard pronunciation. Thus it is that British television chat shows, with their showbiz interviews, are good occasions for observing adoptive RP.

Obviously, adoptive RP merges imperceptibly into mainstream RP. If someone learns to speak exactly like a native RP speaker, then their speech cannot be recognized as adoptive RP. Often, though, this does not happen. The speaker of adoptive RP will in any case normally retain an ability in the native accent of English; and the two accents, native and adoptive, may often come to be related to one another as informal and formal. Thus one crucial characteristic of most speakers of adoptive RP is their lack of control over the informal and allegro characteristics of RP. Native speakers of RP make extensive use of Elision, Assimilation, Smoothing, and other special-context variants, particularly of course in informal contexts; adoptive RP speakers tend to avoid them. Consciously or unconsciously, they may regard such variants as 'lazy' or 'slipshod' and hence incompatible with their 'best' speech, their adoptive RP.

Perhaps the most striking example of this phenomenon concerns /r/ sandhi (vol. 1, 3.2.3). In native-speaker RP it is usual to use sandhi /r/ in the appropriate places, in the environments where it is 'intrusive' (unhistorical, not corresponding to the spelling) just as in those where it is not. But the speech-conscious tend to regard intrusive /r/ as incorrect, and hence attempt to avoid it. As discussed in volume 1 (3.2.3), the typical outcome is the suppression of most sandhi /r/s. Thus we may expect to find sandhi /r/ used freely in mainstream (native) RP, but sparsely in speech-conscious adoptive RP. Pronunciations which I should consider typical of the two varieties are listed in (174). It should be understood that these are to be taken as tendencies, not as absolute differences.

(174)	Mainstream (native) RP	Adoptive RP
more and more	'mɔːr əm 'mɔː	'mɔː ən(d) 'mɔː
Christina Onassis	krɪs'tiːnər əʊ'næsɪs, ə'næsɪs	krɪs'tiːnə əʊ'næsɪs
Brian Howard	'braən 'haəd	'braɪən 'haʊəd
seeing him do it	'sɪɪŋ ɪm 'dʊ ɪt	'siːɪŋ hɪm 'duː ɪt

Among RP speakers the use of /hw/ in *where, wheel* etc. is restricted to the speech-conscious. Thus such avoidance of Glide Cluster Reduction (vol. 1, 3.2.4) tends to be diagnostic of adoptive rather than native RP; though there are occasional native RP speakers who have drilled themselves to use /hw/ as a consequence of becoming speech-conscious through drama training or otherwise.

Speech training of a particularly unrealistic kind may result in what one might call **quasi-RP**. In this variety the incidence of phonemes may well be as in adoptive RP, but certain allophones are selected for their supposed clarity or carefulness rather than for their appropriateness to RP. This is the accent where /t/ tends to be articulated as a median-oral released voiceless alveolar plosive [t] in all phonetic environments – not only in *hat-pin* but even in *atlas* and *chutney* – and where all plosives in clusters are separately released (*doctor, stabbed*). An attempt is made to give full voicing to lenis obstruents in all positions, and the FLEECE and GOOSE vowels, /iː/ and /uː/, are realized as cardinal-type monophthongs. But such a travesty cannot be considered as truly belonging to RP: it properly belongs in Near-RP, to which we turn in 4.1.9.

4.1.4 Variability in mainstream RP

In isolating the tendencies U-RP and adoptive RP we have by no means exhausted the variability of RP. In this section we shall briefly examine assorted phonetic/phonological variables which apply to the accent. Some can be plausibly claimed to be correlated with non-linguistic variables such as social context; for others no known correlation with non-linguistic factors has been discovered.

We have already noted the importance of allegro and special-context variants in mainstream RP. The principal processes involved are the following:

(i) Place Assimilation, e.g. *ten minutes* ['tem 'mınıts], *good girl* ['gʊg 'gɜːl]. A free use of contextual dealveolar regressive assimilation is usually claimed to be associated with a casual style of speech, and it has recently been shown (Ramsaran 1978) that it is indeed **more** frequent in casual speech than in formal speech or monologue, though still frequent in all styles. It is noteworthy that the sub-category of Sibilant Yod Assimilation (e.g. *as you know* ['æʒ jʊ 'nəʊ]) is foreign to some accents within RP, though found in others.

(ii) Elision (preconsonantal Cluster Reduction), e.g. *stand near me* ['stæn nɪə 'miː], *next day* ['neks 'deɪ], *kindness* ['kaınnıs ~ 'kaınnəs]. Ramsaran (1978) has shown that in casual style Elision is less rule-bound; in all styles of speech its frequency increases with a faster pace.

(iii) Unstressed H Dropping, e.g. *tell him* ['tel ım]. In *hotel, historic, hysteria* etc. present-day RP has on the whole restored the /h/ which used to be dropped because of the lack of stress on the initial syllable.

(iv) Syllabic Consonant Formation, e.g. *get along* ['getl̩'ɒŋ]. There is diversity of usage in RP as regards possible constraints upon this rule; thus some speakers, but not all, say *modern* ['mɒdn̩], *satellite* ['sætl̩aıt], *Waterloo* ['wɔːtl̩'uː], *correct* [kr̩'ekt].

(v) Compression, e.g. *to arrive* [twə'raıv], *literary* ['lıtr̩ı]. Although the results of these and similar processes clearly do occur in some kinds of RP, they are by no means general.

(vi) Smoothing (vol. 1, 3.2.9), e.g. *do it at three o'clock* ['dʊ ıt ət 'θrı ə'klɒk], *fire power* ['faə,pɑə]. This is very usual in mainstream RP.

(vii) /r/ sandhi, e.g. *The rota/rotor isn't ready* [ðə'rəʊtər 'ıznt 'redı]. Less common alternative possibilities in RP are [ʔ] sandhi and zero sandhi, ['rəʊtə 'ʔıznt ~ 'rəʊtə 'ıznt]. Ramsaran (1978) found linking /r/ 'frequent' in all styles of speech.

These instances of variability merely reflect variable rules constituting part of the RP speaker's phonological competence. Except as mentioned above, they are not believed to vary significantly from speaker to speaker. But there is other variability in RP which is not of this nature. There are certain differences even in the systemic inventory, as well as in phonetic realization and in lexical incidence.

4.1.5 RP: systemic variability

Systemic differences in RP affect only the vowel system; they concern the long mid back area of THOUGHT–NORTH, FORCE, CURE, and the short front open area of TRAP. The first point mentioned involves the presence or not of contrastive /ɔə/ and /ʊə/, the second that of contrastive long /æː/.

I doubt whether there are any native RP speakers below pensionable age who have contrastive /ɔə/. Where present, this diphthong is found in (some) FORCE words and contrasts with the /ɔː/ of THOUGHT and NORTH. This results in minimal pairs such as *court* /kɔət/ vs. *caught* /kɔːt/, *sore–soar* /sɔə/ vs. *saw* /sɔː/. I have not myself ever had the opportunity of making a detailed study of an RP speaker with this opposition; the transcriptions shown in *EPD* imply that those who use /ɔə/ do in any case not use it consistently in all FORCE words or in any phonetically definable subset of them. Presumably, *worn* and *warn*, *fort* and *fought* are homophones in all varieties of RP without exception. What we have in this older type of RP is thus the lexical diffusion (vol. 1, 1.2.12) of a merger. In contemporary RP the merger may be regarded as complete, FORCE having the same /ɔː/ as THOUGHT–NORTH, so that *court–caught*, *sore–soar–saw*, too, are homophones. The standard work on present-day RP, Gimson 1980, does not include any /ɔə/ in the vowel system.

The question of RP /ʊə/ has been touched on in volume 1 (3.2.7, Second FORCE Merger; 2.2.24 CURE). An RP speaker will usually have at least some words with [ʊə ~ ɔə], i.e. /ʊə/, and they will often furnish one or two potential minimal pairs. But there is a great deal of variation in the lexical incidence of /ʊə/ and /ɔː/ in CURE words, so that it is hardly possible to say of any particular word that it always has /ʊə/ in RP. Many RP speakers say *tour* with a diphthong /ʊə/ distinct from the /ɔː/ of *tore–tor–taw*; but others merge them, variably or categorically. Some can establish the contrastiveness of their /ʊə/ by adducing the items *poor* (vs. *pore–pour–paw*), *moor* (vs. *more–maw*), *yours* (vs. *yaws*), or *sure* (vs. *shore–Shaw*); but there are plenty of RP speakers who pronounce some or all of *poor*, *moor*, *your* and *sure* with /ɔː/, and they are on the increase. Words in which the vowel is preceded by a consonant plus yod are relatively resistant to the shift from /ʊə/ to /ɔː/, e.g. *pure*, *furious*, and *cure* itself; this means that there is a certain tendency to make [ʊə] a

positional allophone of /ɔː/, restricted to the environment Cj__.
(Where the yod is word-initial, /ɔː/ is frequent, as in *your–you're*
/jɔː/, *Europe, Ural*; there is also the matter of the North Yorkshire
river spelt both *Ure* and *Yore*.)

An alternative possibility where the CURE vowel is preceded by
yod is a shift to [ɜː] (which implies a subsystemic merger of /ʊə/ and
/ɜː/ in this environment). Examples are *pure* [pjɜː], *curious* ['kjɜːrɪəs],.
during ['djɜːrɪŋ ∼ 'dʒɜːrɪŋ], *yours* [jɜːz] (compare *yearn* [jɜːn]).
Gimson (1977: xviii) judges this usage 'too idiosyncratic to warrant
inclusion' in *EPD*, a reasonable judgement. The non-idiosyncratic
RP forms are [pjʊə ∼ pjɔə ∼ pjɔː], etc.

The diphthong [ʊə] also arises in RP through Smoothing of the
sequence /uːə/ (vol. 1, 3.2.9), as *fewer, steward, brewery, two o'clock*
['tʊə ˈklɒk]. This means that *fewer* may be a perfect rhyme for *pure*,
steward for *assured*, and *brewery* for *fury*; that *newer* may be identical
with the second half of *manure*, and the first half of *two o'clock* with
tour. However, there is one important difference: the [ʊə] from
Smoothing of /uːə/ is not subject to the possibility of Lowering to
[ɔː]. *Fewer* cannot be *[fjɔː], nor *brewery* *[brɔːrɪ]. One way of
accounting for this interesting fact is through the hypothesis of
ordered rules (vol. 1, 1.2.13): the Lowering of /ʊə/ to [ɔː] is ordered
before Smoothing, so that the output of Smoothing cannot be an
input to Lowering. The only exception seems to be *you're*, if the
usual RP [jʊə ∼ jɔː] is regarded as derived from an underlying *you*
are /juː ɑː/ via [juːə]; but it is perhaps best to regard *you're* as a solid
morph no more derived by general rules from *you* plus *are* than
don't /dəʊnt/ is from *do* /duː/ plus *not* /nɒt/.

The result is in any case to tend to preserve [ʊə] as a phonetic
option in RP, even though its phonemic status is beginning to
become dubious. In beginners' phonetics classes for native English
speakers (mostly of adoptive RP and Near-RP) it is becoming
increasingly difficult to find a satisfactory keyword for /ʊə/, since
any given word may be pronounced with /ɔː/ by over half the class.
Recently I have tried *Ruhr*, which as a foreign word is perhaps
resistant to becoming a homophone of *roar–raw*.

Some RP speakers have a marginally contrastive long /æː/. It
shows up in pairs such as *bad* [bæːd] vs. *pad* [pæd], *glad* [glæːd] vs.
lad [læd]. Long [æː] may also occur before other lenis consonants, as
jam [dʒæːm], *jazz* [dʒæːz]; but it is rare to find contrastive length of

[æ] in environments other than that of a following /d/. There are those who have a large number of minimal or near-minimal pairs, as in the speech of south central England (4.3.7 below); but this is perhaps best regarded as a Near-RP provincialism rather than as a mainstream RP possibility. There are in any case many RP speakers who have no such contrast, making *bad–pad–glad–lad* perfect rhymes. Even those who do potentially make the distinction may in fact make it only in strongly stressed environments.

The commonest basis for the contrast is that monosyllabic adjectives end in [-æːd] but nouns in [-æd]. Hence *bad, clad, glad, mad, sad* have the long vowel, but *cad, dad, fad, pad* the short one. The verbs *add, had* are variable. The adjective *trad*, being a reduction of the polysyllable *traditional*, is short. The opposition is usually retained before *-ly* and the inflectional endings *-er, -est*, so that *badly* fails to rhyme with *Bradley*, while *mad#der* 'more mad' is ['mæːdə], distinct from *madder* '*Rubia* plant, red dye' ['mædə]. It has been hypothesized that the long [æː] in adjectives arose by analogy with the additional vowel length optionally indicating the morpheme boundary in the many past participles in [-V#d], as *awed, ill-starred, studied*. I do not find this convincing; but I have no better suggestion.

4.1.6 RP: distributional variability

As far as concerns phonotactic distribution, there is only one important point of variability in RP: the question of the constraints on vowels and diphthongs before tautosyllabic (intersyllabic) /r/.

It is clear that all the short (checked) vowels can occur in this environment, along with those long (free) vowels and diphthongs whose endpoint is mid or open, namely part-system D (vol. 1, 2.3.4). We can exemplify this by the words *spirit, herald, carrot, sorry, hurry, courier; hero, vary, furry, mascara, story, fury*. Equally clearly, /iː, eɪ, əʊ, uː/ cannot occur stressed in this environment, unless of course there is an intervening major morpheme boundary, as in *key-ring* or *hay-ride*. (It is thus a hesitation about the status of the morpheme boundary that gives rise to the occasional pronunciation of *Jewry* as /'dʒuːrɪ/, instead of the usual /'dʒʊərɪ/, homophonous with *jury*.)

Two kinds of uncertainty arise. One concerns stressed /aɪ/ and (to a lesser extent because only a few unusual words are involved) /aʊ/ and /ɔɪ/. The other concerns vowels of part-systems B and C (vol. 1, 2.3.2 and 2.3.3) in the environment /__'r/.

Consider first words such as *pirate, tyrant, Byron, Giro, thyroid, cowrie, Moira*. An extreme position to adopt would be to say that the only pronunciations possible in RP are those with /-aɪər-, -aʊər-, -ɔɪər-/. Usually, of course, these sequences are reduced by Smoothing to diphthongs or monophthongs: thus *pirate* is ['paərət] ~ 'paːrət] (or [-ɪt]). The current (fourteenth) edition of *EPD*, however, gives /'θaɪrɔɪd/ as a preferred alternative to /'θaɪərɔɪd/, and for *Giro* only /'dʒaɪrəʊ/. (This last entry may well be a mistake, seeing that *biro* is given both possibilities and *tyro* only /'taɪərəʊ/.) For *cowrie* and *Moira* the pronunciations /'kaʊrɪ/, /'mɔɪrə/ are recorded as commoner than, or equally common as, /'kaʊərɪ/, /'mɔɪərə/.

Although for many individual RP speakers (including me) the constraint does operate in its strongest form, it seems therefore that for RP in general it must be stated rather more weakly. Three categories of words seem to be potential exceptions: foreign words (*cowrie*), proper names (*Moira*), and words where the following syllable is not weak (*thyroid*). Yet although all these categories overlap in *Cairo* (Egypt), *EPD* records it only as /'kaɪərəʊ/ (not /'kaɪrəʊ/).

What about the pronunciation of core vocabulary words like *pirate, tyrant, spiral, iris, virus* with /-aɪr-/? I believe it is correct to state that this possibility does not belong in RP, although it is certainly common in Near-RP.

Let us turn now to the question of the distribution vowels and diphthongs in the environment of a following stressed syllable with initial /r/, there being no intervening morpheme boundary. Examples of the words involved are *uranium, eureka, neurotic; irate, ironic, direction*. Can these words have /uː, aɪ/ in their initial syllable in RP?

Certainly the usual RP version of *uranium, eureka, neurotic* has /jʊə'r-/. There is also an alternative with /jʊ'r-/, and the usual possibility of [ɔə] or [ɔː] in place of [ʊə]. *EPD* includes the possibility of /njuː'r-/ in *neurotic* (and other related words such as *neuralgia* and *neurology*), but rules out */juː'r-/ in *uranium* and *eureka*. In various other words morpheme boundaries or related forms exert pressure firmly preventing */-uː'r-/, e.g. *curator, Europa, bureau-*

cracy, juridical, puristic. In *eurhythmic* the etymological morpheme boundary is sufficient to make /juː'r-/ possible alongside /jʊə'r, jʊ'r-/. It seems fair to say that the *neur-* words are possible exceptions to a general phonotactic principle of RP, with /njuː'r-/ etc. perhaps being Near-RP forms now beginning to spread into mainstream RP. Otherwise the sequence /uːr/ within a morpheme is ruled out.

With /aɪ/ there is more diversity. Many RP speakers do have, or can have, the sequence /-aɪ'r-/ in at least some of *irate, ironic, piratical, pyrethrum, direction, spiraea* and other similar words. Equally though, many other RP speakers never have it, pronouncing only /aɪə'reɪt/, /daɪə'rɛkʃən ~ dɪ- ~ də-/ etc. So this is a true case of phonotactic/structural/distributional variability in mainstream RP; it is not known whether the admission or otherwise of the string /-aɪ'r-/ can be correlated with any social parameter.

The problem of the *happy* vowel can be viewed as phonotactic inasmuch as it involves the admission or otherwise of /ɪ/ to the word-final environment. It can also be seen as subsystemic: is the FLEECE vowel, /iː/, a member of the weak-vowel system or not? But it is most conveniently regarded as a realizational variable, and we deal with it in 4.1.7 below.

4.1.7 RP: realizational variability

In this section we discuss only the more striking instances of low-level phonetic (realizational) variability within RP.

The height and degree, of centralization of /ɪ/ and /e/ vary. Relatively close and peripheral qualities are associated particularly, but not exclusively, with old-fashioned RP; relatively open and central qualities are common with younger speakers.

The realization of /æ/ is a matter which currently attracts a lot of popular attention. 'Whatever happened to BBC English?' cried a Sunday newspaper article (Cooper 1978). 'All those female interviewers talking about bunk bulences and Ufrica. I suppose they all grew up in the Sixties . . . when . . . working class became beautiful, and everyone from Princess Unne downwards embraced the Flat A.' The point here is that the newly current [a] is perceptually very similar to the fronted realizations of /ʌ/ which have been around in RP for rather longer. So for those accustomed to pronouncing [bæŋk] the new [baŋk] is readily heard as *bunk* /bʌŋk/ rather than as the intended *bank* /bæŋk/. It may even be the case for some speakers that /æ/ and /ʌ/ are merged, variably at least. It is widely believed that the responsibility for this change of vowel quality rests with the theatrical profession – the article cited above goes on to speak of 'uctors' and 'uctresses' – and this view may well be justified. The pharyngeal stricture associated with the traditional RP [æ] – something which many phoneticians have commented on – does impair voice projection. Teachers of singing, too, have taught [a] as the correct quality for sung /æ/; here there may be Italian influence reinforcing the other considerations.

The lowering and centring of /æ/ is presumably linked to that of /ɪ/ and /e/ mentioned above, though whether in a 'push-chain' or a 'drag-chain' is not clear. It is a change which promises to carry RP further away from both American and southern-hemisphere accents of English.

The starting-points of the PRICE and MOUTH diphthongs, /aɪ/ and /aʊ/, vary considerably. They seem to be getting gradually backer. Older textbooks sometimes explained the quality of cardinal 4, [a], by identifying it with the first element of RP /aɪ/; but so front a quality is now unusual. Jones, too, considered that 'the beginning of the diphthong ranges with different RP speakers from a "middle" ɑ to about a cardinal [a]' (1956: §175). Mainstream RP currently embraces a range from a retracted front [a] to an advanced back [ɑ]. There may even be RP speakers for whom the first element of /aɪ/ is identical in quality with their /ɑː/, namely [ɑ+] – though this is questionable. On the other hand there is also an idiosyncratic pronunciation, probably within RP, which approaches [æɪ]. The starting-point of /aʊ/ also varies from retracted front [a] to nearly fully back [ɑ]. But in RP the starting-point of /aʊ/ is never fronter than the starting-point of /aɪ/.

Rounding of the second elements of /aʊ/ and /əʊ/ is not usually very great in RP. There is now one variant of /aʊ/ where the second element is not only unrounded but also fronted, [i]; this is heard by many as /aɪ/, and has attracted comment. It seems unlikely, though, that the /aɪ–aʊ/ opposition is seriously threatened, notwithstanding comedians' claims that the upper classes are 'ite and abite dine tine'.

Where /aɪə/ or /aʊə/ are smoothed to a phonetic diphthong or monophthong the quality of the first element is preserved. Thus *tire* will usually be somewhat fronter than *tower*, e.g. ['taə ~ 'taː] vs. ['taə ~ 'taː]. But with speakers who use identical qualities for the first elements of PRICE and MOUTH, smoothed /aɪə/ and /aʊə/ may well fall together, making *tire* and *tower* potential homophones. Whether this applies or not, it frequently occurs that smoothed /aʊə/ becomes phonetically identical with /aː/, giving (variable or even categorical) homophones such as *tower–tar, shower–Shah*. These RP Smoothings are sometimes caricatured in spellings such as 'empah' for *empire*. And there must be many who, like me, find the name of the Tower Car Hire Company something of a tongue-twister.

Among the other diphthongs, /eɪ/ shows variability both in the openness of the starting-point and in the degree of diphthongal movement: starting-points in the area bounded by [e, ɛ, ë] all are found in RP. A particularly close starting-point, nearly cardinal 2, is now old-fashioned; an almost monophthongal [ęę ~ ęː] is more recent; both verge on U-RP. The openness of the starting-point of /ɔɪ/ varies, too, ranging from [ɒ] to cardinal [ɔ] or somewhat closer. An old-fashioned variant with an unrounded central starting-point, [ʌɪ], conjures up the image of an elderly clerical headmaster: ['kʌm 'hɪʌ ˌbʌɪ] *Come here, boy!*

The vowel /ɔː/ has been getting less open over the last half-century. Newsreels from the thirties often evidence a cardinal-6-like quality which now seems dated. Perhaps, though, the important change is not so much in tongue height as in the degree of rounding: RP /ɔː/ has become increasingly closely rounded. There are some who have a centring diphthong [ɔə] as a positional allophone for /ɔː/, used in final position, as [sɔə] *saw–sore–soar*. This is, though, perhaps a Near-RP Londonism. On the other side of the vowel area, a monophthongal /ɛə/, i.e. [ɛː], is perhaps a Near-RP northernism if in a stressed final syllable; in other environments, as *careful* ['kɛːfl̩], *bearing* ['bɛːrɪŋ], it carries no such connotations. A particularly open starting-point for /ɛə/, giving [æə], verges on U-RP.

The vowel of GOAT furnishes a well-known example of chronological variation in RP, as the older back [ʠ+ʊ] type gave way to one with a central and usually unrounded starting-point, [ɜʊ ~ əʊ]. One may hazard a guess that the dividing date was the First World War: those who grew up before 1914 had the back type, those who came to adulthood since have the central type. The starting-point of the predominant RP type is identical with the quality of NURSE, i.e. /ɜː/. It follows that a good case can be made for symbolizing it /ɜʊ/. I have retained the more usual notation, /əʊ/, even though it is perhaps open to the objection that the schwa element might be identified with the closish non-final /ə/ allophone in *again*: the 'pinched' quality of such an [ᵊʊ] would not be characteristic of mainstream RP, where the first element of /əʊ/ is definitely opener than half-close. The rounding of the second element of the /əʊ/ diphthong is weak and may be non-existent.

For a time it seemed as if the fronting of the first element of /əʊ/ was continuing beyond [ɜ] towards [ɛ̈ ~ ë̞]. This [ɛʊ] type enjoys some popularity among U-RP and even mainstream RP speakers born between the First and Second World Wars; but it is now widely considered 'affected', and has ceased to be fashionable among younger speakers. It seems as though the [ɜʊ] type, often with very little diphthongal movement and minimal lip rounding, is due to remain the predominant RP variant for some time yet.

A fully back /uː/ was mentioned above as one of the characteristics of U-RP. In mainstream RP it is often somewhat centralized, even to the extent that there is no perceptible difference between the allophone used in the environment /j——/ and the phonemic norm.

The final vowel of *happ*Y is traditionally identified in RP with the /ɪ/ of KIT. Phonetically it may well be indistinguishable from /ɪ/ allophones: a word such as *city* may have two vowels virtually identical in quality and duration. In U-RP, though, the *happ*Y vowel may in fact be rather opener, approaching the quality of DRESS; this applies, for instance, to a certain kind of army-officer speech. Conversely, it appears that recently RP may be beginning to prefer a closer quality, which may come to be identified with the /iː/ of FLEECE rather than with the /ɪ/ of KIT. In particular, speakers of adoptive RP no longer seem to regard ['hæpi], ['sɪti] etc. as regionalisms which should be avoided in cultivated speech. (But see 4.1.9 below.)

Among the consonants, the question of aspiration of /p, t, k/ initially in a stressed syllable has been touched on above (4.1.2), as has the possibility of [ɾ] as the realization of /r/. Mainstream RP has aspirated plosives and approximant /r/ as the norm.

Vocalization of dark /l/ (vol. 1, 3.4.4) is occasionally met with in RP, particularly in the environment of a preceding labial, as *careful* ['kɛəfʊ], *table* ['teɪbʊ]. On the whole, though, L Vocalization must be considered only Near-RP or non-RP, as must forms such as ['mentəl] *mental* (rather than pukka RP ['mentl̩]).

4.1.8 RP: lexical-incidential variability

A glance at *EPD* shows that rather a high proportion of the words it contains are recorded as having more than one pronunciation. Sometimes this is due to the separate recording of forms which are related to one another by one or more of the rules or processes we have discussed elsewhere, as when *mausoleum* is shown as either /ˌmɔːsə'lɪəm/ or /ˌmɔːsə'liːəm/ and *maverick* as either /'mævərɪk/ or /'mævrɪk/. But in many cases it reflects a more genuine variability: words where different speakers clearly have different phonological representations for the same word. Thus some people pronounce *kilometre* /kɪ'lɒmɪtə/, analogously to *thermometer* and *barometer*; others pronounce it /'kɪləmiːtə/, following what to my mind is the more sensible analogy of *centimetre* /'sɛntɪmiːtə/. There is no doubt that both pronunciations should be regarded as belonging to RP, no matter how contemptuous users of one pronunciation may sometimes be of the other. For *garage* the fourteenth edition of *EPD* offers five variants, all within RP: first /'gæraːdʒ/, then less commonly /'gærɪdʒ, 'gæraːʒ/, and further 'occasionally' /gə'raːdʒ, gə'raːʒ/. (Most other authorities consider /'gæraːʒ/ the usual RP form.)

There are several very common words among those having two or more rival forms in RP. They include *again* /ə'gen, ə'geɪn/, *ate* /'et, 'eɪt/, *either* /'aɪðə, 'iːðə/, *Sunday* /'sʌndɪ, 'sʌndeɪ/ (and likewise the other days of the week), *because* (strong form) /bɪ'kɒz, bɪ'kɔːz, bɪ'kəz, bə-/, *quarter* /'kwɔːtə, 'kɔːtə/, *often* /'ɒfən/ (i.e. ['ɒfn̩]), /'ɒftən, 'ɔː-/. In each of these cases the first form quoted appears to be the more usual one in RP.

As mentioned in volume 1 (2.2.7), there are several words which fluctuate in RP between /æ/ and /aː/ (tabulated there as (59')). They include such items as *plastic, masculine, blasphemy, exasperate, transitive* (/æ/ more frequent) and *chaff, lather, pastoral, plaque* (/aː/ more frequent). Formerly *ant* and *contrast* belonged to this category, though they have now settled down as having /æ/ and /ɑː/ respectively.

All kinds of RP retain the opposition between /ɪ/ and /ə/ as reduction vowels, as exemplified in the second syllables of *tulip* vs. *gallop*, *bucket* vs. *ducat*, *solid* vs. *salad*. But there are many types of word where RP speakers differ from one another, some using /ɪ/ and some using /ə/. In all these cases the pronunciation with /ɪ/ is the more conservative, the traditional RP form. This applies, for instance, to words ending in:

1. *-ace* /-ɪs ~ -əs/, as *menace*, *palace*.
2. *-ate* (in adjectives and some nouns) /-ɪt ~ -ət/, as *delicate*, *separate*, *senate*, *chocolate*. (Various nouns in *-ate* have /-eɪt/ as a further variant, tending to become the dominant one, as *magistrate*, *candidate*, *carbohydrate*; with verbs ending in *-ate*, /-eɪt/ is the only possibility, e.g. *create*, *operate*, *to separate*.)
3. *-ible* [-ɪbl̩ ~ -əbl̩], as *visible*, *horrible*; also *-ibility*, as *incompatibility* /ˈɪnkəmˈpætɪˈbɪlɪtɪ ~ ˈɪŋkəmˈpætəˈbɪlətɪ/ (etc.).
4. *-ily* /-ɪlɪ ~ -əlɪ/, as *merrily*, *happily*, *worthily*. In cases such as *readily*, *bodily*, /-əlɪ/ may include the variant [-l̩ɪ].
5. *-ity* /-ɪtɪ ~ -ətɪ/, as *sanity*, *locality*.
6. *-less* /-lɪs ~ -ləs/, *-ness* /-nɪs ~ -nəs/, as *hopeless*, *kindness*, *carelessness*.
7. *-let* /-lɪt ~ -lət/, *-ret* /-rɪt ~ -rət/, as *booklet*, *secret*.

It also applies to words beginning with weakened *be-* (*beneath*, *believe*), *de-* (*depend*, *decide*) and *re-* (*remember*, *return*), and to some words with weakened *e-* (*enough*), though it is perhaps open to question whether pronunciations such as *effect* /əˈfekt/, *except* /əkˈsept/ (homophonous with *affect*, *accept*) properly fall within RP. In the same way, I think it is probably best to regard /əd/ for the allomorph of *-ed* after /t, d/ and /əz/ for the allomorph of *-es* after sibilants as being outside RP, where /ɪd/ and /ɪz/ are used respectively, so keeping *chatted*, *founded*, *dances* and *sauces–sources* always distinct from *chattered*, *foundered*, *dancers*, and *saucers* (which latter do have /-əd, -əz/).

There are many other words exhibiting lexical-incidental variability in RP, as can be confirmed by analysis of the multiplicity of pronunciations recorded in *EPD* (particularly if successive editions are compared). The above are no more than a sample.

Finally it must be admitted that RP is often to be identified by intangibles of rhythm, voice quality, and so on, as much as by the segmental characteristics we have been able to pin down here.

4.1.9 Near-RP

The term **Near-RP** refers to any accent which, while not falling within the definition of RP, nevertheless includes very little in the way of regionalisms which would enable the provenance of the speaker to be localized within England (or even as Australian, New Zealand, or South African). While such an accent may suggest some degree of 'provincialism' ('colonialism') or 'commonness' to those upper-class people who think in such terms, by the generality of the population it will be perceived as indeed 'educated', 'well-spoken', 'middle-class'.

Drawing a boundary line between RP and Near-RP is in many ways a subjective and contentious task. English phoneticians have not infrequently been in implicit disagreement over the problem of the circumscription of RP. Successive versions of the preliminary 'Explanations' of *EPD* reflect Jones's, and later Gimson's, changing views. Windsor Lewis (mimeo) has conveniently summarized a number of writers' views over the last century; he himself argues for a term **General British** to refer to a range of accents which apparently would include my mainstream RP, adoptive RP, and to a considerable extent Near-RP, while excluding U-RP ('any British pronunciations which are associated specifically and only with ... any socially conspicuous background', Windsor Lewis 1972: xiv).

My own opinion, for what it is worth, suggests the following as representative of widespread usages falling outside RP but possibly within one variety or another of Near-RP.

Systemic
1. The absence of any of the phonemic oppositions found in RP. In particular one might mention that between /ʌ/ and /ə/, absent or tenuous in much midlands, northern and Welsh Near-RP (see below, 4.4.2, 5.1.3); and that between /æ/ and /ɑː/, which is tenuous in some west-of-England Near-RP.
2. The presence of any phonemic opposition not found in RP. In

particular, there is the Londonism of an /ɒʊ/ in opposition to the vowel of GOAT (whether we symbolize this latter as /əʊ/ or as /ʌʊ/ is immaterial) – so that *roller* does not rhyme with *polar* (4.2.6 below). Another Londonism makes *pause* and *paws* heterophonous (4.2.5 below). In some other parts of the country a phoneme /ʊ/ is used where RP has the sequence /juː/ and also in some other words, so that for instance *threw* [θrʊ] may be different from *through* [θruː].
3. Neutralization of phonemic oppositions in particular environments, where this does not happen in RP. For example, failure to preserve the three-way opposition /iː–ɪə–ɪ/ before final /l/ (*reel–real–rill*).

Phonotactic distribution
4. Near-RP spoken by those from localities where the local accent is rhotic may, not surprisingly, contain occasional phonetically realized /r/s in the critical non-prevocalic environments. More importantly, Near-RP of this sort may be analysed as including phonological /r/ in NEAR, SQUARE, START, NORTH, FORCE, CURE and *lett*ER, even though the phonetic realization of this underlying /r/ may be [ə], additional vowel length, or zero. In RP *farther* and *father* are perfect homophones: a distinction such as ['fɑəðə] vs. ['fɑːðə] is not RP, but may be heard in the Near-RP of the west of England. The same applies to *spar* vs. *spa*, *nor* vs. *gnaw*, *odour* vs. *soda* and *western* vs. *Weston*. Similarly, *modern* and *trodden* usually form perfect rhymes in RP; but in this type of Near-RP they have [-ɒdən] and [-ɒdn̩] respectively.
5. Relaxation of the constraints against long vowels of part-systems B or C in the environment of a following /r/ within a morpheme, e.g. ['siːr-] in *serious*, ['kjuːr- ~ 'kɪur-] in *curious*, as well as ['paɪr-] in *pirate*, etc., as discussed in 4.1.6 above.
6. Marked degrees of Breaking before a morpheme-final or preconsonantal /l/, as [fiːəl ~ fɪəl] *feel*, [seɪəl] *sale*, [maɪəl] *mile*, [ɔɪəl] *oil*; particularly when this applies word-internally before a suffix beginning with a vowel, as ['fiːəlɪŋ ~ 'fɪəlɪŋ] *feeling*, ['peɪələ] *paler*.
7. Yod Dropping (4.2.13 below) as exemplified variously by [nuː] *new*, [duːk] *duke*, [ɪg'zekətɪv] *executive*, [mænə'f-] *manufacture*.
8. Exclusion of /ɪ, ʊ/ from prevocalic environments, so that the second syllable of *various* or *maniac* is identified as containing the /iː/ of FLEECE rather than the /ɪ/ of KIT. (Since, however, the opposi-

tion between /iː/ and /ɪ/ is neutralized in this environment, it may be unrealistic to make any such identification of a short close [i] in such words.) A pronunciation which leads to the identification of the *happy* vowel with that of FLEECE would traditionally not have been considered to fall within RP, so that ['sɪti] for *city*, ['kɒfi] for *coffee* etc. would be taken as characteristic only of Near-RP or non-RP. Recently, however, such forms have begun to be heard from speakers who on all other grounds would be considered as speaking RP. (See 4.1.7 above.)

Phonetic realization
9. Diphthong shifting (vol. 1, 3.4.2 and 4.2.4 below), including in particular noticeably diphthongal realizations of the vowels of FLEECE and GOOSE, as [wɪip] *weep*, [θrɜ̈iː] *three*, [fɜ̈uːd ~ fɜ̈ːd] *food*; wide diphthongs for FACE and GOAT, [ëɪ ~ ʌɪ] and [ʌʊ ~ ɔʊ] respectively; and a fronter starting-point for the vowel of MOUTH than for that of PRICE, e.g. [aʊ ~ æʊ] but [ɑɪ].
10. Diphthongal [ɔə] in THOUGHT words or, conversely, monophthongal [ɛː] in intonationally prominent monosyllabic SQUARE words, e.g. [lɔə] *law*, [nɒt ˈfɛː] *not fair*, as mentioned in 4.1.7 above.
11. Frequent vocalization of /l/ in non-prevocalic environments, as [bɛʊt] *belt*, [fɔʊs] *false*, ['nʌkʊ] *knuckle*. (See vol. 1, 3.4.4 and 4.2.7 below.)
12. Frequent voiced or glottal realizations of /t/, as ['brɪɾɪʃ] *British*, [geʔ ˈʌp] *get up*. Occasional T Voicing, and Glottalling in certain preconsonantal environments, are found in RP; extensive intervocalic T Voicing and prevocalic Glottalling are not. (See vol. 1, 3.4.5 and 4.2.10 below.)
13. Allophonic lengthening of short vowels when intonationally prominent, as *What do you think of* [ðɪːs]? *The floor was all* [weːt]. Jones (1956: §430) comments on this as a characteristic of 'south-eastern English' and by implication excludes it from RP.

Lexical incidence
14. Use of /ə/ rather than /ɪ/ in suffixes such as *-ed*, *-es*, leading to categorical homophony of pairs such as *tended–tendered*, *offices–officers* (unless there is a duration distinction which could be explained as dependent on an underlying /r/ in the second of each pair, an equally non-RP characteristic). Variable homophony, as

opposed to categorical homophony, may perhaps be regarded as falling within RP. When we combine this with point 8 above, we see that pairs such as *emptied* and *tempted* typically rhyme in RP but not in many kinds of Near-RP or non-RP.

15. Use of /ə/ rather than /ɪ/ in suffixes such as *-age, -in*, as *village* /'vɪlədʒ/, *cabin* /'kæbən/. This includes forms such as ['mɑːtn̩] *Martin*, ['sætn̩] *satin* (RP only ['mɑːtɪn], ['sætɪn]).

16. Failure to make the distinction between verb and noun in words like *experiment, implement*. In RP the verb ends [-ment], the noun [-mənt].

17. Dissimilation of the traditional /gz/ in words such as *exist, examine, exhaust*, to /kz/, usually with preglottalization.

18. The use of the /æ/ of TRAP (however realized phonetically) rather than the /ɑː/ of PALM(−START) in words of the standard lexical set BATH. Lord Curzon's eccentricity in this respect (Nicolson 1927: ch. 8) was evidently an aristocratic idiosyncrasy. Nowadays this is a characteristic of the Near-RP (and the non-RP) of the midlands and north of England. The same applies to the use of /ɒ/ rather than /ʌ/ in *one, once*; and to the use of /ɒ/ rather than /ə/ in unstressed *con-*, as *consider, condition, computer*.

19. Finally, there is the limitless mass of non-standard pronunciations of individual lexical items, ranging from extremely widespread forms such as /'kɒntrɪbjuːt/ *contribute* and /'dɪstrɪbjuːt/ *distribute* (which have now gained a foothold in *EPD*) through other pronunciations resulting from first encountering a word in writing rather than in speech (e.g. /ɪn'ventərɪ/ *inventory*, /'ætrəfaɪ/ *atrophy* – see vol. 1, 1.4.5) down to personal idiosyncrasies (why do I say /'kɔɪn/ for *coin* when everyone else says /kɔɪn/?).

Near-RP shades off into the unquestionably non-RP, accents which are usually localizable, at least in broad terms, and which are discussed in the rest of this chapter, and indeed in the rest of this volume. Characteristics which are certainly not RP nor even Near-RP include, for instance, the absence of an /ʌ–ʊ/ opposition so that *cut* rhymes with *put* (4.4.2 below); general H Dropping, e.g. [ed] *head* (vol. 1, 3.4.1); T Glottalling in the environment of a following syllabic, as ['bʌʔə] *butter*, ['bɒʔl̩] *bottle* (vol. 1, 3.4.5); and non-standard lexical incidence ranging from /'daɪmənd/ *diamond* via the trade unionists' /stə'tjuːtərɪ/ *statutory* and /ɪlek'tɔːrəl/ *electoral* down to idiosyncratic or personal malapropisms like /'vɜːtəsaɪl/ *versatile*.

It is open to question whether it is desirable or possible to draw firm lines of demarcation between RP, Near-RP, and non-RP. The justification for my proposing the term 'Near-RP' is that it conveniently refers to a group of accent types which are clearly 'educated' and situated well away from the lower end of the socio-economic scale, while differing to some noticeable degree from what we recognize as RP. Amongst other advantages, it lets us say that the most prestigious indigenous accents of Australia, New Zealand, and South Africa are not RP (which to an Englishman they clearly are not) but rather the local varieties of Near-RP.

Some people deny that RP exists. This seems to me like denying that the colour red exists. We may have difficulty in circumscribing it, in deciding whether particular shades verging on pink or orange count as 'red', 'near-red', or 'non-red'; the human race disagrees on what to call red, some preferring *rosso* or *krasnyj*, *pupa* or *ruĝa* rather than our *red*; but we all agree in identifying fresh blood as typically having this colour, and almost all have a name for it (Berlin & Kay 1969). Similarly we may hesitate about a particular person's speech which might or might not be 'RP' or 'Near-RP'; we may prefer to call it 'BBC English', 'southern British Standard', 'General British', 'a la-di-da accent' or even 'Standard English', and define it more narrowly or more widely than I have done; but anyone who has grown up in England knows it when he hears a typical instance of it.

4.2 London

4.2.1 Introduction

In view of its position in England as the political capital and the largest city, it is not surprising that London is also its linguistic centre of gravity. Not only did its courtly and upper-class speech lay the historical basis for Standard English and – in many respects – for RP, but its working-class accent is today the most influential source of phonological innovation in England and perhaps in the whole English-speaking world.

The traditional working-class dialect of London is known, like

its speaker, by the name **Cockney**. This dialect is associated particularly with the innermost suburbs of east London, the East End –
Bethnal Green, Stepney, Mile End, Hackney, Whitechapel, Shore-
ditch, Poplar, Bow – and a true Cockney is supposed to be someone
born within the sound of Bow Bells. As a dialect, Cockney is
characterized by its own special vocabulary and usages, including
an extensive development of rhyming slang. Many of these have
spread as slang or colloquialisms into other varieties of English,
e.g. *to be on one's tod, to have a butcher's, a yobbo.*

But it is with the pronunciation of Cockney that we are concerned. It constitutes the basilectal end of the London accent
continuum, the broadest form of London local accent. Its most
striking phonetic characteristics are undoubtedly the noticeably
shifted diphthongs and the extensive use of the glottal stop, as
['waɪʔə] *waiter.*

Most working-class Londoners, though, were not born in the
East End and do not qualify as 'true Cockneys' according to the
definition quoted. For centuries London has had another focus of
working-class life south of the river in Bermondsey, Southwark
/'sʌðək/, and Walworth. By the twentieth century London had
become a vast city 60 kilometres across, and all its thirty-two
boroughs have a socially mixed population. Throughout, the
working-class accent is one which shares the general characteristics
of Cockney. We shall refer to this type of accent as **popular
London**. It is very slightly closer to RP than the broadest Cockney.

Asked for examples of the differences between Cockney and an
ordinary working-class London accent – popular London – people
often point to the pronunciation of MOUTH words. Genuine
Cockney, it is felt, uses a monophthong, [mæːf ~ maːf]. Cockneys
go 'aht and abaht'. But popular London speech has a diphthong,
[mæʊf ~ mæʊθ] etc. (This question is discussed further below,
4.2.4.) Another point of difference is believed to be the glottalling of
fricatives, e.g. ['saɪʔə] *safer*, which may well be confined to Cockney
(4.2.11 below).

Several special subvarieties may be detected within popular
London speech. One is 'refayned' accent, a generally unsuccessful
attempt to sound as if one belonged to a higher social class than one
really does, notably by not only avoiding Diphthong Shifting
(4.2.4) but by going too far in the other direction. This type of

accent is nowadays perhaps not so often encountered as it used to be. Another subvariety is Jewish, characterized (at least in its stereotype) by laminal rather than apical realization of /t, d/ and by the use of a velarized labio-dental approximant, a dark [ʋ], for /r/; also, often, by the use of [-ŋg-] in *singer*, etc. (non-NG coalescing, vol. 1, 3.1.2). It is not known whether there are actual geographical differences in pronunciation within London, other than the Cockney vs. popular dimension already discussed and except insofar as different parts of Greater London have populations of differing social-class consistency. Londoners do sometimes claim to be able to recognize such local differences.

Middle-class speakers typically use an accent closer to RP than popular London. But the vast majority of such speakers nevertheless have some regional characteristics. This kind of accent might be referred to as London (or, more generally, south-eastern) Regional Standard. Points of difference between it and RP might typically include greater allophonic variation in the GOOSE vowel (*two* compared with *tool*) and the GOAT vowel (*go* compared with *goal*), less Smoothing in words such as *fire* and *power*, *being* and *doing*, a certain amount of T Glottalling in prevocalic environments, and a readiness to use [i] rather than [ɪ] in *happy* words. So London Regional Standard might have [tʉː, tuːɫ, gɜʊ, gʌ-oɫ, fɑ+ɪə ~ fa-ɪə, pa-ɤə ~ pɑ+ɤə, 'brɪɪŋ, 'dʉʉɪŋ, ðæʔ'ɪz, 'hæpi], as against RP [tuː, tuːɫ, gɜʊ, gɜʊɫ, fa-ːə, pɑ+ːə, 'brɪŋ, 'dʊɪŋ, ðæt 'ɪz, 'hæpɪ].

It must be remembered that labels such as 'popular London', 'London Regional Standard' do not refer to entities we can reify but to areas along a continuum stretching from broad Cockney (itself something of an abstraction) to RP.

4.2.2 The vowel system

The strong vowel system of London English can be represented as shown in (175). (The phonemic symbols chosen reflect speech varieties intermediate between RP and Cockney.)

(175)

ɪ		ʊ		ii			ʉː			iə		(uə)
e				ʌɪ	ɔɪ		ʌʊ	ɔː		eə	ɜː	ɔə
æ	ʌ	ɒ			ɑɪ		æʊ	ɒʊ		ɑː		

In this vowel system the oppositions /ɔə–oː/ and /ʌʊ–ɒʊ/ disappear as one approaches RP. The actual realization of most items varies considerably among different sectors of the population and, to a lesser extent, in different phonological environments; this is discussed below. Lexical incidence is as shown in (176).

(176)

KIT	ɪ	FLEECE	ii	NEAR	iə
DRESS	e	FACE	ʌɪ	SQUARE	eə
TRAP	æ	PALM	ɑː	START	ɑː
LOT	ɒ	THOUGHT	oː, ɔə[1]	NORTH	oː, ɔə[1]
STRUT	ʌ	GOAT	ʌʊ	FORCE	oː, ɔə[1]
FOOT	ʊ	GOOSE	ʉː	CURE	ʊə[2]
BATH	ɑː	MOUTH	æʊ	NURSE	ɜː
CLOTH	ɒ[3]	PRICE	ɑɪ	*lett*ER	ə
*happ*Y	ii[4]	VOICE	ɔɪ	*comm*A	ə

[1] depending on phonetic context; see below.
[2] otherwise /ʉːə/, or /oː ~ ɔə/; see below.
[3] old-fashioned /oː/.
[4] see below.

The vowel system of London English is thus almost isomorphic with that of RP, not only *qua* system but also as regards lexical incidence. Systemically, the important point of difference is the presence in most kinds of London English of the additional phonemes /ɔə/ (as a consequence of the THOUGHT Split, discussed below, 4.2.5) and /ɒʊ/ (resulting from the GOAT Split, 4.2.6 below). In both cases we see the phonologization of what was previously a matter of allophonic variation, in which a precipitating factor is L Vocalization. Thus London speech usually has minimal pairs such as *bored*, with /ɔə/, vs. *board*, with /oː/; in RP, it will be recalled, all THOUGHT–NORTH–FORCE words (by definition) have /ɔː/, so that *bored* = *board*. And in London speech *polar*, with /ʌʊ/, typically fails to rhyme with *roller*, with /ɒʊ/, while in RP all GOAT words have /əʊ/ and these words constitute a perfect rhyme. London speech also tends to exhibit various pre-/l/ vowel neutralizations.

Distributionally, the principal difference stems from the fact that the *happ*Y vowel is to be equated with that of FLEECE in the local accent of London, but with that of KIT in RP; though, as we have seen, RP may be beginning to change in this respect.

In lexical incidence, there are various traditional Cockney forms such as /əˈgɪn/ *again*, /ˈɪndʒɪn/ *engine*, /gɪt/ *get*, /ef/ *if*, /ketʃ/ *catch*;

but the standard-incidence forms /ə'gʌɪn, 'endʒɪn, get, ɪf, kætʃ/ all occur as alternatives in working-class London speech and are of course usual in middle-class speech. Other traditional oddities of lexical incidence may well have died out, such as the /æ/ forms of *celery, very,* and *yellow* recorded by Matthews (1938: 170) but not found by Sivertsen (1960: 70). Others live on even in middle-class speech, as /θɹi'etə/ *theatre* (RP /'θɪətə/), *only* with no /l/.

4.2.3 Monophthongs and centring diphthongs

The phonetic qualities of London short vowels do not differ greatly from those found in RP. That of KIT may be somewhat more central at times, [ɪ], and those of TRAP and LOT somewhat less open, [ɛ] and [ɔ] respectively. The most striking difference here occurs in the quality of STRUT, which in a London accent is a front vowel ranging from a fronted [ɐ+] to a quality like that of cardinal 4, [a], thus [lav] *love,* (Cockney) [dʒamʔ't⁵apʰ] *jumped up.*

In the environment of a following voiced consonant, particularly /d/, noticeably closer, tense allophones are often encountered, with a palatal offglide, thus [beⁱd] *bed,* [bɛːⁱd] *bad.* The last form also exemplifies the considerable lengthening which characterizes London /æ/ in such environments.

In final position, very open realizations of /ə/ may be encountered in broad Cockney: ['dɪnɐ] *dinner,* ['mærɐ] *marrow.*

The monophthongs /ɑː/ and /ɜː/, in START–BATH–PALM and NURSE respectively, are often much the same in London speech as in RP. The former has a fully back variant, qualitatively equivalent to cardinal 5, which Beaken (1971) claims characterizes 'vigorous, informal' Cockney. The NURSE vowel, /ɜː/, is on occasions somewhat fronted and/or lightly rounded, giving Cockney variants such as [ɜ+ː], [œ̈ː].

The centring diphthongs are /ɪə/ in NEAR, /eə/ in SQUARE, /ɔə/ in some THOUGHT–NORTH–FORCE words (see below, 4.2.5), and the recessive /ʊə/ in CURE, increasingly merged with /oː ~ ɔə/. Phonetically, /ɪə/ has a noticeably closer starting-point in popular London speech than in RP, almost [iə]. The /æʊ/ of MOUTH is also a centring diphthong in broad Cockney, as discussed below, 4.2.4. All of these diphthongs have monophthongal variants, of the types [ɪː, ɛː, ɔː, ʊː, æː]. No rigid rules can be given for the distribution of monophthongal and diphthongal variants, though the tendency seems to be for the monophthongal variants to be commonest within the utterance, but the diphthongal realizations in utterance-final position, or where the syllable in question is otherwise prominent. Triphthongal realizations also occur, and are perceived as very strongly Cockney; they too are restricted to sentence-final position, as in the following examples (from Beaken 1971): ['œʊvr'ɪjɐ] *over here*, ['aʔpstɛjəz] *upstairs*, ['flɔ̣ːʊ̆əz] *floors*, ['kləinɪʔ 'æjəʔ] *clean it out*.

4.2.4 The Diphthong Shift

The FLEECE and GOOSE vowels tend to be diphthongal in London: [ɪi ~ əi] and [ʊʉ ~ əʉ]. The precise quality may vary considerably, and along more than one dimension of variation. The starting-point for FLEECE is typically rather open, anything from [ɪ̞] in popular London to [ə] or even [ɐ] in Cockney. Sometimes this first element has been described as less prominent than the second element [i], so that the diphthong is a crescendo one ('rising'), thus ['bə̆ibə̆i'sə̆iː] *BBC*. It seems to me, though, that diminuendo ('falling') diphthongs are the norm in Cockney, thus ['bəibəi'səːi]. The distinction between the two types is not always at all easily perceptible. In the south-eastern suburbs Bowyer (1973) found no opener starting-point than [ɪ̞] (cf. the common RP type with a starting-point [ɪ̝]); he regards opener starting-points, e.g. [ə], as typical of 'genuine' East End Cockney as distinct from suburban working-class popular London. The earliest reference to this [əi] diphthong appears to be Shaw's representation of the alphabet in Cockney as 'I, Ber-ee, Ser-ee, Der-ee, Er-ee ...'. I have chosen to use the notation /ɪi/ for this phoneme in London speech in general: this must stand for qualities ranging phonetically from Cockney [əi] to elocuted [iː].

In a similar way, the starting-point for the GOOSE diphthong ranges from [ʊ] to [ə], the latter being the most Cockney-flavoured. Here, too, the diphthong may sometimes perhaps be a crescendo one. The endpoint is characteristically noticeably less back than the RP norm, being centralized, [ü], or central, [ʉ]. Typical Cockney qualities are thus [ə̆ʉ, əü], while popular London has qualities such as [ɪü, ə̣ü, ʊ̜ü]. There are also monophthongal varieties such as [ʉː], perhaps with little lip rounding, [ɨː], and [ʊː]. Hudson & Holloway

(1977) found that the environment of a following nasal, as *soon*, clearly favoured a monophthongal realization; diphthongal realizations were favoured by a following lenis consonant, as *move*, or the environment __ # C, as *two people*, and overwhelmingly by the environment __ # V, as *two apples*. They found the commonest diphthongal realization to be [ʊü], though working-class boys, and to some extent working-class girls, used what they write as [ʏu] instead; the commonest monophthongs were [u:] (working-class) and [ü:] (middle-class). On the other hand Bowyer (1973), who studied only isolated words elicited by questionnaire, reports no monophthongs at all for the GOOSE words *boo* and *boot*. Sivertsen regards monophthongs as typical only of unstressed non-final syllables, commenting, 'diphthongization is not equally strong with all speakers, but it seems to be characteristic of an unguarded style of speech' (1960: 81). She also emphasizes the crescendo nature of this diphthong in the Bethnal Green Cockney she studied, and claims that when lengthened it is never *[ə:ü], only [ɜ̈ü:]; the monophthongal variant, furthermore, is (as she points out) qualitatively identical with the endpoint rather than the starting-point of the diphthong. I have, however, certainly myself heard a lengthened diphthong of the [ə:ü] type.

The notation I have chosen for London GOOSE is /ʉ:/. As with /ɪi/, though, the phonemic notation /ʉ:/ covers a considerable range of actual phonetic realizations. In particular, the phonetic range of Cockney /ʉ:/ overlaps with that of RP /əʊ/. Hence Cockney *soup* may sound identical to RP *soap* when both are pronounced [səʊp] (Gimson 1980: §7.25).

The vowel of London FACE is /ʌɪ/. (In this notation the symbol /ʌ/ must be interpreted in an elastic way as reflecting the quality of STRUT, a central or front vowel in London speech.) The corresponding RP vowel is /eɪ/; a London accent has an opener and more central first element, so that the diphthong ranges from popular London [ɛɪ] or [ʌɪ] (= [ɜ̈ɪ, ɐɪ]) to broad Cockney [æɪ ~ aɪ]. The social significance attached to the realization given to this vowel was the inspiration of the song in *My Fair Lady* where Eliza Doolittle succeeds in replacing her stigmatized native *The r*[aɪ]*n in Sp*[aɪ]*n st*[aɪ]*s m*[aɪ]*nly in the pl*[aɪ]*n* with the elegant *r*[eɪ]*n in Sp*[eɪ]*n*. Again, there is a phonetic overlap with RP here: Cockney /ʌɪ/ overlaps with RP /aɪ/, so that Cockney *paint* may sound identical to RP *pint*.

In PRICE the London vowel tends to be backer than that of RP: I write it /ɑɪ/, as against RP /aɪ/. The phonetic quality of the first element of the diphthong characteristically ranges from central to fully back, [ɑ+] to [ɑ]; in more vigorous, 'dialectal' Cockney it may also be rounded, [ɒ]. In Cockney, too, the second element may be reduced or absent (with compensatory lengthening of the first element), so that we have variants such as [ɑ+ə, ɑ+:]. This means that pairs such as *laugh–life*, *Barton–biting* may become homophones: [lɑːf], ['bɑːʔn̩]. But this neutralization is an optional, recoverable one.

The starting-point of the CHOICE diphthong is characteristically rather closer in London speech than in RP: [ɔɪ ~ oɪ].

The shifts in the starting-points of these various fronting-closing diphthongs are presumably related, perhaps as a push-chain: as the FACE vowel opened to [ʌɪ], PRICE had to back to [ɑɪ], whereupon CHOICE closed to [oɪ] to maintain the perceptual distance between them. And the reason for the first change, [eɪ] to [ʌɪ] in FACE, may have been the diphthonging of FLEECE to [ɪi ~ əi]. The outcome is a counter-clockwise shift in the starting-points of the fronting-closing diphthongs, which we may refer to briefly as the Diphthong Shift (as discussed in volume 1, 3.4.2). It has gone further in broad Cockney than in general popular London speech. We can diagram it (somewhat simplified) as (177).

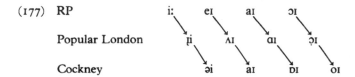

(177) RP   iː   eɪ   aɪ   ɔɪ

    Popular London   ɪi   ʌɪ   ɑɪ   ɔɪ

    Cockney   əi   aɪ   ɒɪ   oɪ

The backing-closing diphthongs are also shifted in London speech. We have already discussed GOOSE. With GOAT the starting-point is shifted opener and possibly fronter; with MOUTH it is shifted fronter and possibly closer, as well as reducing or even losing its second element. The overall effect is thus a kind of clockwise shift of starting-points.

The vowel in Cockney GOAT typically starts in the area of London STRUT, [æ ~ ɐ], which we write [ʌ] for convenience. The endpoint may be [ʊ], but more commonly is rather opener and/or lacking any lip rounding, thus being a kind of centralized [ÿ] (henceforward in this discussion written simply [ʏ]). There is also a monophthongal variety, a frontish [ʌː], reflected by eye-dialect spellings such as 'nah' or 'nuh' *no*. And there is also a diphthongal variant gliding to a front rounded endpoint, [ʌø] or [œ̈ø]; this has a flavour of 'refined' Cockney, and Beaken (1971) found it to be used by girls only. In non-prominent environments a monophthongal [œ̈] is sometimes encountered. The broadest Cockney variant approaches [aʊ]. All of these variants are covered by our phonemic symbol /ʌʊ/, thus /ˈfʌʊn ˈ(h)ʌʊm/ *phone home* etc. The question of the splitting off of /ɒʊ/ (the GOAT Split) is discussed below, 4.2.6.

The MOUTH vowel is one which is widely believed to constitute a touchstone for distinguishing between 'true Cockney' and popular London. In the former it is supposed to be a monophthong of the type [æː], in the latter a closing-backing diphthong of the type [æʊ] (or without lip rounding, [æɤ]). Thus the phrase *half a pound* might be pronounced [ˈɑːf ə ˈpæːn] in Cockney, [ˈhɑːf ə ˈpæʊnd] in popular London, and of course [ˈhɑːf ə ˈpa-ʊnd] in RP. But the dividing-line between Cockney and other forms of popular London speech is not as sharp as this implies; and there are several other variants current. One is a centring diphthong, [æə], another is an opener monophthong, [aː]. Both of these are working-class variants. And middle-class Londoners on the fringe of RP may use a particularly back starting-point, [aʊ], in order to be sure of avoiding the vulgar [æʊ]. Elocutionists, after all, are supposed to concentrate extensively on the phrase *How now, brown cow?* with its four MOUTH words. Hudson & Holloway (1977) found diphthongs commoner than monophthongs in MOUTH for all their social groups, usually [æɤ] but with middle-class boys [ɑ+ʊ]; among those who used monophthongs, [æː] was restricted to working-class boys while [aː] was used to some extent by all other groups. But since their different social groups were also drawn from different parts of the London area, this difference may be in reality geographical rather than social–sexual. Nevertheless, one recurrently finds monophthongal variants characterized as 'rough' or 'coarse'; Sivertsen (1960, 66) ascribes it only to 'men and boys of a less polished type'.

It is noteworthy that in Cockney the MOUTH vowel, ending as it does in a phonetically mid or open quality, [æː ~ æə], is subject to intrusive /r/ (vol. 1, 3.2.3). It can be heard in phrases such as [æːr ˈɒʊd ə jəʉ] *How old are you?*, [ˈnæər ɪiz ˈdanɪʔ] *Now he's done it.*

Thus the shift in the starting-points of the back-closing diphthongs in London speech is on the whole clockwise, as shown in (178).

(178) RP   αʊ˙   əʊ   u:

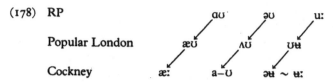

    Popular London   æʊ   ʌʊ   ʊɵ

    Cockney   æ: a–ʊ   ɘɵ ~ ɵ:

In particular, the starting-point of PRICE is very considerably backer than that of MOUTH, [αɪ] etc. vs. [æʊ] etc., whereas in RP it is fronter or perhaps identical, but definitely not backer, as shown in (179).

(179) RP   αɪ   αʊ

    Popular London   æʊ   αɪ

We may refer to this phonetic development as the PRICE–MOUTH Crossover – a by-product of the Diphthong Shift.

4.2.5 The THOUGHT Split

The vowel of THOUGHT (merged of course with NORTH and FORCE) is closer in London speech than in perhaps any other accent of English. Qualities around cardinal 7, [o:], are by no means unusual. It is presumably London speech which is responsible for the drift of RP THOUGHT to a closer quality which has taken place over the past fifty years. In broader popular London speech, however, the THOUGHT vowel is not merely rather close, it is also diphthongal. The direction of the diphthongal glide depends on phonological environment. In a checked syllable it is closing, [ǫʊ ~ oʊ], but in a free syllable centring, [ǫə ~ ɔwə]. Thus on the one hand we have [sǫʊs] *sauce–source*, [lǫʊd] *lord*, ['wǫʊʔə] *water*, and on the other [sǫə] *saw–sore–soar*, [lǫə] *law–lore*, [wǫə] *war–wore*. The foregoing represent broad Cockney pronunciations; in intermediate London accents the qualitative difference is characteristically not so great, though it is usually present in some degree, e.g. [lo:d] *lord*, [lɔ:] *law–lore*.

The distribution of the [o: ~ oʊ] and [ɔə] types is not, however, entirely complementary, at least on the phonetic level. There are two complicating factors: morpheme boundaries and L Vocalization. The latter leads to potential homophones such as *pause–Paul's*, *water–Walter*, and is discussed further below (4.2.7). The former is discussed directly.

We have seen that a word such as *bore* is pronounced with a variant of the [ɔə] type. This is retained when an inflectional ending is added. Thus *bored* is pronounced [bɔəd], and is distinct from *board*, which is [boːd]. Similarly, *pour* and its homophones *paw* and *pore* are [pɔə], and this opener quality is retained in *pours–paws–pores* [pɔəz]. But *pause* is [poːz]. Cockney has a dialectal form of *yours*, namely *yourn* [jɔən]; its pronunciation implies that it is perceived as containing a morpheme boundary (*my* : *mine* :: *your* : *yourn*), and it is phonetically distinct from *yawn* [joːn].

In middle-class speech this opposition typically remains at least potentially distinctive. Minimal pairs such as *bored–board* may be considered diagnostic for a 'modified London' accent as against non-regional RP, although the phonetic difference may be very slight, [ɔ̞ː] vs. [o̞ː]. Accordingly I have treated the opposition as established in London English and have recognized /ɔə/ and /oː/ as distinct phonemes. (The latter might equally be written /ou/ or /ɔu/.) The process leading to the establishment of distinctive /ɔə/ vs. /oː/ may be referred to as the THOUGHT Split.

It will be seen that the THOUGHT Split yields opposing phonetic qualities not unlike those which distinguish FORCE from NORTH–THOUGHT for old-fashioned RP, a contrast which we write as /ɔə/ vs. /ɔː/ (4.1.5 above). But it is important to note that the two possible types of opposition have rather different spreads of lexical incidence, as shown in (180):

(180)	Older RP, with /ɔə/ vs. /ɔː/	London, with /ɔə/ vs. /oː/
board, force, port . . . (1)	ɔə (ɔː)	oː
bored, four, pours . . . (2)	ɔə	ɔə
bawd, form, pause . . . (3)	ɔː	oː
draw, for, paws . . . (4)	ɔː	ɔə

– where (1) comprises FORCE words with the vowel in a checked syllable, (2) FORCE in a free syllable, (3) NORTH and THOUGHT checked, and (4) NORTH and THOUGHT free. The older-RP vowels in type (1) appear to have a somewhat inconsistent incidence.

4.2.6 The GOAT Split

The London GOAT vowel, as discussed above (4.2.4) is typically a wide closing diphthong. We have seen that the variability of the starting-point on the vertical dimension has social-class connotations (RP /əʊ/ vs. London /ʌʊ/), while within RP variability of the starting-point in the horizontal dimension has generational and other social connotations ([oʊ], [ɜʊ] and [ɛʊ] types). In London, however, horizontal variability of the starting-point must until recently have been allophonic but has now on the whole become phonemic. This allophonic variation involved the use of a diphthong of the [ɒʊ] type in the environment of a following dark /l/ (i.e. in the environments —lC and —l#), as *bold, roll, goal,* in what was once complementary distribution with the [ʌʊ] type in all other environments.

The complementarity of the distribution of [ɒʊ] and [ʌʊ] was upset by two factors: morphological regularization and L Vocalization.

The allophonic rule given above means that a verb such as *roll* is pronounced with [ɒʊ] when occurring in isolation or in final position. Its past tense is [rɒʊłd] *rolled,* its 3sg. pres. form [rɒʊłz] *rolls.* But in the *-ing* form the /l/ is clear (being prevocalic), so the appropriate diphthong is [ʌʊ], as [rʌʊlɪŋ] *rolling.* And when the base form itself occurs before a syntactically close-knit word beginning with a vowel, then it too takes the form [rʌʊl], as *roll up* ['rʌʊl 'ʌp]. Hence the morpheme *roll* comes to have two rather different phonetic forms, [rɒʊł] and [rʌʊl]. Verbs such as *roll* begin to seem irregular in their *ing*-form: [rɒʊł], but [rʌʊlɪŋ].

Now there are otherwise no English verbs with irregularities in the *-ing* form. So pressure begins to make itself felt to regularize this irregular verb. People start to use the pronunciation [rɒʊlɪŋ] instead of [rʌʊlɪŋ]. And since *roller* is obviously related to *roll* they start to pronounce it too with [ɒʊ] in place of the earlier [ʌʊ].

There are other words containing the sequence /ʌʊl/ where no such morphological considerations apply. The name *Roland* is one; it remains ['rʌʊlənd]. The word *polar* is another (its connection with *pole* being evidently not appreciated by Londoners): ['pʌʊlə]. Hence we now have a non-rhyming pair *roller–polar* ['rɒʊlə] vs. ['pʌʊlə]; compare also ['rɒʊlɪŋ] *rolling* vs. ['rʌʊlənd] *Roland.* In football, the player who stands in the *goal* [gɒʉɫ] is the *goalie*, now ['gɒʉli]; he no longer rhymes with *slowly* ['slʌʊli]. A straight minimal pair for many speakers is *wholly* ['hɒʉli] vs. *holy* ['hʌʊli]. A phoneme split has occurred, and we must recognize distinct phonemes /ɒʉ/ and /ʌʊ/ in London English. This accords with native speakers' intuitions.

The development of L Vocalization (see next section, 4.2.7) leads to further pairs such as *sole–soul* [sɒʉ] vs. *so–sew* [sʌʊ], *bowl* [bɒʉ] vs. *Bow* [bʌʊ], *shoulder* ['ʃɒʉdə] vs. *odour* ['ʌʊdə], while associated vowel neutralizations may make *doll* a homophone of *dole* [dɒʉ], compare *dough* [dʌʊ]. All this reinforces the phonemic nature of the new opposition and increases its functional load. It is by now well established in all kinds of London-flavoured accent, from broad Cockney to Near-RP.

The phonetic quality of /ɒʉ/ ranges from the common [ɒʉ ~ ɔo] type implied by the phonemic notation I use to a broad Cockney [aʏ] type (distinguished from /ʌʊ/ mainly by an opener first element) and a modified-regional [əo] type.

4.2.7 Vowel plus /l/

London /l/ is very susceptible to vocalization in syllable-final position (vol. 1, 3.4.4). Typical examples of this are [fɪo] *fill*, [fɪod] *field*, [foʊ] *fall*, ['pʰiːpo] *people*. The phonetic result of this development is typically a close back vocoid of the type [o, ʊ]. It seems most commonly to be rounded, although some investigators report unrounded [ɣ] after front vowels, as [fɪɣ] *fill*. L Vocalization is a sound change still very much in progress; speakers are by no means consistent. They fluctuate between using a lateral consonant and a vocoid; if they use a vocoid it may be unrounded or rounded; and they may restrict L Vocalization to preconsonantal and absolute-final environments, i.e. ___(#)C (*fall down*) and ___|| (*fall.*), or they may extend it to word-final prevocalic environments, ___ # V (*fall off*). Beaken (1971) even found children vocalizing /l/ before a word-internal morpheme boundary plus vowel, as ['foʊɪn] *falling*; but this has not yet been observed in adult speech, where internal linking /l/ remains, thus ['foʊlɪn ~ 'foːlɪŋ].

The vocalization of syllabic [ɫ], i.e. the use of a monophthongal vocoid to realize /əl/, seems to be particularly common: ['pʰiːpo] *people,* [ˈdʒʌgo] *juggle,* [ˈpɑːsoz] *parcels.* In a word-final prevocalic environment, the syllabic is perhaps more readily vocalized than the non-syllabic: [ˈsii ðə piipo ˈɒf] *see the people off.*

L Vocalization is overtly stigmatized, being disapproved of by the speech-conscious. It is also socially sensitive. In their study of the speech of young adolescents, Hudson & Holloway (1977) found that in the environment __C# (*milk, pulse* etc.) the lateral consonant variant [ɬ] was associated particularly with middle-class girls, and the vocoid variants [ʊ] etc. with working-class children in general. Bowyer (1973) found vocoid variants usual in the speech of his two groups of informants ranked as 'broadest' (furthest from RP), occasional in the speech of the third-broadest group, and entirely absent from the speech of the least broad (most RP-like) group; there was a highly significant correlation between these groupings and occupational class. In his broader groups Bowyer also encountered occasional instances of clear [l] in the vocalizing environment; he correctly interprets these as 'hyper-reaction against the use of vocoid allophones'.

In broad Cockney, and to some extent in general popular London speech, a vocalized /l/ is entirely absorbed by a preceding /oː/: i.e. *salt* and *sort* become homophones, and likewise *fault–fought–fort, pause–Paul's, Morden–Malden, water–Walter* (someone from the East End has told me that until he learnt to read and write he always thought his name was *Water*). Sometimes such pairs are kept apart, in more deliberate speech at least, by a kind of length difference: [ˈmɔʊdn̩] *Morden* vs. [ˈmɔʊːdn̩] *Malden*. It was, however, clearly wise of the railway authorities to ensure that the local stations in these adjacent parts of south London are named in such a way as to be distinct in more than just this respect: *Morden, Morden Road, Morden South,* but *New Malden, Malden Manor.*

We have seen that a preceding /ə/ is also fully absorbed into a vocalized /l/. The reflexes of earlier /əl/ and earlier /ɔː(l)/ (/oː(l)/) are thus phonetically similar or identical; speakers are usually ready to treat them as the same phoneme. Thus *awful* can best be regarded as containing two occurrences of the same vowel, /ˈoːfoː/ (compare its RP form [ˈɔːfl̩], phonemicized as /ˈɔːfəl/). The difference between *musical* and *music-hall,* in an H-Dropping broad Cockney, is thus nothing more than a matter of stress and perhaps syllable boundaries: /ˈmjʊʉzɪkoː/ vs. /ˈmjʊʉzɪkˌoː/.

With the remaining vowels a vocalized /l/ is not absorbed, but remains phonetically present as a back vocoid in such a way that /Vl/ and /V/ are kept distinct. But in the environment of a following non-prevocalic /l/ (whether or not actually vocalized) most vowels are subject to extensive allophonic effects and neutralizations. The precise range of these neutralizations is a matter of some uncertainty: different phoneticians have reported different sets of neutralizations. No doubt there are local geographical and generational differences within London; and there are certainly stylistic differences, inasmuch as many pairs which readily fall together in casual running speech can equally readily be distinguished by a speaker who directs his attention to the matter.

The clearest and best-established neutralizations are those of /ɪ ~ ɪi ~ iə/ and /ʊ ~ ʉ: ~ uə/. Thus *rill, reel* and *real* fall together in Cockney as [rɪʏ], *will* and *wheel* as [wɪʏ], *hills* and *heels* as [(h)ɪʏz]; while *full* and *fool* are [foʊ ~ fʊu] and may rhyme with *cruel* [krʊu]. Before clear (i.e. prevocalic) /l/ the neutralizations do not usually apply, thus ['sɪli] *silly* but ['sɪilɪn] *ceiling–sealing*, ['fʊli] *fully* but ['fʊulɪn] *fooling*.

A pair such as *fill* and *feel* are kept distinct when followed by a vowel in the next morpheme or word: *filling* [-ɪlɪ-] but *feeling* [-ɪilɪ-]. Followed by a consonant or pause, though, they usually neutralize: *fills = feels* [fɪʏz] etc. Similarly, *pulling* [-ʊlɪ-] is distinct from *pooling* [-ʊulɪ-], although *pulled* and *pooled* neutralize as [poʊd ~ pʊud]. (These latter do not rhyme with *mood* etc., which has a much less back vowel, [mʉʉd]; likewise *tool* [toʊ, tʊu] but *two–too* [tʊʉ].) It follows, then, that pairs such as *fill–feel, pull–pool* must be phonologically distinct in the lexicon. The neutralization of their vowels in non-prevocalic position is a synchronic process. Hence the underlying form is readily recoverable, and speakers can easily make a distinction even in the neutralizing environment if they are motivated to do so.

Between /ɪi/ and /iə/ matters are not so clear. There is only one common word which in RP ends in /ɪəl/, namely *real*. The RP distinction between *real* /rɪəl/ and *reel* /riːl/ seems to be quite foreign to any kind of London accent, including middle-class Modified Regional and Near-RP. Londoners studying phonetics and doing transcription exercises often transcribe *field* as /fɪəld/ (RP /fiːld/). But they are clear that it is distinct from *filled* /fɪld/.

In some broader types of Cockney the neutralization of /ʊ ~ ʉː ~ ʊə/ before non-prevocalic /l/ may also involve /oː/, so that *fall* becomes homophonous with *full* and *fool* [fɔo]. Beaken (1971), when investigating how well children could tell apart minimal pairs pronounced by other children in the same school in east London, had to drop the pair elicited by picture stimuli of a *ball* and a *bull*, since it became clear that these were not a minimal pair for /oː/ and /ʊ/ in the local Cockney but rather homophones.

Comparing the broadest East End Cockney with RP, we see that L Vocalization together with these close back vowel neutralizations and the absorption of vocalized /l/ into the vowel leads to the arrangement of incidence shown in (181).

(181)   Broad Cockney   RP

Broad Cockney		RP
	pours, bore	
ɔə	*wars, nor*	ɔː
	paws, bored	
	pause, board	
	Paul's, bald	ɔːl
oː	*pulls, full*	ʊl
	pools, fool	uːl
	ap*ples,* mid*dle*	l̩

The other pre-/l/ neutralization which all investigators agree on is that of /æ ~ ʌɪ ~ æʊ/ (the vowels of TRAP, FACE, and MOUTH respectively). Thus *Sal* and *sale* can be merged as [sæʏ], *fail* and *foul* as [fæʏ], and *Val, vale–veil* and *vowel* as [væʏ]. The typical pronunciation of *railway* is ['ræʊwʌɪ]. This neutralization too is restricted to non-prevocalic position: the stressed vowels of *palace*, *sailing*, and *howling* remain distinct. An exception to this principle reported by Sivertsen (1960) is that in broad Cockney there are certain prevocalic word-final occurrences of [æl] where [ʌɪl] might be expected: ['ælən'θʌndə] *hail and thunder*.

According to Sivertsen, /ɑː/ and /ɑɪ/ (the START–BATH–PALM and PRICE vowels) can also join in this neutralization. They may on the one hand neutralize with respect to one another, so that *snarl* and *smile* rhyme, both ending [-ɑɤ], and *Child's Hill* is in danger of being mistaken for *Charles Hill*; or they may go further into a fivefold neutralization with the one just mentioned, so that *pal*, *pale*, *foul*, *snarl* and *pile* all end in [-æɤ]. But these developments are evidently restricted to broad Cockney, not being found in London speech in general.

A neutralization discussed by Beaken (1971) and Bowyer (1973), but ignored by Sivertsen (1960), is that of /ɒ ~ ʊʊ ~ ʌ/ (LOT, GOAT as discussed above, and STRUT). This too is restricted to the environments /__l(#)C/ and /__l‖/. It leads to the possibility of *doll*, *dole*, and *dull* becoming homophonous as [dɒʊ] or [da‑ɤ]. My own impression is that the *doll–dole* neutralization is rather widespread in London, but that involving *dull* less so.

Where the /l/ is morpheme-final the underlying vowel is recoverable, as discussed above in connection with *feel* and *fill*: *d*[ɒ]*lling herself up*, *d*[ʊʊ]*ling it out*. Where the /l/ is followed by a consonant within the same morpheme it is not, and a Cockney speaker cannot predict from his own speech whether the RP vowel in words like *old*, *bolt*, *solve* is that of GOAT or that of LOT. In fact it is /əʊ/ for the first two but /ɒ/ for the third. Hypercorrection by Londoners may well be the origin of the much-commented-on rise of the pronunciations *s*[əʊ]*lve*, *inv*[əʊ]*lve*, *rev*[əʊ]*lving* by middle-class speakers, in place of the traditional (and still more usual) *s*[ɒ]*lve*, *inv*[ɒ]*lve*, *rev*[ɒ]*lving*.

One further possible neutralization in the environment of a following non-prevocalic /l/ is that of /e/ and /ɜː/ (DRESS, NURSE), so that *well* and *whirl* become homophonous as [wɛʊ]. The only investigator to mention this is Beaken (1971), whose speakers were East End children.

4.2.8 Further remarks on vowels

It is quite common for a vowel plus a following nasal (/m/, /n/ or /ŋ/) to coalesce into a nasalized vowel. Thus we may have [əʔ'ʌõ] *at home*, [wẽʔ] *went*, [ə'pãːʔ n̩ə 'ɑːf] *a pint and a half*, [θæ̃ʔ] *thank*, [əlõ'wæɪ] *a long way*, ['sʌmθĩk, 'sʌðĩk, 'sãɪŋʔ, 'sʌmĩk] *something* (a word with a wide range of pronunciations, the underlying representation being generally /'sʌmθɪŋk/). The precise conditions under which this coalescence may occur are not well understood. As can be seen, it often involves the loss of opposition of /Vm/ vs. /Vn/ vs. /Vŋ/. In these cases the resultant vowel nasality is phonologically relevant, inasmuch as it signals the presence of an underlying nasal consonant.

Another, weaker, type of nasality may occur in Cockney without phonological relevance. This nasality is merely a component of the characteristic local voice quality; it is found particularly in the environment of nasal consonants, but also sometimes elsewhere: [əðɛɪ 'lãɪʔ] *as they like*, ['pʌ̃ʔnə̃ɪ] *Putney*, ['fʌ̃nĩ 'ĩnĩʔ] *funny, isn't it?*, [wɛ̃n 'ʌp] *went up*. The word ['dʒẽʔõmə̃n] *gentleman* exemplifies both types of nasality; that on the first vowel may well be stronger than that on the second and third, and it alone has phonological relevance.

Reduction of /ʌʊ/ to [ə] in unstressed final syllables is characteristic, in London as elsewhere, of the broadest ('roughest') kind of speech only (vol. 1, 2.2.25). Examples are ['bærʌʊ ~ 'bærə] *barrow*, ['jelʌʊ ~ 'jelə] *yellow*, etc.; the [ə] in such words, being final, may well be as open as the starting-point of the diphthong with which it alternates, both being of the [ɐ] type. There are three other points of interest to be made in this connection.

First, the resultant [ə] qualifies as an environment triggering intrusive /r/: *tomat*[ər] *and cucumber production*. Secondly, it has been demonstrated by Beaken (1971) that young Cockney-speaking children acquire the unreduced /ʌʊ/ forms first, and only subsequently learn to reduce the diphthong to [ə] when appropriate. Thus the typical four-year-old's pronunciation of *barrow* is ['bæʊʌʊ], although the commonest adult Cockney form is ['bærə]. Thirdly, some instances of [ʌʊ → ə] reduction may be seen as a special case of a wider process of vowel reduction applying within the utterance in rapid speech, a process whereby both stressed and unstressed syllables may have their vowels subject to the following neutralizations (all examples from Beaken 1971):

/ɪ, iɪ, iə/	neutralize as	/ɪ/:	['nɪðə'ʃɒʔps] *near the shops*
/e, eə/	"	" /e/:	[we'wəiɑ] *where WE are*
/æ, ʌɪ, æʊ/	"	" /æ/:	[dæn'steəz] *downstairs*
/ə, ʌʊ, ɜ:/	"	" /ə/ or sometimes /ʌ/:	['fɑɪwəʔks] *fireworks*
			[dᶻʌʔ'nʌːʊ] *don't know*

/ɒ, ɔə/   "   " /ɒ/: [sˈfɔðɛn] *I was four then*
/ʊ,ɐː, oː/   "   " /ʊ/: [ˈwɔʔˈjʊævɪn] *what are* YOU *having?*
[ˈmetˢʊˈθɪŋz] *metal things*

We have also seen (4.2.4 above) that /aɪ/ and /ɑː/ may be neutralized as /ɑː/.

These reductions are found mainly in the less prominent syllables within the utterance. Even where the neutralizations do not take place, it would seem that the main phonetic distinction in Cockney between pairs such as *his–here's, merry–Mary, at–out, Polly–poorly* is one of duration.

The *happ*Y vowel in London speech is usually to be equated with the /ɪi/ of FLEECE. Phonetically it ranges from a diphthong [əi] in broad Cockney through [ɪi] to a monophthongal [i] in a middle-class local accent. Thus *coffee* may be [ˈkɒfəi], [ˈkɒfɪi] or [ˈkɒfi]. The last-mentioned is the careful pronunciation within a London accent, and so constitutes an important point of difference vis-à-vis traditional RP, which has [ˈkɒfɪ]. Yet pronunciations of the latter, RP, type are by no means uncommon among Londoners of all social classes, usually in alternation with the forms mentioned above; the [ɪ] forms are perhaps particularly characteristic of non-prominent positions in the utterance. This implies that the *happ*Y vowel, although underlyingly to be identified with that of FLEECE, is like it subject to potential neutralization with the KIT vowel, thus being often pronounced [ɪ] in running speech.

The vowel in the CLOTH words is usually /ɒ/, as in England in general. The traditional Cockney vowel, however, is /oː/. Sivertsen treats the choice between /ɒ/ and /oː/ as chronologically determined: 'in the older generation /ow/ [my /oː/, JCW] is the usual variant ... before the voiceless fricatives /f θ s/ ... however, the younger generation more frequently use forms with the simple peak /o/ [my /ɒ/, JCW] ..., and these are considered by the older generation, too, to be more correct' (1960: 78–9). While this description of the situation is in general justified, Beaken (1971) has shown that although younger children consistently use /ɒ/ older ones sometimes acquire the /oː/ forms later on as informal variants in certain words only (notably *off* and *gone*).

Listing the points of difference he found between the local accent of the London borough of Bromley and RP, Bowyer (1973) includes 'less reduction of /aɪə, aʊə/ than in RP'. In his test word *tyre* he found a preference for [ɑ+ɪə ~ a–ɪə] and an absence of the [a–:ə ~ a–:] he rightly considers typical of RP. Similarly in *tower* he recorded only triple-target vocoids of various timbres, and never double- or single-target [ɑːə ~ ɑː] (which are what Gimson describes for 'general RP' and 'advanced RP' respectively). Yet 'flahrz' is the Cockney-stereotype eye-dialect for *flowers*, and in her study of East End Cockney Sivertsen has plenty of examples such as ['tˢɑːəd] *tired*, ['lɑːənzɪz] *Lyons's*, ['wɑɑlɪs] *wireless*, ['dɑːrəi] *diary*, [flɛːə] *flower*. Indeed, it follows naturally from the neutralization possibilities discussed above that Smoothings such as these are likely in broad Cockney.

What we have here, then, is a process characteristic of the two ends of the social scale in London speech but not of the majority lying between. Pronunciations such as [fɑːə] *fire* and [pæːə] *power* are found in broad Cockney; pronunciations such as [faːə ~ faː] *fire* and [pɑːə ~ pɑː] (or the same with a fronter starting-point) belong to RP. The phonetic difference between the Cockney and the RP variants rests on the presence or otherwise of the PRICE–MOUTH Crossover. It would appear, though, that most Londoners use unsmoothed forms of the type [faɪə ~ faɪə], [pæʊə ~ pɑʊə].

The vowel [ə] is subject in Cockney to processes of epenthesis and deletion which are not well understood. The typical environment for Schwa Epenthesis is that between a non-initial consonant and a liquid, as ['lʌvələi] *lovely* ('loverly'), ['enərəi] *Henry*, ['æfə'leʔɪks] *athletics*, ['ʌmbə'relə] *umbrella*. These are well-known caricature Cockneyisms, and the corresponding [ə]-less forms are also common in Cockney speech. There are also various words whose pronunciation matches the structural description for Schwa Epenthesis but which are not, as far as I know, ever subject to it – e.g. /'ʌɪproː/ *April*, /'sʌnraɪz/ *sunrise*, /ɪm'brɔɪdə/ *embroider*. So it is not clear whether Schwa Epenthesis is a synchronic variable rule or merely a recessive historical relic.

In respect of Syllabic Consonant Formation, popular London speech seems, in comparison with RP, to tend towards rather more uncoalesced forms, thus typically ['stʌɪʃən] *station* (RP ['steɪʃn]), ['dʌzən] (['dʌzn]), ['sevən] (['sevn]), and often also ['pɑːdən] (RP ['pɑːdn]). Syllabic [l], as we have seen, is potentially subject to vocalization in non-prevocalic environments, merging with /oː/. In careful but London-accented speech the [l] may be restored after a

back vocoid, giving pronunciations of the type ['tˢeɪbʊl] *table* alongside broad Cockney ['tˢæɪboʊ], intermediate ['tˢʌɪbɫ ~ tˢʌɪboʊ] and
RP ['tʰeɪbɫ].

In rapid informal speech /ə/ and other unstressed vowels sometimes undergo coalescence with a preceding consonant. This seems
to happen above all in a syllable immediately preceding a stressed
syllable. The result is a kind of syllabic consonant. Examples (from
Beaken 1971) include [fˈɡɒʔ] *forgot*, [ʃ ˈsɛd] *she said*, [n̩ʔ ˈmaʔtʃ] *not
much*. Between fricatives or nasals, the vowel may disappear
entirely, leaving a long consonant as the realization of two now
contiguous consonants: ['pʰəisːəv] *pieces of*, [ɪnːˈnɜːʂrəi] *in the nur-
sery*. But the instances which strike my ear most forcefully, and
which as far as I can see are not mentioned by the writers on
Cockney, involve the deletion of /ə/ in the environment of a preceding glottalled /t/. Examples are ['bɛʔ æv əˈnʌvə wʌn] *better have
another one*, ['soʊ ə 'bɪʔ və 'dʒʌŋɡoː] *it's all a bit of a jungle*, ['bæːʔ 'æːr
əɡʌʊ] *about a(n) hour ago*, ['bæːʔ 'wɪɪk] *about a week*, ['ɡɛʔ 'pɛə
'sændoːz] *get a pair of sandals*. As the last three examples illustrate,
the deleted /ə/ may have been the entire phonological realization of
the indefinite article. (The last example also includes an instance of
Compression, leading to the loss of the entire phonological realization of the preposition *of* /ə(v)/.)

4.2.9 The consonant system; [h]

The consonant system of London English is essentially isomorphic
with that of RP, both as a system and in the phonotactic distribution
of the consonants constituting the system. It is true that tendencies
exist towards the absence from the system of /h/ and of the dental
fricatives /θ, ð/, towards the neutralization of the oppositions
between /p, t, k/ in final position, and towards the exclusion of /l/
from non-prevocalic environments; but all of these matters are
subject to variability. The last-mentioned, for instance, has been
dealt with above (4.2.7); in this case variability in the use of lateral
and vocoid articulations in places where other accents have non-
prevocalic /l/ means that we should be premature if we claimed for
Cockney a consonant system with /l/ restricted to prevocalic
environments and a vowel system augmented by a set of new diphthongs /ɪʊ, ɛʊ, æʊ . . ./ (*milk, shelf, sales* . . .). Given another century,

though, things may well have progressed so as to justify such conclusions.

H Dropping has been dealt with in volume 1 (3.4.1). It is of course common in popular London speech, though strongly stigmatized by teachers and the speech-conscious. But pairs such as *heat–eat, harm–arm* appear to be phonologically distinct, even if they are often phonetically identical, (ii?, ɑːm]. As Sivertsen puts it (1960: 141), 'most adult informants know where there "should" be [h], but even when they are on their guard there are apt to be "slips" and erratic pronunciations, the same words being sometimes pronounced with and sometimes without [h]'. In the somewhat formal circumstances of an interview, Bowyer (1973) found that all his Bromley informants had a contrastive [h] with the approved lexical incidence. Sivertsen, on the other hand, working with working-class informants in the Cockney heartland of Bethnal Green, goes on to conclude that 'in really colloquial style its presence or absence cannot be considered contrastive; it may be missing in words where RP has it, and on the other hand it may occur where it is paralleled by no segment in RP, but never consistently one way or the other'. She considers that [h], like prevocalic [ʔ], is to some extent a stylistic marker of emphasis: e.g. [ˈnʌʊ ɑɪ ˈhʌɪnt] *no, I ain't*, [ɜː ˈhɛrənz] *her errands*, [ɑɪ ˈlɑɪʔ ˌhɪʋz] *I like eels*.

4.2.10 Plosives: affrication, glottalling, tapping

The voiceless plosives /p, t, k/ of London English are typically aspirated, affricated, preglottalized, glottalled, or voiced, or more than one of these, depending on phonetic environment and social factors.

Aspirated [pʰ, tʰ, kʰ] must be considered the phonemic norm, more than in most other kinds of English: London /p, t, k/ are often given this realization even in the intervocalic and final environments, e.g. *upper, utter, rocker, up, out, rock*, where RP is traditionally described as having the unaspirated variants. The only environment where unaspirated [p, t, k] are at all common in a popular London accent is that following /s/, as *spin*. Furthermore – in broad Cockney at any rate – the degree of aspiration is typically greater than in RP, and may often also involve some degree of affrication.

Affrication may be encountered in initial, intervocalic, and final position. In the latter it is usually preglottalized, as [aʔpɸ] *up*, [ɑːʔtˢ] *art*, ['na‑ θɪŋʔkˣ] *nothing*. Non-finally affrication of /p/ is rare, but examples for /t/ and, to some extent, /k/ abound, e.g. [tˢəi] *tea*, [kˣoʊ] *call*, ['betˢəi] *Betty* (the latter differing from ['betsəi] *Betsy* in having a shorter fricative element). Sometimes the voiced plosives, too, are affricated – particularly /d/, as [dᶻɪʔkˣ] *Dick*, [bædᶻ] *bad*.

Preglottalization and glottalling are found in many kinds of English (see the discussion in volume 1, 3.4.5). Yet the glottal stop is widely regarded as a sound particularly characteristic of Cockney. Matthews (1938: 80) even goes so far as to assert that 'the chief consonantal feature of the dialect is the prevalence of the glottal stop'. It is certainly plausible to suppose that one of the principal factors contributing to the apparently recent geographical spread of T Glottalling is the influence of London English, where it is indeed very common.

In the speech of East End schoolchildren Beaken (1971) found /p, t, k/ 'almost invariably glottalized' in final position. This may be preglottalization (with or without affrication), in which there is a glottal closure made slightly before the oral one, overlapping with it, and released before it: [ʌʔp] *up*, [kæʔt] *cat*, [sɒʔk] *sock*. Or it may involve the use of a glottal closure only, without any oral closure – what I have called glottalling: ['fɪlɪʔ] *Philip*, [ɑ'lɪʔɪʔ] *I lit it*, [ə 'bʊʔ] *a book*. This latter implies the neutralization of the place-of-articulation oppositions, so that for example *whip*, *wit*, and *wick* might all be pronounced homophonously as [wɪʔ]. Bare [ʔ] is, how-ever, much commoner as a realization of underlying /t/ than of /p/ or /k/. With Beaken's young schoolchildren, the ratio of bare [ʔ] to other realizations was 20:1 for /t/, 1:1 for /k/, and 1:2 for /p/ (word-final position only). Even the middle-class, older school-children studied by Hudson & Holloway (1977) realized word-final /t/ as bare [ʔ] in over 80 per cent of cases where the next word began with a consonant (though where the next word began with a vowel this dropped to 20 per cent for middle-class girls, with a succes-sively larger proportion for middle-class boys, working-class girls, and working-class boys; the last-mentioned group had well over 90 per cent of final /t/ as [ʔ] preconsonantally (*tha[ʔ] sort*), as against 75 per cent prevocalically (*tha[ʔ] end*).) However, in the more formal circumstances of an interview, and the less Cockney locality of an outer suburb, Bowyer (1973) found that only five of his thirty-four informants used [ʔ] for final /t/; they were all among those classified as having the broadest accent.

The use of [ʔ] for word-final /t/ before a word beginning with a vowel is one characteristic distinguishing an educated London accent from traditional RP, e.g. [ðæʔ 'ɪz] *that is*, [kwaɪʔ 'ɪizi] *quite easy*. But, as is evident from the figures quoted above, other pronunciations are also common in an educated London accent.

Where word-final /p, t, k/ are preceded by a nasal, the use of [ʔ] as a realization for the stop does not involve real loss of opposition, since place-of-articulation information can be inferred from the nasal, thus [læmʔ] *lamp*, [wenʔ] *went*, [tæŋʔ] *tank*.

Word-internally, a variety of realizations are again found for intervocalic /p, t, k/. If not glottalized, they are in Cockney usually aspirated, as mentioned above. Hudson & Holloway found 46 per cent of /t/ in this environment to be [tʰ], and none to be unaspirated [t]. Otherwise common realizations include [ʔb̥], [tˢ ~ ʔ ~ ɾ], and [kˣ]. The first mentioned, a preglottalized devoiced lenis plosive, is found at all three places of articulation, though more commonly for the bilabial than for the alveolar or the velar, thus [pʰʌɪʔb̥ə] *paper*, and also ['lʌɪʔd̥ə] *later*, ['bʌɪʔg̥ə] *baker*. But the oral stop component of these variants may be reduced to a secondary articulation or – particularly in the case of /t/ – disappear altogether. It is questionable whether a labialized glottal stop in the middle of *paper*, a velarized glottal stop in the middle of *baker*, and a plain (or alveolarized?) glottal stop in the middle of *later* are auditorily different, even though their articulations may not be identical.

A bare [ʔ] as the realization of word-internal intervocalic /t/ is one of the most stereotyped characteristics of Cockney, as ['bʌʔə] *butter*, ['woːʔəlʊʉ ən 'sɪʔii ˌlaɪn] *Waterloo and City Line*. As such, it suffers some degree of overt stigmatization. In the speech of the schoolchildren studied by Hudson & Holloway, only 17 per cent of /t/s occurring in this environment were realized as [ʔ] (though this no doubt was influenced by the fact that the subjects were being interviewed on tape by an outsider). Indeed, there is another variant which also has a strong claim to be considered 'typically Cockney', namely the voiced tap (T Voicing, vol. 1, 3.3.4) [ɾ], as ['bʌɾə] *butter*, ['ʃæəɾɪd] *shouted*. It is also common intervocalically across word boundaries where the syntactic linkage is close:

[(')ʃʌˈʌp] *shut up*, [ˈgɒɾɪʔ] *got it*. The use of [ɾ] appears to be connected with the rate at which the person is speaking, since [ɾ] does not occur in slow speech, in hesitation, or before pause. Interestingly, though, Sivertsen claims that this alveolar tap (or 'flap', as she calls it; she writes it [ṭ]) is regarded by her Bethnal Green informants as 'the normal, "correct" variant' (1960: 119); she continues, 'the alveolar stop, at least when it is strongly affricated in [the environment 'V⸺V], is looked upon as being too "posh" for a Cockney to use: [ˈbetˢə] *better* is "posh", [ˈbeṭə] is normal, and [ˈbeʔə] is "rough"'. Even rougher is a variant she does not mention, namely zero: in broad Cockney this is sometimes found even in intervocalic environments, e.g. [beə], [lɪo] *little*. Sivertsen also reports the [ʔ] allophone of /t/ as being much commoner with men than with women, a claim that has been confirmed by later research. Thus Beaken found that the proportion of [ʔ] (including 'incomplete' and 'glottal creak' subvarieties) to [tʰ ~ tˢ] in this environment was 73:4 in boys' speech, as against 46:14 in girls' speech; that is, that boys pronounced [ˈbʌʔə], etc., over eighteen times as often as they pronounced [ˈbʌtʰə] or [ˈbʌtˢə], whereas girls did so only just over three times as often. Hudson & Holloway found that for /t/ in this same environment the percentage of [ʔ] realizations for middle-class children was well under 10, for working-class girls 40, and for working-class boys 80. But the T Glottalling rule is probably variable for all speakers: in the circumstances of one-word questionnaire answers, Bowyer (1973) found only 6 per cent of his entire Bromley sample glottalizing intervocalic /p, t, k/, and only 12 per cent using T Voicing – the relevant minority in each case being drawn from among the 'broadest' respondents.

T Glottalling is also common in various other intersonorant environments, although T Voicing is apparently not. In this respect a preceding /l/, whether vocalized or not, seems to behave just like a vowel, e.g. [jʉ ˈspoɪʔ ɪʔ] *you spoilt it*, [ˈgɪʊʔi] *guilty*. It is also common to find [ʔ] in the environment /n⸺V/, as [ˈpʌɪnʔɪn] *painting*; though here, of course, an underlying /n/ is often realized as vowel nasality, e.g. [ˈwẽʔ ˈdæʊn] *went down*. In the environment of a following non-syllabic nasal or /l/, glottalling is usual in all kinds of London accent, e.g. [ˈʌʔmɪnstə] *Upminster*, [ˈpʌʔni] *Putney*, [ˈskɒʔlənd] *Scotland*. Some would consider that this usage also falls within RP; though most would not, refusing to recognize as RP any pronunciation lacking the characteristic lateral release plus trans-itional voiceless lateral affrication of ['skɒ(ʔ)tˡlənd]. Popular views on correct or careful pronunciation would also require the mainten-ance of the place-of-articulation opposition in pairs such as *lightly* vs. *likely*, in London speech readily neutralized as ['laɪʔli].

   Where the nasal or lateral following /t/ is syllabic (i.e. for /t/ in the underlying environments /__ən, __əl/), T Glottalling is subject to sharply differing social evaluations according to whether the syl-labic sonorant is in fact nasal or lateral. Where it is lateral, the use of [ʔ] is felt to be strongly Cockney-flavoured, and subject to a similar evaluation to that of intervocalic [ʔ]. This applies independently of whether the underlying /əl/ is realized as one segment or as two, vocalized or not. Examples are ['lɪʔo 'bɒʔoz] *little bottles* (with fol-lowing vocalized [ɫ]), ['lɪʔ]'ɪʔ]əi] *Little Italy* (with following syllabic clear [l]). In mesolectal speech such variants would tend to be avoided (at least part of the time) in favour of ['lɪtl] etc. (or indeed, in 'posh Cockney', ['lɪtˢəl]). But in the environment of a following syllabic nasal T Glottalling seems to be subject to no such negative popular evaluation: pronunciations such as ['bʌʔn̩] *button*, ['hæʔm̩] *happen*, ['tɒʔnəm] *Tottenham* are extremely widespread, and may again possibly be considered to extend into RP. On the other hand, the pronunciation of *-ing* as /ən/ (vol. 1, 3.4.6) gives rise to forms such as ['kʌʔn̩] *cutting*, ['weɪʔn̩ ~ 'wʌɪʔn̩] *waiting*, ['stɒʔm̩] *stopping*, which clearly do not belong in standard speech.

   Glottalling of /k/ in the environment of a following [n] means that broad Cockney may neutralize the opposition between /t/ and /k/ in this position: compare ['reʔn̩] *reckon* and ['θreʔn̩] *threaten*. But a pair such as *beaten–beacon*, although they may be rendered homophon-ously as ['briʔn̩], may nevertheless also be kept apart by speakers in more careful styles, e.g. as ['briitˢən], ['briikˣən].

   In certain words where intervocalic /t/ might be expected, [d] is sometimes encountered – a slower, more deliberate articulation than the tapped [ɾ] which we have already mentioned as one of the possibilities for intervocalic /t/. The [d] variant seems to be an informal alternative in certain common expressions, including *sort of, whatever, get/got it/up, little, hospital* ['ɔspɪdoʊ].

   Cockney [ʔ] can also function as the realization of /d/ in the environment __*C, where * stands for a syllable boundary or word boundary. As such it is an alternative to the commoner [d] variant.

Examples are ['breʔ n̩ 'bʌʔə] *bread and butter*, ['eʔwəʔ 'kʌɪm] *Edward came*, ['guʔ 'guʊd] *good God*. It is particularly common in the negative modals *couldn't, didn't, hadn't, needn't, shouldn't, wouldn't*: [ɑ 'dᶻɪʔnʔtˢ] *I didn't*, ['wuʊʔənja–] *wouldn't you?* From a taxonomic-phonemic point of view, one would probably have to say in such cases that these particular morphemes have variant allomorphs ending in /t/ instead of /d/, and that the [ʔ] realizes this /t/ rather than /d/ directly. But in view of the examples previously quoted (*goo*[ʔ] *God* etc.) I prefer to regard the [ʔ] as a lexically-restricted variant realization of final /d/.

In informal speech Cockney /t, d/ are often elided in non-prevocalic environments, including some where RP could not elide them, e.g. ['dæzgənə] *Dad's going to . . .* , ['tˢɜːn 'lɛf] *turn left*.

4.2.11 Glottalling of other consonants

Although the use of [ʔ] for /t/ is widespread in all kinds of popular London speech, its use for other consonants is perceived as being broader, more Cockney, 'rougher'. We have already seen the possibility of its realizing /p/, /k/, and /d/ in final environments. It can also on occasion realize /f/, /v/, /θ/ and /ð/, i.e. any of the anterior-most fricatives.

Examples of its use for /f/ are ['sʌɪʔə] *safer*, ['dɪʔrən] *different*, [də 'wɑɪʔ ən də 'kɪdz] *the wife and the kids*, ['ta–ʔno 'pɑːʔk] *Tufnell Park*, ['duː jəsɛuʔ ə 'fʌɪvə–] *do yourself a favour*. Instances illustrating its use for /v/ mostly involve the word *of*, as [əʔ 'koʊs] *of course*, [ə 'bɒʔləʔ 'wɪskəi] *a bottle of whisky*; but also ['gɪʔəm] *give 'em*. . . . The sequence [æʔə] can represent both *had to* and *have to*.

It is important to emphasize that these are by no means the usual realizations of /f/ and /v/ in these environments. On the contrary, the examples just quoted were gleaned from many hours of listening; the more usual pronunciations of the phrases concerned would involve [f] or [v] respectively.

Examples of [ʔ] representing /θ/ or /ð/ are even rarer, though they do occur: e.g. [sæːʔ'end] *Southend*, ['a–ʔə] *other*. On tape I have the phrase *on the other side of the water* pronounced as [ɒn i 'a–ʔə 'sɑɪʔ ə ə 'woʊʔə], where [ʔ] represents successively /ð/, /d/, and /t/; and the phrase could well have been pronounced, still in Cockney, with [v ~ ð], [d], and [tˢ ~ ɾ] respectively in place of [ʔ].

The pronunciations ['ɑːʔə], ['ɑːʔə'nʊʉn], broad-Cockney variants of the more usual ['ɑːftə], ['ɑːftə'nʊʉn] etc., *after, afternoon,* are not to be taken as instances of [ʔ] realizing an underlying /ft/ cluster. Rather, these forms represent a 'dialectal', historically long established /f/ -less pronunciation, /'ɑːtə(-)/. The spelling *auternoone* is recorded in a text of 1578, and pronunciations of the type ['ɑːtə(-)] are widespread in midland and southern dialects (E. J. Dobson 1968: §423). In the mid-nineteenth century Mayhew represents Londoners as saying *arter* and *arternoon.*

4.2.12 Fricatives

Another of the very well known characteristics of Cockney is **TH Fronting**. It involves the replacement of the dental fricatives, [θ, ð] by labiodentals, [f] and [v] respectively. This makes *thin* a homophone of *fin,* [fɪn], and *brother* ['brʌvə] rhyme with *lover.* It is reflected in eye-dialect spellings such as *fings, bovver, wiv.* TH Fronting happens readily to the voiceless fricative in all environments, but to the voiced one only when non-initial. Thus we get [friː] *three,* ['ɑːfə] *Arthur,* [bɑːf] *bath,* ['fɑːvə] *father,* [smʊʉv] *smooth;* but for *this* usually not *[vɪs], only [dɪs] or various other possibilities discussed below.

It is wrong to suppose that TH Fronting implies a systemic difference between Cockney and other accents (only six items plus /h/ in the fricative system, as against eight plus /h/). Dental fricatives are used, at least sporadically, by all native adult Londoners, barring only those with speech defects. Even the broadest-speaking Cockneys clearly have /θ/ and /ð/ as items in their (underlying) phonemic inventory. But for the broader speakers underlying /θ, ð/ are subject to the variable rule of TH Fronting, leading to their frequent realization as [f, v] (etc.). Putting this another way, speakers have the ability to distinguish *free* and *three, fought* and *thought, lava* and *lather,* given the appropriate social context and motivation. Thus [foʊʔ] may represent the realization either of /foːt/, past tense of /faɪt/, or of /θoːt/, past tense of /θɪŋk/ [θɪŋk ~ fɪŋk ~ θɪʔk ~ fɪʔ . . .]. As the first it has no alternative pronunciation with [θ], but as the second it does.

If [θ] and [f] were stylistic alternatives realizing the same underlying phoneme /f/ in all cases, we should have frequent hypercorrections such as * [θɑɪv] or * [θɑɪð] *five*, * [leθt] *left*, etc. Except to a small extent in the speech of young children, such hypercorrections are virtually unknown. Beaken (1971) found that by the age of nine children were able to alternate [f] and [θ], [v] and [ð] in the appropriate stylistic way for underlying /θ, ð/, without using hypercorrect dentals for underlying /f, v/. Words such as *feather* constitute a special case, where the difficulty of having /f/ and /ð/ so close to one another does lead to the hypercorrection ['θeðə].

Punners can rely confidently upon their audience's awareness of the possibility of TH Fronting. Advertisements for beer award the brand in question 'thirst prize', or declare that 'for the southerner, it's the guv'nor'.

For initial /ð/ in working-class speech, if a dental articulation is used it may well be frictionless, i.e. the approximant [ð̞] rather than the fricative [ð]. Other possibilities are [d], [l], and [ʔ]; so *this* may be any of [ðɪs, ð̞ɪs, dɪs, lɪs, ʔɪs]. All these variants may occur in absolute initial position, in apparently free variation. Hudson & Holloway found avoidance of variants other than the fricative [ð] to be characteristic of their middle-class subjects (and hence, implicitly, the use of the other variants to be characteristic of the working-class subjects).

Where a word beginning with /ð/ follows closely after one ending with a consonant, certain coalescences or other sandhi forms are widespread. After an alveolar consonant the realization of /ð/ may be zero: [ɪz'æʔ'oʊlə] *is that all the...?* Alternatively, there may be prolongation of the alveolar articulation: ['ræːnːə] *round the....* A further, very common alternative is the coalescence of an alveolar plus /ð/ into a single dental consonant with the remaining features of the original alveolar (/sð/ → [s̪], etc.); thus ['gɒt̪ə] *got the*, [ɪn̪ə] *in the*. In this case the difference in pronunciation between *seen the book* and *seen a book* may be just that one has [n̪], the other [n].

Word-initially after a word ending in a consonant, [d] and zero are also common for /ð/. Where the preceding word ends in [ʔ], /ð/ may be realized as a creaky onset to the following vowel, as ['lɑːʔ'a̰æʔ] *like that.*

It appears that in previous centuries Cockney exhibited not Fronting but Stopping of /θ, ð/. This is evidenced by many spellings of the type *Tursday* (*Thursday*) and *furder* (*further*). Except in the case of initial /ð/ this kind of pronunciation is now probably obsolete; though Sivertsen, whose informants were born before the turn of the century, did find just two unambiguous instances in her data, namely *thousand* with [tʰ-] and *bathe* with [-d] (1960: 124). But the usual Cockney forms of these words have [θ ~ f] and [ð ~v] respectively. The pronunciation of the place-name *Bethnal Green* as ['beʔnoʊ 'grəin] is sometimes adduced as an example of /t/ for /θ/; but it is better seen as a further example of the independently attested glottalling of /θ/ (see above, 4.2.11).

The speech of London children often seems to exhibit neutralization of the /s/ vs. /z/ opposition, with [s]-type articulations being used for both. This applies particularly to verb endings, plurals, and function-words such as *was, because*. Hence *knees* can optionally be homophonous with *niece* [nəis], or *purrs* with *purse* [pɜːs]. Adults do not generally neutralize the opposition, though /z/ of course has voiceless allophones [z̥] in appropriate environments just as in other accents, the phonological contrast being realized in the duration of the preceding vowel and/or in the lenis vs. fortis quality of the consonant itself.

The typical Cockney quality of /ʃ, ʒ/ seems to be somewhat 'clearer' (more palatal, less lip-rounded) than that of RP.

4.2.13 Yod phenomena

The only consonants which /j/ follows freely in clusters are /p, b, v, g/, as *dispute* [dɪs'pjʊɐt], *beautiful, view, argue*. It is also common in clusters after /m, f, k/, although Sivertsen reports occasional Yod Dropping as ['mʉːzɪk] *music*, [fʉː] *few*, [kʉː] *Kew* (though in London speech these too normally have [-j-]).

Where RP has an alveolar stop plus yod, Cockney traditionally exhibits Yod Dropping (as in GenAm, vol. 1, 3.3.3), e.g. [tʉːn] *tune*, [dʉːk] *duke*, [nʉː] *new*. Comments on the prevalence of this type of pronunciation in London are to be found from the eighteenth century onwards; and writers as recent as Matthews (1938: 172) and Sivertsen (1960: 143–4) regard it as the contemporary Cockney norm, though always of course alongside the approved RP-type variants with [tj-, dj-, nj-]. In the environment /n___/ this Yod Dropping is still commonly heard in working-class London speech; further examples are ['nʉːtroʊ] *neutral*, [nʉː'mʌʊniə] *pneumonia*. But in the environments /t___, d___/ there seems to have occurred a switch in Popular London speech towards Yod Coalescence (vol. 1,

3.1.10) instead. Neither Beaken (1971) nor Bowyer (1973) find any cases whatsoever of Yod Dropping after /t/ or /d/. This is all the more striking in the case of Beaken, inasmuch as his survey of primary-school children was based on a school in the East End quite close to Bethnal Green, where Sivertsen had carried out her survey of Cockney speakers who were perhaps some seventy years older. Beaken reports that the typical pronunciation of words such as *tune, due* is now [tʃʊʉn, dʒʊʉ]. The only variants are the elegant alternatives [tj-, dj-]. Bowyer, studying adults in a prosperous south London suburb, reports that *tune* commonly had [tʃ-] for his two lower social groups, and varied between [tʃ-] and [tj-] for his two higher groups. In *new*, the variant with bare [n-] was restricted to his two lower groups, and even with them was less common than [nj-]. Hurford (1967), studying three generations of East Enders, speaks merely of 'variation' between [tʃ] and bare [t] in *tune*, etc.; he suspects it may be lexically conditioned. It is not known why Yod Coalescence has displaced Yod Dropping as the broad-Cockney norm. This does seem to have been an unusually abrupt switch. It is possible, though, that the [tʃ-, dʒ-] forms have long existed in south London (as they are known to have in Surrey – see for example Wright 1905, s.v. *Tuesday*), and that from there they have spread to other parts of London, displacing the (typically East Anglian) forms with bare [t-, d-].

Awareness of the fact that Yod Coalescence is somewhat stigmatized leads to hypercorrection in would-be elegant speech, with the use of [tj, dj] in place of [tʃ, dʒ] in words such as *chew, June*. A small child told Beaken, [ɜ ˈdjʌs ˈnaɪ̃] *I'm just nine*.

In rapid informal speech Yod Coalescence with fricatives takes place on a wider scale than in RP: that is, final /s/ or /z/ coalesces with initial /j/ of the following word, yielding [ʃ] or [ʒ] respectively, as [ˈwɒʔ kˣalə ˈʒɔː heə] *What colour's your hair?*. This can even take place across an elision, whether of a vowel or of a consonant: [ˈlɑʃɪə] *last year* (/t/ elided), [wɒʔˈklɑʃəʉ ɪn] *What class are you in?* (/ə/ are elided).

4.2.14 Prosodic features

The voice quality of Cockney has been described as typically involving 'chest tone' (rather than 'head tone') and as being 'rough' and 'harsh', involving abrupt alternations in the amount of energy involved. This is contrasted with the RP of Kensington or Mayfair, described as being characterized by velvety smoothness. As always, it is difficult to sort out stereotype from reality in such impressionistic depictions.

More objectively, it is clear that popular London speech has even less lip activity than RP. Only /w/ and the /ɔ:/ of *ball* /bɔ:/ involve any significant rounding.

Mention has already been made of vowel nasalization. Another factor contributing to the overall voice-quality effect of Cockney and popular London speech is the preponderance of 'sloppy' plosive releases – heavy aspiration or affrication. The only plosive which is typically released abruptly is the glottal one, [ʔ]; and its high frequency of occurrence, realizing a variety of phonological possibilities, adds its own characteristic flavour to the overall voice-quality impression.

The intonation of London English is very much the same as that of RP. The only pattern which has come to my attention as distinctively Cockney is a falling tone on the question tag *eh?*

Rhythmically, one striking London characteristic is the tendency to lengthen utterance-final syllables. In such a syllable, there may be an impression of stress, and the vowel may be prolonged, as [ˈkʰanʔˌtrii:] *country*, or in some cases subjected to additional gliding (above 4.2.4). If the final segment is a plosive, then preglottalization and affrication can considerably extend its effective duration, as [ˈɑ:ʔtˢ] *art*. Even [ʔ] can be aspirated in this utterance-final environment, as [ˈɑ:ʔʰ]; ejective realizations of /p, t, k/, too, are restricted to this environment, as [ˈɑ:ʔt']. All these variant possibilities mean that it takes longer than it would otherwise to articulate the final consonant.

London English seems to allow deletion of [ə] in ways that most other accents do not. This applies even to the indefinite article before vowels (where the standard form is *an*), e.g. [ˈgɪv s ˈbæʊʔ ʔæ:ə] *Give us about an hour* (4.2.8 above).

4.2.15 Literary Cockney

A fair number of writers have offered literary representations of Cockney speech. Alongside the many humorists aiming merely at comic effect there are two important literary figures who have done this: Charles Dickens and George Bernard Shaw.

Undoubtedly there are many readers of Dickens who, lacking first-hand acquaintance with Cockney, have formed their ideas about its nature from the usages and spellings with which the writer supplies Sam Weller (*Pickwick Papers*) and his other Cockney characters. It is therefore worth emphasizing that Dickens's Cockney is a literary stereotype which was seriously out-of-date at the time he wrote and is now wholly obsolete. This stereotype makes great play, for example, of the supposed interchange of [v] and [w]:

'Ah, dear!' moaned Mrs Gamp, sinking into the shaving chair, 'that there blessed Bull, Mr Sweedlepipe, has done his wery best to conker me. Of all the trying inwalieges in this walley of the shadder, that one beats 'em black and blue.' [. . .] 'Sech is life. Vich likeways is the hend of all things!'
(*Martin Chuzzlewit*, ch. 29)

'I'm a-goin' to leave you, Samivel, may boy, and there's no telling ven I shall see you again. [. . .] A thousand things may have happened by the time you next hears any news o'the celebrated Mr Veller. [. . .] I may trust you as vell as if it was my own self. So I've only this here one little bit of adwice to give you . . . !
(*Pickwick Papers*, ch. 23)

As long ago as 1836 Smart, the author of a work entitled *Walker Remodelled*, calls the interchange of *w* and *v* 'the habit of a more distant generation of Cockneys'. On the other hand Wyld (1936: 292) remembers the substitution of [w] for [v] as a jocular pronunciation among middle-class adults in 1870–80, the inference being that this was, or had until recently been, a characteristic of lower-class London speech of the day. But in any case it must be doubtful whether actual interchange of [v] and [w] (not only *walley* for *valley*, but also *vich* for *which* above) was ever as widespread in London as the novelists (not only Dickens) make out. At the present time it is utterly obsolete.

Dickens's Cockney lacks any indication of such matters as Diphthong Shift, L Vocalization, and T Glottalling, all of which are of great importance in the phonetics of contemporary London speech.

Shaw's Cockney presents a picture much closer than Dickens's to contemporary reality. Shaw knew a little of phonetics, which he discusses with vigorous interest in the preface to *Pygmalion* and in the note 'English and American dialects' appended to *Captain Brassbound's Conversion*. The character Drinkwater in the latter play has his Cockney pronunciation indicated throughout by special spellings:

Weoll, waw not? Waw not, gavner? Ahrs is a Free Tride nition. It gows agin us as Hinglishmen to see these bloomin furriners settin ap their Castoms Ahses and spheres o hinfluence and sick lawk hall owver Arfricar. Daownt Harfricar belong as much to huz as to them? thets wot we sy. Ennywys, there ynt naow awm in ahr business. All we daz is hescort, tourist, hor commercial. Cook's hexcursions to the Hatlas Mahntns: thets hall it is. Waw, its spreadin civlawzytion, it is. Ynt it nah?

(Captain Brassbound's Conversion, act I)

The stage instructions at the start of the play include the following specification of Drinkwater's 'dialect':

His dialect, apart from its base nasal delivery, is not unlike that of smart London society in its tendency to replace diphthongs by vowels (sometimes rather prettily) and to shuffle all the traditional vowel pronunciations. He pronounces ow as ah, and i as aw, using the ordinary ow for o, i for ā, ă for ŭ, and ĕ for ă, with this reservation, that when any vowel is followed by an r, he signifies its presence, not by pronouncing the r, which he never does under these circumstances, but by prolonging and modifying the vowel, sometimes even to the extreme degree of pronouncing it properly. As to his yol for l (a compendious delivery of the provincial eh-al), and other metropolitan refinements, amazing to all but cockneys, they cannot be indicated, save in the above imperfect manner, without the aid of a phonetic alphabet.

As can be seen from the extract quoted, Shaw does attempt to indicate the results of the Diphthong Shift. He also suggests special pre-/l/ allophones (*weoll* for *well*), but not L Vocalization. There is no hint of T Glottalling. H Dropping and hypercorrect /h/ insertion are ludicrously exaggerated. Some of the vowel representations can be accounted for only in the light of Shaw's own Anglo-Irish background, e.g. *waw* for *why*: [wɑː], the broadest Cockney form of /wɑɪ/, may sound like Dublin 'waw', though it is considerably different from RP /wɔː/. And there are not a few special spellings which might equally well be used of RP (*ahrs* for *ours*) or indeed of almost any accent of English. In *Candida* the Cockney character Burgess is shown as saying *moddle* for *model*; since the only distinctively Cockney pronunciation of such a word would be of the type ['mɔdɔː], with median rather than lateral release of the [d], this spelling is the opposite of reasonable.

4.3 The south

4.3.1 Introduction

The south of England falls naturally into three general areas: the home counties, East Anglia, and the west country.

The so-called **home counties** are the counties adjacent to London and into which London has extended; they are London's 'exurbia'. They comprise Kent, Surrey, Sussex, Hertfordshire, and Essex, together with at least some parts of Buckinghamshire, Berkshire, and Bedfordshire. They are dominated, linguistically as well as in other matters, by London, and their urban speech has strong affiliations to that of London. Even many of their rural villages are inhabited largely by people who work in London; and they are dotted with 'new towns', built since 1945 and populated mostly by former Londoners. Nevertheless, traditional local speech patterns do persist in many more rural areas; in Sussex and Kent, for example, they may be readily recognized by their rhoticity.

East Anglia comprises Norfolk and Suffolk, together with adjacent parts of Cambridgeshire and Essex. It has two large urban centres, Norwich and Ipswich. The local accents, which are non-rhotic, are discussed in sections 4.3.2–4 below.

Linguistically speaking, the south may be said to extend up as far as the isogloss marking the northern limit of the FOOT-STRUT Split in popular speech. This runs from the Severn estuary in the west to the Wash in the east (4.4.2 below). Except at its western extremity, a rather similar path is traced by the isogloss marking the northern limit of BATH Broadening in popular speech (4.4.3 below). Thus in a broad local accent of the south *cup* is [kʌp ~ kəp] and *glass* is [glɑːs ~ glaːs], whereas further north they are of the types [kʊp] and [glas] (map, fig. 8).

The core of the **west country**, the west of England, is formed by the cider counties of Gloucestershire, Avon, Somerset, and Devon, with Bristol as the main centre of population. In the far south-west, Cornwall stands somewhat apart: not only does it have its own separate traditions, but a Celtic language, Cornish, was formerly spoken there (and is now the subject of attempts at revival). Nearer London, the transitional area of Wessex comprises Dorset,

335

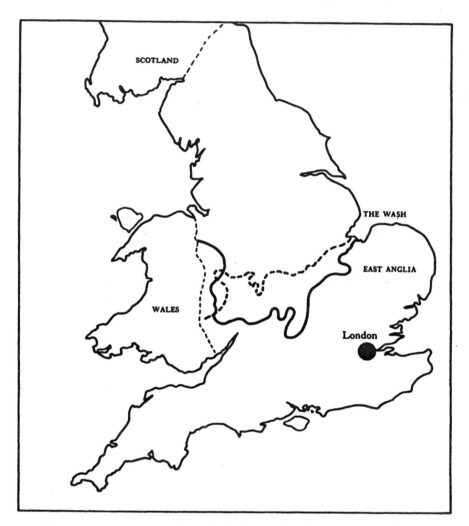

Fig. 8   Approximate southern limits in broad local accents of unsplit
FOOT–STRUT (solid line) and flat BATH (broken line) (from Chambers &
Trudgill 1980)

Hampshire, Wiltshire, and perhaps post-1974 Oxfordshire.
Rhoticity is the most striking distinguishing feature of west-
country accents, which are discussed in sections 4.3.5–8 below.

As everywhere in England, the range of accents to be heard in any
particular locality spans the gamut from the broadest local accent
up to Near-RP and RP. This implies that by no means every native

of the west country, for example, pronounces every historical /r/, nor does every native of East Anglia have all or even any of the characteristic East Anglian phonetic features.

4.3.2 East Anglia: vowels

An East Anglian accent is like that of London, and like RP, in having a firm opposition between STRUT and FOOT (/ʌ/ vs. /ʊ/), in having undergone BATH Broadening (*bath* = [baːθ] etc.), and in being entirely non-rhotic (except very occasionally in the speech of the oldest people). Yet East Anglian speech – particularly that of Norfolk and eastern Suffolk – sounds very different from that of London and the home counties. Some of the main features responsible for this difference are as follows.

1. In East Anglia the Long Mid Mergers (vol.1, 3.1.5) are not complete. Among the FACE words, a distinction of the type [eː ∼ eə] in *name, paper, face* versus the type [æɪ] in *nail, way, eight* has been reported in the older rural dialects of Norfolk and Suffolk; it is, however, sharply recessive, with younger people generalizing to both subsets of words a diphthong varying from [æɪ] to an RP-type [eɪ]. With the GOAT words, the corresponding distinction is more widely retained, giving minimal pairs such as (182).

(182) [ʊu] = /uː/ [ʌu]
    < Middle English /ɔː/ < Middle English /ɔu/
    moan *mown*
    sole *soul*
    nose *knows*
    toe *tow*

In Norwich itself there is even a distinction made very often between two senses of *no*, as ['nʌu ðæs nʊu 'gʊd] *No, that's no good*. Leaving aside this particular item, a consistent distinction between the two subsets of GOAT words seems generally to be made in working-class Norfolk accents (e.g. in Norwich and King's Lynn), but to be increasingly lost the further up the socio-economic scale one goes and the nearer geographically one gets to London. In a 1975 survey, working-class informants in Ipswich (Suffolk) and Colchester (Essex) were found not to make the distinction, having *moan – mown* etc. as homophones (Trudgill & Foxcroft 1978).

2. The vowel in GOOSE words is in general a central [ʉː ∼ əʉ], e.g.

do [dʉː], *soon* [sʉːn]. Thus the contrast between GOOSE and GOAT is normally retained, e.g. as *two* /tʉː/ vs. *toe* /tuː/. But in Norwich, at least, certain GOOSE words fluctuate between the expected /ʉː/ and the /uː/ typical of (certain) GOAT words. This means that pairs such as *soup–soap, moon–moan, boot–boat* may be homophonous, /suːp, muːn, buːt/.

3. To complicate matters still further, some GOAT words can be pronounced with the /ʊ/ of FOOT rather than with /uː/. Thus *boat* can be [bʊt], *road* [rʊd], etc., making perfect rhymes of *boat* and *foot*, or *road* and *hood*. Other examples include *comb, bone, oats, whole, home, froze*. Overall, though, the pronunciation is sharply recessive. Certain GOOSE words, too, may sporadically appear with /ʊ/, especially in Suffolk, thus *bloom* /blʊm/, *tooth* /tʊθ/.

These three points together mean that East Anglian accents typically differ from RP in a way which involves considerations both of system and of lexical incidence among the back close vowels: four phonemes (/ʌu, uː, ʉː, ʊ/) are spread over the three lexical sets GOAT, GOOSE, FOOT.

4. The vowels of NEAR and SQUARE are variably merged. Words of both sets may be pronounced with a vowel of the type [ɛː ~ ɛə], and there are potential homophones such as *rear–rare, fear–fair, here–hair, idea–I dare*. The distinction is, however, often preserved in the most formal styles of speech, as well as by middle-class speakers in all styles; and it has been argued that a 'deep' (phonological) opposition remains even for speakers who habitually merge the two vowels on the phonetic level. This is shown by the finding that in working-class Norwich speech, in the more colloquial styles, NEAR words have on average a slightly opener vowel than SQUARE words, e.g. *fear* [fɛː], *fair* [fɛ̝ː] (Trudgill 1974: 123).

5. Yod Dropping is very widespread, and extends to virtually all environments except word-initial. Thus /j/ is typically absent not only after alveolars (*suit, resume, tune, duke, new*) but also after labials (*pure, beauty, music, few, view*), velars (*accuse*) and /h/ (*huge*). Because, no doubt, of pressure from RP, which always has /j/ in such words, Yod Dropping is certainly variable; but it is not at all unusual for there to be homophony in pairs such as *do–dew* /dʉː/, *mute–moot* /mʉːt/, *cute–coot* /kʉːt/. The working-class pronunciation of *Hughes Hall* in Cambridge is usually /(h)ʉːz (h)ɔːl/, identical with *whose haul*.

In CURE words where historically there was a /j/ the Norwich vowel is the /ɜː/ of NURSE, e.g. *sure* /ʃɜː/. Yod Dropping therefore makes potential homophones also out of pairs such as *pure–purr* /pɜː/, *cure–cur* /kɜː/. (Even for those who pronounce a /j/ in *pure* and *cure*, these pairs still typically rhyme, as *pure* /pjɜː/, *purr* /pɜː/.)

6. The process of Smoothing (vol. I, 3.2.9) is carried further in Norwich speech than in RP. It is not known how far it is characteristic of the rest of East Anglia, but in Norwich it has been established that there are common pronunciations such as the following:

(i) *fire* [faː], *trying* [trɑːn]; *tower* [tɑː], *allowing* [əˈlɑːn];
(ii) *seeing* [sɛːn];
(iii) *saying* [sæːn], *player* [plæː];
(iv) *booing* [bɔːn ~ bɜːn]; *going* [gɔːn]; *employing* [-plɔːn];
(v) *knowing* [nɒːn].

Bearing in mind that Norwich -*ing* is popularly /-ən/, we see that we have the following subprocesses:

(i) /æiə, æʉə/ → [ɑː]; the output vowel is usually distinct from the [aː] of START–PALM–BATH, so that *fire* ≠ *far* as [fɑː] vs. [faː], although they may merge under pressure from RP, in which they are phonetically the other way round;

(ii) /iːə/ →[ɛː]; the output vowel is identical with that of NEAR and SQUARE (see above);

(iii) /æiə/ → [æː]; this vowel [æː] occurs only as the result of Smoothing;

(iv) /uːə, oiə/ → [ɔː]; this output vowel is phonetically identical with the /ɔː/ of NORTH–FORCE–THOUGHT and some CURE words, e.g. *tour* /tɔː/; /ʉːə/ → [ɜː], phonetically identical with the /ɜː/ of NURSE; so that *booing* may end up phonetically identical with either *born* or *burn*;

(v) /ʌʊə/ → [ɒː]; this vowel [ɒː] occurs only as the result of Smoothing.

It is clear that the formal rules for Norwich Smoothing are somewhat more complicated than those for RP. At the same time they tend to justify a phonological analysis which treats the vowel of NEAR, for example, as underlyingly /iːə/ or even /iːr/ – a matter we shall not pursue here.

7. In Norfolk, though apparently not in the rest of East Anglia, the LOT vowel has an unrounded variant, ranging phonetically from

[ɑ] to [a–]. This may or may not involve a variable phonetic merging with START (so that *box* = *barks* = [ba–·ks]). Currently, however, this unrounded variant is giving way to a rounded [ɒ] in urban Norwich. It has been shown that the change to [ɒ] is spearheaded by middle-class women and working-class men (see further in volume 1, 1.4.5).

8. In certain environments the vowel of DRESS may be centred to a quality of the type [ɜ] or [ʌ]. The principal environment in which this occurs is before a final or preconsonantal /l/, as in *tell*, *bell*, *healthy*; it is also found in the environment preceded by a labial and followed by [ʔ] in a penultimate syllable, as *better*, *metal*. Although reported from rural East Anglia in the 1920s, this tendency is evidently an innovation in Norwich, since Trudgill's survey of that city, carried out in 1968, showed the central variant to be very much commoner with the under-twenty age group than with older informants.

9. Lastly, there seems to be a tendency for closing diphthongs in East Anglia to have a fully close vowel, [i] or [u], as the second element, rather than the [ɪ] or [ʊ]-type endpoint found in RP and other accents.

4.3.3 The Norwich vowel system

Bearing in mind the points mentioned in 4.3.2, and excluding those phonetic vowels which arise only as a result of Smoothing, we can set out the Norwich vowel system as (183). Lexical incidence is as shown in (184). It seems typical of most of East Anglia, though it must be borne in mind that deviations in the direction of RP and/or Cockney are to be expected.

(183)

ɪ ʊ	iː		ʉː uː			
ɛ ʌ		oi		ʌu	ɛː ɜː ɔː	
æ ɒ	æi ʌi		æʉ		aː	

(184)

KIT	ɪ	FLEECE	iː	NEAR	ɛː	
DRESS	ɛ	FACE	æi	SQUARE	ɛː	
FAT	æ	PALM	aː	START	aː	
LOT	ɒ	THOUGHT	ɔː	NORTH	ɔː	
STRUT	ʌ	GOAT	ʌu, uː, (ʊ)	FORCE	ɔː	
FOOT	ʊ	GOOSE	ʉː	CURE	ɜː, ɔː	

BATH	aː	PRICE	ʌi	*happ*Y	[i]
CLOTH	ɒ, ɔː	CHOICE	oi	*lett*ER	ə
NURSE	ɜː	MOUTH	æʉ	*comm*A	ə

4.3.4 East Anglia: consonants and prosodic features

T Glottalling (vol. 1, 3.4.5) is widely established in East Anglia – not just in urban accents, but also in rural speech. In Norwich the use of [ʔ] or [tʔ] has been shown to increase as one moves towards casual speech from more formal styles, as one descends the social class scale, and as we consider word-final environments (e.g. *hat*) rather than those which are word-internal (e.g. *butter*).

East Anglian /l/ is still a lateral consonant in all positions. In the older rural speech of Norfolk it is clear in all positions; elsewhere, and in the current urban speech of Norwich, it is allophonically clear/dark as in RP. L Vocalization (vol. 1, 3.4.4) does not yet appear to have made inroads far into East Anglia.

Historical /h/ is preserved in rural Norfolk and Suffolk, and also to some extent in Essex. This sets East Anglia proper apart from adjacent Cambridgeshire and Hertfordshire, where H Dropping is (variably) usual in working-class accents. However, in urban Norwich it is clear that H Dropping has long been a sociolinguistic variable just as in most other parts of England.

But it is a prosodic feature that furnishes one of the most typical characteristics setting East Anglian accents apart from those of elsewhere. This is a special kind of rhythm which involves extreme lengthening of stressed long vowels, and the compensatory reduction or elimination of certain unstressed vowels, as *thirty-two* ['θɜːːʔˈtʉː].

4.3.5 The west country: rhoticity and its consequences

The preservation of historical /r/ in all environments is the best-known phonetic characteristic of the west of England. Full rhoticity is to be observed in any kind of broad western accent, and extends well up the social scale in cities such as Bristol, Exeter, or (to a lesser extent) Southampton. Plymouth and Bournemouth, large cities with very mixed populations, seem to have more variable rhoticity or even none. Traces of variable rhoticity may be found as close to London as Reading (Berkshire).

Rhoticity in the west means that the vowels of NURSE and *lett*ER are r-coloured, [ɜ:] and [ɚ] respectively; while in START, NORTH, FORCE, NEAR, SQUARE, and CURE there is either an r-coloured vowel or else a diphthong/triphthong in which r-colouring is absent at the outset but increases as the vocoid progresses, with [ɚ] as the final element. It is difficult to establish firm rules for the alternation between these two phonetic types; on the whole, though, the [Vɚ] type seems commoner with front vowels (NEAR, SQUARE) and/or word-finally under nuclear stress, while the [Vʴ] type seems commoner where neither of these factors operates. We shall in any case regard both types as phonemically /V:r/.

The phonetic quality of /r/ is retroflex, [ɻ], in most of the west country: this applies both to consonantal /r/ and to the r-colouring of vowels just discussed (so that [ɚ] above is more precisely [ɜʴ]). As recorded in *LAE*, the isogloss separating retroflex from post-alveolar /r/ runs from about Bristol to Portsmouth; the retroflex area covers Hampshire, Wiltshire, Dorset, Somerset, Devon, and Cornwall.

There is a phonemicization problem with the vowels before /r/. Contrasts such as *nearer–mirror, fairy–ferry* seem always to be preserved, so that the vowels of NEAR and SQUARE cannot be identified with /ɪ/ and /ɛ/ (as they can in most American accents). As long as 'postvocalic' /r/ is retained as such we are not justified in recognizing phonemes such as /ɪə/ or /ɛə/ (since they would occur only before /r/, where other long vowels would be ruled out). Extra phonemes /iʳ, eʳ/, as sometimes proposed, are uneconomic. So the best solution seems to be to treat [ɪːɚ], etc., in NEAR as /iːr/, and [ɛːɚ], etc., in SQUARE as /ɛɪr/ (i.e. as the vowel of FACE plus /r/). The only difficulty here is the rather big phonetic difference sometimes between /ɛɪ/ in FACE words and in SQUARE words. Similar considerations apply to the other r-coloured vowels or r-diphthongs. There seem to be different answers in different places to the question whether the [ɜ:] of NURSE can be identified with (i) the vowel of STRUT plus /r/, and (ii) the unstressed vowel of *lett*ER (which is often rather long). It seems that in some accents, at any rate, all three can be identified as realizations of the same sequence /ər/.

Among middle-class speakers in the west one often finds a kind of pronunciation which seems rhotic in its underlying essentials, even though there may be no 'postvocalic' /r/ phonetically realized as such. Speakers of this type may, for example, have a centring diphthong in START words, e.g. *bar* [bɑə] (but *spa* [spɑː ~ spaː]). They may have a similar vocalic distinction in pairs such as *nor* vs. *gnaw*, *court* vs. *caught*, or *western* vs. *Weston*; and they may have [ən] rather than the usual [n̩] in *modern* and *pattern*.

On the other hand it is also quite common to find instances of hyper-rhoticity in the west. In particular, *comm*A words may be found with final [ɚ] (not only when the following word begins with a vowel, as in the 'intrusive /r/' of RP, but in any environment), e.g. *china* ['tʃɒɪnɚ], *banana* [bə'naːnɚ]. This also applies in some areas to words where RP has final unstressed /əʊ/, e.g. *window* ['wɪndɚ]. In the word *yellow*, *LAE* records [ɚ(ː)] very widely in the west country (though not in Avon or Gloucestershire).

Hyper-rhoticity also occurs sporadically in PALM words, by false inference in words learnt from RP or other non-rhotic source accents. Examples include *khaki* ['kaːrki], *Chicago, camouflage* ['kaməflaːrdʒ].

4.3.6 The west country: other consonants

Almost as well known as rhoticity, as a diagnostic for a west-country accent, is the use of a voiced fricative in words whose standard pronunciation has initial /f, θ, s, ʃ/, e.g. *farm* [v-], *thimble* [ð-], *seven* [z-], *shepherd* [ʒ-]. This Initial Fricative Voicing is by now sharply recessive, and nowadays more frequently encountered in pseudo-dialect songs about ['zʌɪdɚ] from ['zʌmɚzɛt] than in authentic unstudied speech. It seems in any case never to have affected the whole set of lexical items that begin with fricatives, and even the old-fashioned rural dialects reported in *LAE* show great inconsistency from one word to another. In the *LAE* maps Initial Fricative Voicing never reaches north-eastwards beyond a line drawn from Hereford to Hastings; it is also nearly always absent from western Cornwall. Initial Fricative Voicing never gives [ð-] in words where there is a following /r/, as *three, thread*; here, /dr-/ occurs instead.

The voicing feature is also affected in another characteristic of traditional western speech: the lenis articulation of medial obstruents and of those which are final after a weak vowel. Forms such as *jacket* ['dʒaˑgëd] have often been reported from Devon; and

LAE shows *butter* with [d] everywhere south-west of a line from Weston-super-mare to Portsmouth. I am not convinced, however, that this lenis articulation necessarily involves the loss of opposition between, say, /k/ and /g/ or /t/ and /d/: *jacket* may still be at least potentially distinct from *jagged*. Kingdon (1939c) transcribes the local pronunciation of *Exeter* as [ɛksëḏəɹ], implying that the alveolar plosive corresponding to RP /t/ is lenis but devoiced or voiceless. But the possibility of T Voicing of a more familiar kind complicates the picture. It is by no means clear how the western leniting of obstruents interacts with the use of a voiced tap in words such as *butter, beautiful, hospital* (that is, for /t/ in the environments 'V—V, 'Vl—V, 'Vn—V), which is certainly very common in urban areas such as Bristol.

Glottalling of intervocalic and final /t/ is another possibility which is frequently found in a Bristol accent, as [lɒʔ, lɒʔs] *lot, lots*, ['bʌʔən] *button*, ['dɜːʔi 'wɔːʔɚ] *dirty water*. I have heard occasional T Glottalling in adolescents from as far west as Redruth (Cornwall), where it is nevertheless probably a very recent innovation.

It has been claimed that final /k/, too, can be realized as [ʔ] in Bristol speech, so that there is variable homophony of pairs such as *lot–lock* [lɒʔ], *rots–rocks* [ɹɒʔs] (Weissmann 1970: 222).

Optional Elision of final /t, d/ applies in a wider range of following environments than in RP; e.g. in Bristol [sæːn] *sand*, [ɹɛs] *rest*, in sentence-final position.

Bristol is the home of another famous consonantal characteristic, Intrusive /l/. This consists in the addition of /l/ to words which would otherwise end in [ə] (e.g. *banana, tomorrow*: i.e. words belonging to the standard lexical set *comm*A, or those ending in RP unstressed /əʊ/; but those belonging to *lett*ER, of course, have /-ər/). This makes *area* a homophone of *aerial* ['ɛːɹjəɫ]. Intrusive /l/ is not a sandhi phenomenon: it can apply equally to a word which is sentence-final or in isolation, and it varies allophonically between clear and dark according as the following segment is or is not a vowel. It has given rise to many jokes. Bristol is 'the only city in Britain to be able to turn ideas into ideals, areas into aerials, and Monicas into monocles', where a father had 'three lovely daughters, Idle, Evil and Normal', where a local girl learning to dance was heard to say 'I can rumble but I can't tangle' (quotations from Robinson 1971). Thus derided and stigmatized, Intrusive /l/ seems always to have been a pretty local phenomenon, not occurring beyond the boundaries of Avon; even within them it is by now quite rare. Its origin must presumably lie in hypercorrection after the loss of final /l/ after /ə/, a hypothesized ['æpə] for *apple*. When the /l/ was restored under pressure from standard accents, it was added analogically to all words ending in [ə]. Bristol itself was once Bristow.

H Dropping is sociolinguistically variable in most parts of the west country just as elsewhere in England. It is certainly so in urban Bristol, although the city lies within a relic area shown in *LAE* as retaining historical /h/.

4.3.7 The west country: vowels

In general, vowel length is not as important phonologically in the west as it is in other parts of England. Traditionally short vowels are lengthened in many environments, so that one may have pronunciations of the type [dɪːd] *did*, [stɛːm] *stem*, [flaˑʃ] *flash*, [tɒˑp] *top*, [pʊˑs] *puss*. This applies particularly when such monosyllables are phrase-final and intonationally prominent.

In most rural western speech the TRAP vowel is qualitatively [a] rather than [æ]. This is also not uncommon in urban speech, though Bristol and Southampton seem to have [æ]; so also, according to *LAE*, do patches of Somerset and Hereford-and-Worcester. Since the vowel of BATH and, in some areas, that of START typically have this same quality [a], any phonemic distinction of the type illustrated by *gas–grass, carry–starry* would have to depend on duration alone. Since, as we have just seen, short vowels tend to be lengthened, it follows that in a west-country accent the phonemic contrast corresponding to RP /æ/ vs. /ɑː/ is absent or variable. This is a matter which has by no means been properly investigated. I have, though, certainly come across Gloucestershire speakers who rhyme the pairs just quoted, and say *bad* with the same [aː] as *father*. *LAE* shows an area of Devon, Somerset and Dorset with [aˑ] in *carrots*. And I have been initially misled into taking a Plymouth man for a northerner on the basis of a shortish [a] in *last*. Thus although the deviation from the RP long–short opposition may be in either direction, the point is that the distinction of length among front/central open vowels tends to be missing. (This does not apply in the speech of Southampton or Bristol, where the opposition between TRAP and BATH is retained, as *gas* [gæs] vs. *grass* [græːs ~ graːs] etc. But see further below.)

The standard lexical set PALM poses a problem here. In the west *palm* itself often retains its historical /l/, and is pronounced [palm]; likewise *calm* and other words. The town of *Calne* (Wiltshire) is locally [kaɫn], though [kɑːn] in RP. This [a] is probably to be identified with the vowel of LOT, so that *palm* is phonemically /pɒlm/. However, there are also many PALM words with no historical /l/ (and no orthographic *l*). Mostly, these seem to have the same vowel as BATH, i.e. [aː ~ æː]. This would apply, for example, to *tomato* and *banana* in most west-country accents. In Southampton they, like BATH words, have [æː] in working-class speech, varying sociolinguistically with a backer vowel, towards [ɑː], among the middle class.

The next complication is the possibility of differential lengthening of [a ~ æ] in TRAP words, giving contrasts such as *bad* [bæːd] but *pad* [pæd]. As we have seen (4.1.5), some RP speakers make this kind of distinction, which is marginally contrastive. So, it seems, do people in much of Wessex. A native of Hampshire, Fudge (1977), lists a large number of such pairs, including *sand* vs. *strand*, *drab* vs. *crab*, *jam* vs. *sham*, *standing* vs. *landing* (the first in each pair has the long vowel). Thus in working-class Southampton speech words such as *bad*, *sand*, *drab* have in effect been transferred from the lexical set TRAP to BATH. But in middle-class speech the BATH words, as mentioned above, have a backer vowel; some, therefore, can make a three-way distinction of the type *hand* [æː] vs. *land* [æ] vs. *command* [ɑː], or *Sam* vs. *Spam* vs. *psalm*. A word of caution here: there is a good deal of disagreement among different individuals as to which TRAP words have the short vowel and which the long. It does seem possible, though, to make the generalization that the long vowel is particularly common in 'expressive' or 'informal' words. In any case, the opposition does not have a very high functional load.

The possibility in a (lower-)middle-class accent of deleting postvocalic /r/ under the influence of the RP norm raises still further complications. According to Fudge, the result in START words is a long vowel or centring diphthong fronter than that of (middle-class) BATH: he writes *farce* [fa–əs], as against *pass* [pɑ+ːs]. There is thus at least the possibility of a four-way distinction of the type *man* [mæːn] vs. *pan* [pæn] vs. *barn* [baən] vs. *Calne* = *Khan* [kɑːn]. In some areas, though – parts of Devon and Cornwall, for instance – START has a back vowel, [ɑːɻ]; so even when derhoticized it tends to remain backer than the [aː] of BATH.

The LOT vowel, too, calls for comment. It often appears to be unrounded in the west, being qualitatively [ɑ], much as in the Irish Republic or the United States. This is certainly the way the LOT vowel is realized in the popular stereotype of a west-country accent; strangely, though, *SED* records throughout the west not [ɑ] but [ɒ] (i.e. a rounded vowel). The *LAE* maps for *holly* and *fox* (Ph38, Ph39) exemplify this, with in each case a rounded vowel shown for all west-country localities except one. Of course, the auditory difference between a fully back [ɑ] and [ɒ] is very slight, and it may well be a matter of free variation.

There are thus some west-country accents where an [ɑːɹ] in START words is to be phonemically identified as /ɒr/, i.e. as the [ɑ(ː)] of LOT plus /r/, rather than as /ar/, i.e. as /r/ following the [a(ː)] of TRAP, BATH, and words like *father* or *tomato*.

There is a large patch of Wessex where (in old-fashioned rural dialect, at least) we find the vowels of NORTH and START merged, since both *corn* and *darn* have [aɻ] (*LAE* maps Ph48, Ph19).

The vowels of FOOT and GOOSE are fronted in rural Devon speech, spilling over into adjacent parts of Somerset and Cornwall: *LAE* shows *foot* as [fʏt] and *goose* as [gʏːs]. The latter may also have something of a closing diphthong, of the type [øʏ].

The FACE and GOAT vowels are monophthongal, [eː] and [oː] respectively, in the more old-fashioned kind of Devon and Cornwall speech. Nowadays, though, there as elsewhere, there is a tendency for these monophthongs to be replaced by diphthongal qualities.

The PRICE and MOUTH diphthongs frequently exhibit Crossover (4.2.4 above). It is difficult to make any general statement about west-country PRICE, since it ranges widely over qualities such as [əɪ, ʌɪ, ɑɪ, ɒɪ]. The opposition vis-à-vis CHOICE is apparently usually, though not always, retained. The typical qualities for MOUTH are perhaps [æʊ] and [ɐʊ]. Near London, however, *LAE* shows [ɛʊ] as prevalent. To my ear the second element nowadays is definitely fronted and unrounded, giving [ɛɪ ~ eɪ], so that in Hampshire and the home counties *down* tends to sound like RP *deign*, and *out* like

RP *eight.* Investigations by C. Capell (unpublished) in High Wycombe (Buckinghamshire) in 1978 showed that some older working-class speakers there in fact had variable neutralization of the MOUTH–FACE opposition, and could indeed pronounce *out* and *eight* as homophones, [ɛɪʔ].

In much west-country speech the question arises whether there is any phonemic opposition between the STRUT vowel and the weak [ə] of *about* or *salad.* (The final vowel in *comma, window,* etc., may constitute other instances of [ə], though as we have seen they also occur as /ər/ and, in Bristol, as /əl/.) The *LAE* maps imply that a phonetic difference is generally present, with [ʌ]-type vowels in *butter* everywhere except on the Gloucestershire–Avon border, where [ə] occurs instead. But this does not preclude the possibility of stressed [ʌ] and unstressed [ə] being allophones of the same phoneme. Whether this analysis is the correct one is tricky to determine; I am inclined to think that for west-country local accents it usually is. Support comes from words whose stress pattern may fluctuate according to prosodic considerations: for example, *Cheltenham,* with a slower or phrase-final form ['tʃɛlt,nʌm] and a faster or phrase-internal one ['tʃɛltnəm]; or similarly *moment* ['moʊ,mʌnt] ∼ ['moʊmənt]. And it may be the case that *an ending* and *unending* cannot, in a west-country accent, be uttered with identical stress patterns as they can in RP; thus the [ə] of the former and the [ʌ] of the latter are not in direct contrast in the same environment.

4.3.8 The Bristol vowel system

The Bristol vowel system can be set out as (185), with incidence as (186). In view of the phonetic variability in duration we have referred to, no phonemic length-marks are used here. As can be seen, the Bristol system is considerably closer to RP than one would find in a west-country rural accent.

(185)

I ʊ	i		u		
ɛ ʌ	ɛɪ ɔɪ		ɔʊ	3 ɔ	
æ ɒ	ɑɪ	aʊ	a		

(186)

KIT	ɪ	FLEECE	i	NEAR	ir [ɪɻ]	
DRESS	ɛ	FACE	ɛɪ	SQUARE	ɛɪr [ɛɻ]	
TRAP	æ	PALM	a	START	ar [aɻ ~ aɾ]	
LOT	ɑ	THOUGHT	ɔ	NORTH	ɔr [ɔɻ ~ ɔɾ]	
STRUT	ʌ	GOAT	ɔʊ	FORCE	ɔr	
FOOT	ʊ	GOOSE	u	CURE	ur ~ ɔr	
BATH	a	PRICE	ɑɪ	happY	i	
CLOTH	ɒ	CHOICE	ɔɪ	lettER	ər [ɚ]	
NURSE	ɜr [ɝ]	MOUTH	aʊ	commA	ə ~ əl	

A Smoothing rule gives optional variants of diphthong plus weak vowel plus sonorant, as follows: *pale* [pɛːɫ], *player* [plɛːɻ], *playing* [plɛːɪn]; *mile* [mɑːɫ], *tired* [tɑːɻd], *crying* [kɻɑːɪn]; *hole* [hoːɫ], *lower* [loːɻ], *going* [goːɪn]; *power* [pɑːɻ].

4.4 The north

4.4.1 Introduction

From a linguistic point of view, the population of England is about equally divided between the north and the south. If we exclude the small number of RP speakers (who are scattered throughout the whole country), about half of the English speak with some degree of northern accent.

'Northern' in this sense might more precisely be glossed 'midlands or northern'. We cross from the south to the linguistic north at the point where we pass the northern limits (in broad local accents) of the FOOT–STRUT Split and of BATH Broadening (both further discussed below, 4.4.2–3). In a northern accent, then, *put* and *putt* are typically homophones, [pʊt], while *gas* and *glass* rhyme perfectly, [gas, glas].

This means that the linguistic north comprises not only that part of England which is ordinarily called the north (i.e. from the Scottish border south as far as a line from the Mersey to the Humber), but also most of the midlands. It includes, for example, the Birmingham–Wolverhampton conurbation, Leicester, and Peterborough.

There is a further difficulty with the term 'northern'. For

349

historically-oriented dialectologists, a 'northern' dialect is one located north of a line from the Lune to the Humber – a descendant of the Old English of Northumbria rather than that of Mercia, Wessex, or Kent. They refer to dialects from the areas around Manchester and Leeds as 'north midland'. But in contemporary everyday language, the 'north midlands' means places like Stoke-on-Trent or Chesterfield; and Leeds and Manchester are not in the 'north midlands', but in the 'north'. Accordingly I have decided not to employ the traditional dialectologists' nomenclature for these areas. Instead, I call everything from the Severn–Wash line north-wards 'the (linguistic) north'. Within it we can distinguish, as we move away from London and towards the Scottish border, (i) the midlands, (ii) the middle north, and (iii) the far north.

The **midlands** comprises the east and west midlands. The east midlands includes the large cities of Leicester and Nottingham, whose local accents are in many ways similar to those of the middle north. The west midlands includes the modern county of the same name, centred on the Birmingham–Wolverhampton conurbation. Its local accent is rather different (4.4.5 below). There is also a north-western transitional area including Stoke-on-Trent and Derby.

The **middle north** includes the densely populated industrial belt straddling the Pennines from Manchester through Hudders-field, Bradford, and Leeds, to Sheffield. The local accents within this area – the modern counties of Greater Manchester, West Yorkshire, and South Yorkshire – show considerable resemblances to one another; we shall take them as 'typical' northern accents. The modern counties of Merseyside and Lancashire differ in certain important respects: we discuss them in 4.4.8 and 4.4.10 below.

As far as population centres are concerned, the **far north** means Tyneside and Tees-side. The accent of the former differs from typical northern accents considerably more than that of the latter (4.4.11). Tyneside is the Newcastle-upon-Tyne conurbation, the modern county of Tyne and Wear, the home of the accent com-monly referred to as 'Geordie'. Tees-side centres on Middles-borough and the modern county of Cleveland. Between them is County Durham, with an accent referred to locally as 'Pitmatic'.

It is in the north of England that traditional-dialect (vol. 1, 1.1.3) survives most strongly. It is probably also true that local differences in dialect and accent as one moves from valley to valley or from village to village are sharper in the north than in any other part of England, and become sharper the further north one goes. Harold Orton, the guiding spirit behind the *SED*, came from County Durham, and became well-known through his study of the dialect of his native village (Orton 1933); and many of his associates in this project were also northerners, inspired no doubt by the dialectal diversity around them.

4.4.2 The STRUT words

As we have seen, the two most important characteristics setting northern local accents apart from southern ones are (i) the absence of the FOOT–STRUT Split, i.e. the lack of a phonemic opposition between the vowels of FOOT and STRUT; and (ii) the absence of BATH Broadening, i.e. the use in BATH words of the vowel of TRAP.

The isogloss for the FOOT–STRUT Split runs from the Severn estuary in the west to the Wash in the east. The area in which FOOT and STRUT have the same vowel comprises all of England north of this line except for (i) a part of Salop and Herefordshire, along the Welsh border, and (ii) northernmost Northumberland (including the town of Berwick-on-Tweed), which though politically English is linguistically Scottish. (See map, fig. 8.)

This, then, is the area where – in the broadest local accents, if not necessarily in higher-status speech – *put* is a homophone of *putt*, and *could* (strong form) a homophone of *cud*. As we saw in volume I, 3.1.7, this can essentially be traced historically to the failure of the FOOT–STRUT Split, the split of Middle English short /u/ into two phonemes. Further south, further west, and further north this split was carried through, so that in the south of England, in Wales, and in Scotland we now have a six-term system of short vowels (*A* vowels). In the north of England it did not take place, so that a five-term system was preserved.

Nevertheless, the prestige norm (RP) exhibits the six-term system. This means that everywhere in the north of England there is sociolinguistic variation between a more local, overtly less prestigious, five-term system, with the same /ʊ/ in both FOOT and STRUT, and the national, overtly more prestigious, six-term system which makes a distinction between the /ʊ/ of FOOT and some kind of unrounded and opener vowel in STRUT. It appears that the further north one goes, the higher up the social scale is the crossover between a five-term system and a six-term system located. In the West Midlands conurbation, in fact, it is probably true to say that all speakers do to some extent have a STRUT vs. FOOT opposition, but that it is variably neutralized and sometimes of uncertain incidence. In Cannock, Staffordshire, a survey found that all except the lowest of the five social classes recognized in the survey had the opposition; even the speakers in the lowest class did make some variable and inconsistent use of it, pronouncing, for instance, [ʌ] in *bud* and *butter* but [ʊ] in *rubber* (Heath 1980). Further north, though, broad working-class speakers certainly do not have any control of a FOOT vs. STRUT opposition, which is associated with 'good' speech only. In the far north, the five-term short vowel system extends well up the social scale, and would be quite usual, for instance, in a lower-middle-class Newcastle-upon-Tyne accent.

In accents or pronunciation styles intermediate between the broad (with [ʊ] in STRUT) and RP (with [ʌ]), there are commonly two phenomena characteristic just of such intermediate stages. One is the use of qualities for the STRUT vowel which are distinct from the [ʊ] of FOOT but nevertheless perceptually different from any realization of RP /ʌ/; the other is the hypercorrect avoidance of [ʊ] in FOOT words. (See discussion in Chambers & Trudgill 1980: ch. 8.)

Such intermediate qualities for the STRUT vowel include a vocoid somewhat opener than [ʊ], namely a mid back [ɤ]; the unrounded equivalent, [ɤ]; and a half-open vocoid, unrounded or slightly rounded, similar to cardinal [ʌ] (and therefore somewhat different from RP /ʌ/, which is usually central rather than back). They also include a mid or half-close [ə], central and unrounded.

The last-mentioned possibility, stressed [ə] in STRUT, seems to be particularly characteristic of northern Near-RP, with pronunciations such as *cup* [kəp], *brother* ['brəðə]. Naturally, its use tends to imply the absence of any opposition between STRUT and the /ə/ of weak syllables. This is typically revealed by the lack of distinction between the strong and weak forms of *but, does, must, us*. Alternatively, northern Near-RP may have stress-sensitive allophonic variation between [ʌ] and [ə], which entails the appearance of seemingly weak forms even for words such as *up* and *one*, which have no RP weak forms – an alternation conveniently diagnosed by the pronunciation ['sʌmwən] *someone* (RP: ['sʌmwʌn]; other northern forms include not only ['səmwən, 'sʊmwʊn], but also [-wɒn]).

By 'the hypercorrect avoidance of [ʊ] in FOOT words' is meant the use of some opener vocoid not only for STRUT but also for FOOT: pronunciations such as *sugar* ['ʃəgə ~ 'ʃʌgə], *butcher* ['bətʃə ~ 'bʌtʃə], *cushion* ['kəʃn̩ ~ 'kʌʃn̩]. In STRUT words, after all, the use of an opener quality, [ə ~ ʌ] etc., does represent a genuine modification of a broad northern accent towards RP, and as such is readily adopted by the upwardly-mobile speaker who starts off with a five-term *A* vowel system. In FOOT words, however, it constitutes a movement away from the phonetic quality of RP /ʊ/.

It seems that hypercorrect ['ʃʌgə], etc., may arise as the result of the individual speaker's poshing-up of his accent through the strategy of adopting the new, opener, realization for all instances of his underlying /ʊ/ (both STRUT and FOOT); or it may in some cases have become institutionalized as a widespread form located sociolinguistically between the broad northern and RP pronunciations, both of which are phonetically ['ʃʊgə].

Summing up, then, (187) tabulates the typical possibilities for STRUT and FOOT in the north of England.

(187)		STRUT	FOOT	
	Broad	[ʊ]	[ʊ]	One phoneme, /ʊ/
Intermediate	{	[ə ~ ʌ]	[ə ~ ʌ]	One phoneme; realization modified
		[ə ~ ʌ]	[ʊ]	Two phonemes; incidence may be erratic
	RP	[ʌ]	[ʊ]	Two phonemes, /ʌ/ vs. /ʊ/

And of course there are many speakers whose pronunciation varies between these possibilities according to contextual style.

4.4.3 The BATH words

In the north of England the words belonging to the standard lexical set BATH (vol. 1, 2.2.7) are very generally pronounced with the same short open vowel as TRAP, namely /a/ (= RP /æ/); thus *laugh* [laf], *path* [paθ], *example* [ɛgˈzampl]; etc.; *glass* [glas] rhymes with *gas* [gas]. Unlike the accents of the south of England, the local accents of the north are thus flat-BATH accents.

At its eastern end, the isogloss marking the northern limit of

BATH Broadening (vol. 1, 3.2.6) coincides with the FOOT–STRUT isogloss. Towards the west, as mentioned in 4.3.7 above, the phonemic opposition between short and long open vowels (TRAP vs. START–PALM) becomes variable or absent, and it is therefore phonologically meaningless to ask which vowel phoneme, short or long, is used in the BATH words. With many Gloucestershire speakers, for example, we find long [aː] used not only in *glass* but also in *gas*, the lengthening thus being purely allophonic; so that, although there is a long vowel here in BATH words, this accent lacks the essential factor in BATH Broadening, which is the making of a distinction between BATH words and TRAP words. If we consider merely phonetic lengthening in BATH words, ignoring the question of its phonemic status, we find its geographical extent delimited by an isogloss running more or less horizontally across the country from west to east, from Salop to the Wash, passing just to the south of Birmingham and Leicester but to the north of Northampton. For most of its path it is thus somewhat to the north of the FOOT–STRUT isogloss. (See map, fig. 8.) Northampton, Wellingborough, and Kettering lie between the two major isoglosses.

As one has come to expect, the isoglosses for any two particular BATH words, as revealed by *SED*, tend not to coincide exactly. The line for *aunt*, for example, lies well to the north of the line for *last* (map, fig. 9). Places that lie between these two single-word isoglosses – Birmingham, for example – have /aːnt/ but /last/.

Retention of a short vowel in BATH words extends much further up the social scale than does the retention of unsplit /ʊ/. In Cannock the BATH vowel was found to be a consistent short /a/ in the three lowest social classes, variable for the next-to-highest, and long /aː/ only for the highest of the five social classes recognized in the study (Heath 1980). There are many educated northerners who would not be caught dead doing something so vulgar as to pronounce STRUT words with [ʊ], but who would feel it to be a denial of their identity as northerners to say BATH words with anything other than short [a].

One or two of the BATH words are particularly susceptible to Broadening as a result of their association with school and school-inspired standards of correctness. An instance is *master*, often pronounced /ˈmaːstə/ by northerners who would nevertheless pronounce *plaster* and *disaster* with short /a/. The fact that the traditional-dialect form of this word often has the FACE vowel (thus

	phonetically short vowel in *aunt* Ph 174		phonetically short vowel in · *half* Ph 10 (excluding a few sporadic cases further south)
	phonetically short vowel in *last* Ph 4		

Fig. 9   Isoglosses for some BATH words (after *LAE*). *Note*. The county boundaries shown are those prior to the local government reorganization of the 1970s

/ˈmeːstə/ etc.) no doubt also contributes to the fact that the 'typical' northern form /ˈmastə/ is not quite as widespread as one might otherwise expect.

For the word *half* the long vowel is the rule rather than the exception in the north. The short-vowel pronunciation is virtually confined to Northumberland and Tyne and Wear. (Northern traditional-dialect mostly has [e:] or [ɔ:].) With varying degrees of emphasis, the same applies to the other words listed in (59c) of vol. I, 2.2.7: if we were considering their pronunciation in England alone, and leaving North America out of account, we should place *half, can't, banana*, etc. in the PALM set rather than in BATH.

4.4.4 Other vowels

The absence of a FOOT–STRUT Split means, as we have seen, that northern accents typically have five rather than six vowels in part-system A. They are the /ɪ, ɛ, a, ɒ, ʊ/ of KIT, DRESS, TRAP, LOT, and FOOT–STRUT respectively. Except in the West Midlands, all five tend to be somewhat opener than in RP. In particular, /a/ is not of the [æ] type, but a fully open vowel somewhere between front and central [a ~ a–]; thus *back* [bak], *bad* [bad], *damp* [damp]. The LOT vowel, too, is generally fully open: it is [ɒ], perceptibly opener than mainstream RP /ɒ/. (In Lincolnshire, however, this does not apply: *SED* writes [ɔ] there, as against [ɒ] in most other places.) In Northumberland traditional-dialect there is also a fronted [œ] type in some LOT words.

Neither /ɒ/ nor /ʊ/ is necessarily very rounded in northern speech. The latter may indeed often be of the [ɤ] type; as explained above, there are in any case sociolinguistic reasons why a rounded [ʊ] tends to be replaced by an unrounded and less close quality.

In the first paragraph of this section the assertion was made that a five-term short vowel system is the broad northern norm. In some areas, though, there is evidence for the existence of an additional short vowel in the system, a stressable /ə/ (quite apart from the possible use of [ə] in STRUT words). Phonetically, this is a half-close [ə] or [ɪ]; it occurs mainly in NURSE words, and seems to have originated as a positional variant of /ɪ/ or /ɛ/ in the vicinity of /r/, though this consonant may then have been vocalized or disappeared. Thus in Dent (a village formerly in Yorkshire, now in Cumbria) it is recorded for such words as *very, terrible* [tɪbl], *birk* 'birch' [bɪk ~ bɪrk], *girs* 'grass' [gɪs], *red*, as well as in *not* [nɪt], which may have originated as a restressed weak form (data from Hedevind 1967). *SED* shows [kəs] as the most widespread form for *curse* (*cuss*) in Yorkshire traditional-dialect. Where the traditional vowel system already includes this /ə/, the task of 'improving' one's accent by incorporating a FOOT–STRUT Split becomes one of transferring certain /ʊ/ words to /ə/, rather than one of introducing a completely new stressed-vowel quality into the system.

The CLOTH words have short /ɒ/ throughout the north.

The FLEECE Merger (vol. 1, 3.1.6) has not been carried through everywhere in the north. Particularly in traditional-dialect, but also to some extent in less extreme varieties of northern speech, one can find the historical opposition preserved. Thus in a broad swathe through the middle north *meet* is [miːt] but *meat* may be [mɪət]. In the Dales of North Yorkshire the distinction is rather *meet* [məɪt] vs. *meat* [mɪət]; in Staffordshire, *meet* [mɛɪt] vs. *meat* [miːt]. The Long Mid Mergers (vol. 1, 3.1.5) have, on the whole, been carried through, so that pairs such as *mane–main, daze–days* are homophonous. Long Mid Diphthonging (vol. 1, 3.1.12) has applied only in the midlands and, to a limited extent, in the urban speech of the middle north; so the FACE words are still very commonly pronounced with a long monophthong, half-close or somewhat lowered and retracted from cardinal 2, thus *gate* [geːt ~ gë̞ːt]. In the east of the middle north and in Lincolnshire a centring diphthong is usual in traditional-dialect, thus *gate* [gɛət]. In the far north, too, to the north of a line from the Lune to the Humber, the FACE words typically have centring/opening diphthongs, either the [ɪə] of *meat* or an opener [ea ~ ɪa ~ jɛ]. In the traditional-dialect of Dent, *dale* is [deal ~ dial], but *deal* is [diël].

The old velar fricative of words like *weigh, reign, straight* (vol. 1, 3.1.3) has left its traces rather widely in the north. Thus *LAE* shows *weigh* as [wɛɪ] nearly throughout the region, contrasting with the [eː ~ ɛə] of *way* and of most other FACE words. Even in the urban accents of the middle north *eight* may fail to rhyme with *late*, [ɛɪt] vs. [leːt]. But as the diphthonging of FACE spreads under the influence of RP and other accents, the distinction is increasingly lost.

Similarly, PRICE words which once had a velar fricative (shown by *igh* in their spelling) have a middle north traditional-dialect form in which the vowel is not the /aɪ/ of most PRICE words but the /iː/ of FLEECE: thus *night* [niːt], *right* [riːt], etc. This is shown in eye-dialect by spellings such as *good neet, all reet*. As traditional-dialect disappears, so these /iː/ pronunciations are supplanted by the standard forms with /aɪ/, and *night* comes to rhyme with *bite* rather than with *beet.* (There is also the possibility of a traditional-dialect vowel in *night*, etc., which differs both from that of *bite* and from that of *beet*.)

As far as the vowel in the bulk of PRICE words is concerned, the general picture presented by the north is of a progression from a back starting-point, [ɑ ~ ɒ ~ ɔ], in the midlands via a front [a] in the middle north to a less open [ɛ] in the far north. At the two extremes, the endpoint of the diphthong is close, [ɪ ~ i]; but in much of the middle north the diphthong is a very narrow one, not moving much beyond [ɛ], and often being (variably?) monophthongal. Thus the three most typical realizations of the PRICE diphthong seem to be [ɑɪ] in the midlands, [aɛ] in the middle north, and [ɛɪ] in the far north; so that *price* appears as [prɑɪs], [praɛs], and [prɛɪs] respectively. (Particular developments in Birmingham and Newcastle-upon-Tyne are discussed below.)

The vowels in part-system C exhibit a somewhat similar pattern, though simpler. The Long Mid Mergers, as mentioned above, have on the whole been carried through, at least in the midlands and the middle north, so that pairs such as *throne–thrown*, *nose–knows* are more often than not homophonous. The quality of this merged GOAT vowel is [ɔʊ ~ ʌʊ] in the midlands, [oʊ ~ əʊ] in some of the urban middle north, and otherwise either a monophthongal [o: ~ ǫ:] or, along the east coast and in the far north, a centring/opening diphthong [ʊə ~ oə]. (For Tyneside [ø:] etc., see below.) To the north of the Lune–Humber line, these back vowels are displacing or have displaced the traditional-dialect vowel, which (in words deriving from northern Middle English /a:/) is a front diphthong [ɪə ~ ɪa ~ ea]. Thus in Dent the traditional-dialect pronunciation of *stone* is [steǎn]; but 'in polite speech' the pronunciation [stǫ:n] is used instead (Hedevind 1967: §2.24). (Both of these pronunciations sound very different from RP [stəʊn], which justifies our claiming that [steǎn] belongs to 'northern traditional-dialect' and [stǫ:n] to a 'northern accent'.)

Another traditional-dialect vowel of certain GOAT words is [ɔɪ], restricted to South and West Yorkshire and central Lancashire. Examples include [kɔɪt] *coat*, ['kɔɪlɔɪl] *coal-hole*.

Some northern accents, like most traditional-dialect of the middle and far north, include a diphthong of the [ɔʊ ~ ɒʊ ~ ʌʊ] type which contrasts both with the [ɔ:] of words like *jaw* and also with [aʊ] and [o:]. It tends to be used in THOUGHT words which historically contained a velar fricative, such as *daughter, bought,* and *thought* itself. It is very typically found in the items *owt* (*aught*) and *nowt* (*naught*), the non-standard local equivalents of *anything* and *nothing*. It may also be used in GOAT words such as *cold, roll, blow, own*. Thus some have /aʊ/ vs. /ɔʊ/ vs. /oː/ in *out* vs. *owt* vs. *oat;* *now* vs. *know* vs. *no*. But others have *out* and *owt* identical as /aʊt/, *know* and *no* /noː/.

The vowel of MOUTH furnishes one of the most important iso-glosses in northern traditional-dialect. This is the line stretching across the country from Cumbria to Humberside, the line dividing the middle north from the far north. To the north of it, the Great Vowel Shift (vol. 1, 3.1.1) did not apply to Middle English /uː/, so that pronunciations such as [uːt] *out*, [kluːd] *cloud*, [kuː] *cow*, etc., remain. (GOOSE words, on the other hand, have [ɪə] in this dialect, so that pairs such as *shoot* [ʃɪət] and *shout* [ʃuːt] remain in principle distinct.) To the south of the line, the Great Vowel Shift has given the usual types [aʊ] etc. in MOUTH and [uː] etc. in GOOSE. (These types are of course also encountered in the far north, where they represent the ousting of traditional-dialect forms by more standard ones.)

In the midlands and the middle north MOUTH is generally of the [aʊ] type, although there is quite a bit of phonetic variation. It seems possible that the monophthongal types to be heard in some accents of the middle north, [aː ~ ɑː], are synchronic stylistic variants of diphthongal types. Fronted starting-points, [ɛʊ], etc., are not nearly as common as in the south of England, although [æʊ] may be heard in Sheffield (South Yorkshire). Parts of southern Lancashire and Greater Manchester (e.g. Bolton, Oldham) have an unusual type [ɐʏ ~ ʌʏ], with a fronted second element, thus [mʌʏθ] *mouth*.

The GOOSE vowel is mostly [uː ~ ʊu] much as in RP. In some of Greater Manchester and adjacent parts of Lancashire and Cheshire there is also a fronted [ʏː] type. A diphthongal realization, ranging variably to [əu], is characteristic not only of Birmingham and some other urban speech but also of the very rural northern Yorkshire Dales and Dentdale: [təu] *two*.

Some speakers retain a contrastive /ɪu/ diphthong, as in *blue* [blɪu], *suit* [sɪut]. This appears to be quite sharply recessive in the face of the RP /uː ~ juː/ types, so that the tendency is to lose the historical distinction between *threw* and *through*.

Traditional-dialect possibilities in GOOSE words include (i) [ɪə ~ ɪʏ ~ ɪʊ] to the north-east of the Lune–Humber line, thus [gɪəs] etc. (rhyming in some places with *grease*); (ii) [ʊɪ] in West and South Yorkshire, thus [gʊɪs]; and (iii) [ɛʊ] in parts of Derbyshire and Staffordshire (in the northern midlands), thus [gɛʊs].

In part-system D the number of contrasting vowels does of course depend very much on the fate of historical /r/; but rhoticity in northern accents is quite sharply restricted geographically (as discussed in 4.4.8 below). All northern vowel systems include at least a long open /aː ~ ɑː/, a mid or open back /ɔː/, and a mid central or front /ɜː ~ ɛː ~ ɛə/. The non-rhotic accents often also include contrastive /ɪə/ and /ʊə/, although with the latter both its lexical incidence and its distinctness from /uːə/ are somewhat variable.

The vowel of PALM and START varies from a front [aː] to a back [ɑː]. The front variety may be identical in quality with the /a/ of TRAP, differing from it only in length, as [pak] *pack* vs. [paːk] *park*; or it may be somewhat less front. This type predominates in the middle north, including the broad urban accents of Leeds and Manchester. The backer type, [ɑː], is like RP /ɑː/ or even backer. It is this type which characterizes the speech of such midlands cities as Stoke-on-Trent and Derby, as well as that of Newcastle-upon-Tyne in the far north. Here *car park* is [ˈkɑː pɑːk], and the qualitative difference from [pak] *pack* is very noticeable.

Some THOUGHT words, as discussed above, may have /ɔʊ/. Others never do: items such as *walk* and *straw* are said with /ɔː/ everywhere, excepting only the traditional-dialect of the far north, which has /aː/ in these words (4.4.11 below). As traditional-dialect /ɔʊ/ recedes, *thought* itself and similar items come to be said with the same /ɔː/ of *walk* and *straw*. The vowel /ɔː/ is also the one used in the standard lexical set NORTH, as *short* /ʃɔːt/; increasingly, too, it comes to be used in FORCE words. In the latter set, though, an older pronunciation persists, particularly in the middle and far north; this involves the use of [ʊə ~ oə], as *door* [dʊə ~ doə] (now also [dɔː]).

In the middle north, /ɔː/ is often fully open in quality, [ɒː]. This is understandable, given the [ö̞ː] realization of GOAT and the pressure to preserve a clear distinction between GOAT and THOUGHT, as [lö̞ː] *low* vs. [lɒː] *law*. Compare also the word *jaw-bone* [ˈdʒɒːbö̞ːn], which sounds almost like RP '*jar-born*' /ˈdʒɑːbɔːn/.

The NURSE vowel is often much as in RP, [ɜː]; but a closer

variety, [ə: ~ ɨ:], is characteristic of some urban accents in the western midlands (Birmingham, Stoke-on-Trent), thus ['ɨ:θwɨ:m] *earthworm*.

In some areas NURSE and SQUARE are merged, so that *pair* is homophonous with *purr*, *staring* with *stirring*, and *fairy* with *furry*. This is a well-known characteristic of Scouse, the broad accent of Liverpool and Merseyside; it extends to adjacent parts of Lancashire and to some at least of Greater Manchester (for example, Wigan, my home town). Although the question has not been adequately investigated, I have the impression that there are various other parts of the north (Leicestershire, West Midlands, Lincolnshire?) where there is at least variable merging of NURSE and SQUARE. The quality of the merged vowel is generally [ɜ:] (like RP /ɜ:/ of NURSE), thus ['mɜ:rɪ] *Mary*, ['fɜ: 'ʃɜ:z] *fair shares*. But it may also be [ɛ:], [ɛə], or something intermediate. In Liverpool the most characteristic qualities are reported to be the centralized front monophthongs [ë:] and [ɛ̈:]; but [ɛ:] and [e:] also occur (Knowles 1978: 84). Pronunciations such as [nɛ:s] *nurse* might be looked on as hypercorrections.

Where the SQUARE vowel is distinct from NURSE it is nevertheless frequently monophthongal, [ɛ:].

The [iə ~ ɪə] of the standard lexical set NEAR can often be identified as a contrastive /ɪə/ (though not, of course, in rhotic accents, where it is a positional allophone of /i:/ in the environment of a following /r/). The more conservative northern accents, though, use disyllabic or varisyllabic pronunciations of the type [fi:ə] *fear*, [bi:ə] *beer*, which is best regarded as a phonemic sequence /i:ə/. Word-internally before /r/, in words such as *serious*, *period*, these accents usually have simple /i:/ with no following /ə/. These pronunciations are clearly recessive in the face of RP-type pronunciations with [ɪə] = /ɪə/.

Generally similar considerations apply to the [uə ~ ʊə] of CURE. Here the most conservative accents have /u:ə/ or even /ɪuə/: the item *sure* in *SED* exhibits a complicated patchwork of [u:ə, ɪuə, uə, ʊə, oə, ɔ:ə] and other types. The situation is more complicated than that of NEAR because of the all-England trend towards merging /ʊə/ with /ɔ:/ (vol. 1, 3.2.7), making *sure* homophonous with *shore* and *Shaw*.

The Cumbrian speaker mentioned in volume 1 (p. 217) thought that the disyllabic pronunciations [bi:ə], [ʃu:ə] for *beer* and *sure* were 'ugly', but found centring diphthongs with a centralized starting-point, [bɪə, ʃʊə], 'posh'. Her own pronunciation (perceived as 'ordinary') had monosyllabic [iə, uə] with peripheral starting-points, thus ['dʒuəri] *jury*, [biə] *beer*. In SQUARE and FORCE words she used long monophthongs, as ['stɔːri] *story*, ['fɛːri] *fairy*. Very much the same kind of thing is described for the working-class speech of Cannock, nearly two hundred miles to the south.

The other northern vowel which calls for mention is the *happ*Y vowel. In the heartland of the north – places such as Manchester and Leeds – this vowel is [ɪ], clearly to be identified phonemically with the /ɪ/ of KIT. This is one important respect in which a typical northern local accent agrees with RP, while southern accents differ. In Leeds the word *happy* is pronounced ['apɪ] at the bottom of the sociolinguistic continuum, ['hæpɪ] at the top: but the difference lies in the first two segments alone.

There are areas of the north where the *happ*Y vowel is even opener, approaching the /ɛ/ of DRESS. This applies, for instance, to the speech of Nottingham: ['sɪtɛ̈] *city*. But in the peripheral north, a closer vowel is used, often to be identified phonemically with the /iː/ of FLEECE: this applies, for instance, to the speech of Birmingham, Liverpool, Newcastle-upon-Tyne, and Scunthorpe, which lie respectively to the south, west, north, and east of the [ɪ]-using area.

In traditional-dialect, of course, lexical incidence differs sharply from that of standard accents. Ignoring this, there are also a few types of word where northern accents, too, characteristically exhibit a difference of vowel incidence as compared with RP or other accents. Thus *one* is /wɒn/ in parts of the north, rather than the expected /wʊn/ (RP /wʌn/); the /wɒn/ area includes Birmingham, Stoke, Liverpool, Manchester and Sheffield. Further east and north there is indeed /wʊn/, it having in some places dis-placed traditional-dialect forms such as /jan/. In a somewhat more restricted area, *once, among, none* and *nothing* may also be encountered with /ɒ/. Another difference of lexical incidence con-cerns the FOOT and GOOSE words. Several words with the spelling *-ook* retain the historical long vowel in much of the north, thus /buːk/ *book*, /kuːk/ *cook* etc; although still widespread, these forms are recessive in the face of the standard /ʊ/ forms. Conversely, in Birmingham *tooth* has /ʊ/ (RP /tuːθ/).

Northern speech tends to retain strong vowels in certain

environments where RP and other accents show weakening. Notable among these are Latin prefixes such as *ad-*, *con-*, *ex-* when pretonic. A list of examples is given in (188). The geographical area over which strong-vowel prefixes extend is not precisely known: clearly, though, it excludes Birmingham but includes the middle north.

(188)	Northern form	RP form	orthography
	adˈvans	ədˈvɑːns	*advance*
	kɒmˈpjuːtə	kəmˈpjuːtə	*computer*
	kɒnˈsɪdə	kənˈsɪdə	*consider*
	kɒnˈtɪnjuː	kənˈtɪnjuː	*continue*
	ɛgˈzamɪn	ɪgˈzæmɪn	*examine*
	ɛkˈspɛkt	ɪkˈspɛkt	*expect*
	ɒbˈdʒɛkt	əbˈdʒɛkt	*object* (v.)

In the middle north and far north phonologically long vowels (i.e. part-systems B, C, D) tend to be phonetically long under all conditions. A word like /ʃiːp/ *sheep* thus has a vowel of greater duration in a northern accent than in RP or a southern accent; and the rhythm of a word such as /ˈmiːtɪŋ/ *meeting* is rather different.

4.4.5 Two vowel systems

We can pull the preceding sections together by stating the complete vowel systems of two representative accents of the linguistic north: those of Birmingham (West Midlands) and Leeds (West Yorkshire).

The Birmingham vowel system is shown in (189). It combines London-like shifted diphthongs in part-systems B and C with a northern part-system A.

(189)	ɪ	ʊ	iː				uː	(ɪə)		(ʊə)
	ɛ	(ʌ)		ʌɪ	(ɔɪ)		ʌʊ	ɛː	3ː	ɔː
	a	ɒ			ɒɪ	æʊ				ɑː

Phonetically, /ɪ/ is very close, [ɪ]; /iː/ and /uː/ have variants ranging through [ɪi, ʊu] to [əi, əu]; /æʊ/ has a variant [æə]; /3ː/ is [əː ~ ɪ̈ː]. The oppositions between /ʊ/ and /ʌ/, and between /ɒɪ/ and /ɔɪ/, appear to be variably neutralizable, perhaps as phonetically intermediate [ɤ], [ɒɪ]. For the possible /ɪə/ and /ʊə/, see above. Incidence is as shown in (190).

(190)

KIT	ɪ	FLEECE	iː	NEAR	iːə (~ ɪə)
DRESS	ɛ	FACE	ʌɪ	SQUARE	ɛː
TRAP	a	PALM	ɑː	START	ɑː
LOT	ɒ	THOUGHT	ɔː	NORTH	ɔː
STRUT	ʊ (~ ʌ)	GOAT	ʌʊ	FORCE	ʌʊə (~ ɔː)
FOOT	ʊ	GOOSE	uː	CURE	uːə (~ ʊə ~ ɔː)
BATH	a	PRICE	ɒɪ	*happ*Y	[i]
CLOTH	ɒ	CHOICE	ɒɪ (~ oɪ)	*lett*ER	ə
NURSE	ɜ	MOUTH	æʊ	*comm*A	ə

This system applies generally to the West Midlands, including the Black Country around Wolverhampton, though there are apparently some speakers who merge SQUARE and NURSE. (The Black Country is linguistically notable for its retention of traditional-dialect forms such as have disappeared from the rest of the midlands.) The broad accent of Cannock (Staffordshire), as described by Heath (1980), differs mainly by having [ɛɪ, ɔʊ] for FACE and GOAT, with peripheral starting-points, and [ɑɪ] for PRICE, with an unrounded starting-point, rather than the Cockney-like [ʌɪ, ʌʊ, ɒɪ ~ ɔɪ] to be heard in Birmingham.

Seventy kilometres to the north, the Potteries accent of the Stoke-on-Trent conurbation lacks the London–Birmingham Diphthong Shift: FACE and GOAT have narrow diphthongs, [eɪ] and [əʊ] respectively, and PRICE has [aɪ]. The Stoke /əʊ/ in GOAT has a closer starting-point than the identically transcribed RP diphthong; it also has a positional allophone of the [ɔʊ] type in the environment of a following /l/.

The Leeds vowel system is shown in (191).

(191)

ɪ	ʊ	iː			uː	ɪə	ʊə
ɛ		eː	(ɛɪ)		oː	ɛː	3ː ɔə
a	ɒ	aɪ		ɔɪ	aʊ (ɔʊ)	aː	ɔː

Phonetically, /ɔː/ is very open; the diphthongal movement in /aɪ/ may be slight, [aɛ], or even absent. For the possibility of contrastive /ɛɪ/ and /ɔʊ/ in certain FACE and THOUGHT words, see above. Incidence is as shown in (192).

(192)

KIT	ɪ	FLEECE	iː	NEAR	ɪə
DRESS	ɛ	FACE	eː (~ ɛɪ)	SQUARE	ɛː
TRAP	a	PALM	aː	START	aː

LOT	ɒ	THOUGHT	ɔː	NORTH	ɔː
STRUT	ʊ	GOAT	oː (~ ɔʊ)	FORCE	ɔː (~ ɔə)
FOOT	ʊ	GOOSE	uː	CURE	ʊə (~ ɔː)
BATH	a	PRICE	aɪ	happY	ɪ
CLOTH	ɒ	CHOICE	ɔɪ	lettER	ə
NURSE	ɜː	MOUTH	aʊ	commA	ə

This system applies generally to the middle north (except for the relic areas of rhoticity): not only to the rest of urban West Yorkshire (Bradford, Wakefield, Huddersfield) but also non-rhotic Greater Manchester (including Stockport) and further – in broad outline – South Yorkshire (Barnsley, Sheffield) and the eastern midlands (Nottingham, Leicester, where, however, FACE and GOAT are diphthongal).

The vowel systems of Liverpool and Newcastle-upon-Tyne are discussed below in the sections devoted to the accents in question (4.4.10, 4.4.11).

4.4.6 Velar nasal plus

In words like *sing, hang, wrong* most accents have a velar nasal as the final segment, e.g. RP [sɪŋ, hæŋ, rɒŋ]. But certain accents of the north are non-NG-coalescing (see vol. 1, 3.1.2); in them such words have a velar plosive phonetically present after the nasal, thus [sɪŋg, (h)aŋg, rɒŋg]. Words never end with [ŋ] in such an accent, at least not after a stressed vowel; and the [g] is retained not only word-finally, but also before a suffix-initial vowel or liquid, thus ['sɪŋgə] *singer*, ['sɪŋgən ~ 'sɪŋgɪn ~ 'sɪŋgɪŋ] *singing*. It follows that *singer*, so pronounced, is a perfect rhyme for *finger*, and *kingly* of *singly*: ['sɪŋgə, 'fɪŋgə; 'kɪŋglɪ, 'sɪŋglɪ] (compare RP ['sɪŋə, 'fɪŋgə; 'kɪŋlɪ, 'sɪŋlɪ]).

The area where this type of pronunciation is dominant comprises most of the western half of the midlands and middle north, including Birmingham, Coventry, Stoke-on-Trent, Manchester and Liverpool; also (uniquely in Yorkshire) Sheffield. The *LAE* map of *tongue* (collected in the phrase *putting your tongue out*) shows [ŋg] for Derbyshire, Staffordshire, and Cheshire, together with the southern half of historical Lancashire (including the modern counties of Merseyside and Greater Manchester) and parts of Shropshire, Worcestershire, Warwickshire, and Leicestershire.

(It also shows a patch of the same in the south of England, namely in Kent.)

It is striking that this [ŋg] pronunciation where it is used at all applies almost throughout the social scale. Only the very small layer of RP speakers at the top have [ŋ] without the following plosive. In Cannock, Heath (1980) found [ŋg] to be used by speakers of all social classes; so did Knowles in Liverpool, where a final stop 'is quite prestigious locally, and is even used by middle-class women' (1978: 86).

In a rather more restricted area (which includes the Potteries of north Staffordshire), [g] is retained even before a following word-internal obstruent, thus [sɪŋgz] *sings*, [rɒŋgd] *wronged*; *Longton*, near Stoke-on-Trent, is locally ['lɒŋgtən]. The sequence nasal plus [g] also remains after an unstressed vowel, as ['rʊnɪŋg] (~ ['rʊnɪn]) *running*. Phonologically, this has the interesting consequence that [ŋ] never occurs except before a following velar plosive, /k/ or /g/, and can therefore without question be regarded as a positional allophone of /n/. From a taxonomic-phonemic point of view, as well as in more abstract models of phonology, Stoke-on-Trent English has no phoneme */ŋ/.

Elsewhere the position is somewhat more complicated. In the Black Country [ŋ] without following [g] is reported as occurring after an unstressed vowel: ['muːvɪŋ], one form of *moving*, used by many who would nevertheless say *sing* with final [g]. In Liverpool bare [ŋ] is the rule before an obstruent within the word, thus [sɪŋz] *sings*, [rɒŋd] *wronged*. This obviously calls for a phonetic rule deleting [g] in the environments in question, and is not fatal (in my view) to the claim that [ŋ] is an allophone of /n/; but it would make this claim unworkable in a strictly taxonomic-phonemic approach, in view of minimal pairs such as [sɪŋz] *sings* vs. [sɪnz] *sins*. In Liverpool, furthermore, Knowles (1974, 1978) has shown that the phonetic facts are actually somewhat more complicated (see below, 4.4.10).

4.4.7 Yorkshire Assimilation

In Yorkshire a special kind of assimilation is to be heard. An example is ['bɛttaɪm] *bed-time*. It arises when a final voiced obstruent comes into contact with an initial voiceless obstruent, either within a compound word or across a true word boundary, and has the effect of completely devoicing the former consonant: thus ['sʊpkəmɪtɪ] *subcommittee*, ['hɛtkwɔːtəz] *headquarters*, [ə 'bɪk 'piːs] *a big piece*, ['laɪf pə'fɔːməns] *live performance*. This is not mere allophonic devoicing, such as is very widespread in English: it involves the complete neutralization of the voicing (fortis/lenis) opposition. So *wide trousers*, having undergone Yorkshire Assimilation, is a perfect homophone of *white trousers* ['waɪt 'traʊzəz], while *frogspawn* ['frɒkspɔːn] sounds identical with an imaginary *frock-spawn*. An underlying /d/, Yorkshire-assimilated, can be realized as [ʔ] just as an underlying /t/ can be: ['oːlʔ 'piːpl] *old people*.

The rule can be formulated as (193).

(193)   Obstruent → voiceless / ___# [voiceless C]

The geographical spread of this Yorkshire Assimilation is not exactly known. It was not investigated (as far as I can tell) by *SED*. It is certainly general throughout West Yorkshire and South Yorkshire, where in the local accent it seems to be virtually categorical as a phonological rule of connected speech. I suspect it to extend to most of historical Yorkshire, i.e. to North Yorkshire, Cleveland, and Humberside as well as West Yorkshire and South Yorkshire.

The accents of Greater Manchester and the West Riding may sound extremely similar one to the other, in spite of the fact that Manchester and Leeds are separated by the geographical barrier of the Pennines and the historical, political, cultural and sentimental boundary of old Lancashire vs. old Yorkshire. This section and the preceding one seem to offer the two most satisfactory diagnostics for distinguishing between them: [g] in *sing* indicates Manchester and the red rose, but [t ~ ʔ] in the first syllable of *Bradford* indicates Leeds and the white rose.

4.4.8 The consonant /r/

Two questions of interest arise in connection with /r/ in the north: the extent of rhoticity, and the possibility of realizations such as [ɾ] and [ʁ].

Lancashire accents are popularly supposed to be rhotic. Yorkshire people often think of this as a typical distinguishing feature between their own speech and that of their rivals on the other side of the Pennines: white rose /'faːmə/, red rose /'faːrmər/. However, this picture is not very accurate. Most urban Lancashire speech (including under 'Lancashire' the modern counties of Merseyside and Greater Manchester) is not rhotic, although *SED* shows an r-coloured vowel in the first syllable of *farmer* not only throughout Lancashire but also in some Yorkshire localities along the Pennines (Swaledale, Lonsdale, Ribblesdale, villages near Halifax and Huddersfield). But the current extent of 'rhotic Lancashire' as an urban accent is very much more restricted: ordinary Liverpool, Manchester, Wigan speech is non-rhotic. The patch of residual urban rhoticity, ever shrinking under the pressure of the non-rhotic majority, now seems to be located to the north of Manchester, in places such as Rochdale and Accrington. It remains also in the country areas around Preston and in the north of the county.

Otherwise, there is some rhoticity in Northumberland (as discussed below in connection with uvularity), and also along the coast of North Yorkshire, Humberside, and Lincolnshire. In the latter areas historical /r/ is lost preconsonantally, but retained (to some extent) in final position, __#, thus ['faːmɔ]. The map in *LAE* (Ph245) shows this feature as extending inland to cover most of Lincolnshire; I have heard it only from fishermen in Flamborough, between Bridlington and Scarborough.

An alveolar tap, [ɾ], seems quite widespread in the north of England as a rival to the usual post-alveolar approximant, [ɹ]. The conditions favouring the use of [ɾ] are not exactly known; I have the impression that the environments in which it occurs most readily are that of a preceding labial (*pray, bright, frog*), a preceding dental (*three*), and intervocalically (*very, sorry, pair of shoes*). Nor is its geographical spread known: I associate it with Leeds and Liverpool rather than with, say, Manchester. (I find no trace of [ɾ] in *SED*.)

The 'Northumbrian burr' consists in a uvular realization of /r/: usually a voiced uvular fricative [ʁ], occasionally a uvular tap or velar fricative. It is found in an area coinciding quite closely with the historical county of Northumberland, though extending also southwards into northern County Durham and northwards just across the Scottish border north of Berwick-on-Tweed, but excluding the Newcastle-upon-Tyne conurbation itself (map, fig. 10). It formed the subject of an intensive study by Påhlsson (1972), who found confirmation of the impression that it is gradually receding, giving way to [ɹ] or (in the case of the non-prevocalic environments)

Fig. 10   Map showing the geographical extent of the Northumbrian burr (from Påhlsson 1972)

zero. (Påhlsson's analysis and presentation are, I find, remarkably difficult to interpret. His findings relate principally to the village of Thropton, near Rothbury, where he reports that 'burrers' constituted a majority among children and adults, but not among young people ages fifteen to twenty-four.)

Both [ɹ] and [ʁ] can affect surrounding phonetic segments. It is the effect of uvular /r/ on a preceding vowel which has historically given rise to forms such as [bɔʁːdz] *birds*, [wɔʁːmz] *worms* in North-

369

umberland: the [ʁ] has not only coalesced with the vowel, making it uvularized, but has also caused it to be retracted from central to back. More surprisingly, it appears that not only post-alveolar/ retroflex /r/, but also uvular /r/, can cause a following alveolar consonant to be realized instead as retroflex (Orton 1939). Where the [ɹ ~ ʁ] is lost as such, the consequence may be minimal pairs such as the [ʃɔt] *shot* vs. [ʃɔʈ] *short*, [maːz] *mows* vs. [maːʐ] *mars* reported for Dentdale traditional-dialect by Hedevind (1967: 73); the retroflex sounds are best interpreted as realizations of synchronically underlying /rC/, and represent the last trace of a vanishing rhoticity.

SED records an alveolar roll, [r], in *red* in northern Cumbria.

4.4.9 Other consonants

There are some kinds of northern accent which have little or no aspiration of /p, t, k/ before a stressed vowel (the environment where most other accents do have aspiration). Impressionistically I associate non-aspiration particularly with the Pennine valleys north of Manchester; I knew someone from Burnley whose name was *Parker* [p=aːkə].

A widespread but stigmatized connected-speech process in the middle and far north involves the use of /r/ instead of /t/ in phrases such as *shut up* [ʃʊɹ'ʊp], *get off* ['gɛɹ 'ɒf]. The T-to-R rule takes as its input /t/ in the environment of a preceding short vowel and a following boundary plus vowel, as shown in (194).

(194)   t → r / [short V] __ # V

Other examples include *but he ain't got it* [bəɹ i 'eɪnʔ 'gɒɹɪʔ] (which I noted in a speaker from Barnsley, South Yorkshire); *what about him?* ['wɒɹ ə'baʊt ɪm], *not having* . . . ['nɒɹ avɪn . . .] (which shows the T-to-R rule triggered after application of H Dropping), *sit on my knee* ['sɪɹɒn mi 'niːi]. The historical origin of the T-to-R rule must lie in the Tapping of /t/ as [ɾ], and then the phonological reinterpretation of [ɾ] as /r/, followed then by the use of the prevailing /r/ variant, [ɹ], in place of the earlier [ɾ]. Very occasionally the rule applies word-internally, as in *what's the matter* ['maɹə]?

Northern pronunciation often lacks the sharp clear/dark allophony of /l/ found in the south and RP. A middle kind of [l] in all

environments can, however, give the impression of being dark
when it occurs in surroundings in which other accents would have a
clear /l/ (e.g. *silly* ['sɪlɪ]) but of being clear when it occurs in surroundings where other accents would have dark /l/ (e.g. *feel* [fiːl]).
The far north tends to have a rather clear variety of /l/ in all
environments.

H Dropping is prevalent in popular accents of the midlands and
middle north, but not of the far north. Newcastle-upon-Tyne is the
only large English city with an accent not characterized by H
Dropping. Historical /hw/ is simplified to /w/ in all English urban
accents (see vol. 1, 3.2.4, Glide Cluster Reduction); /hw/ remains
in some rural areas of the far north.

4.4.10 Merseyside

The accent of the city of Liverpool and its immediate surroundings
(now the county of Merseyside) is known as **Scouse**. This accent is
rather clearly distinct from that of the neighbouring areas. It is
believed to have come into existence in the nineteenth century,
when large numbers of Irish immigrants, as well as a fair number of
Welsh, settled in this corner of the north of England.

As in other parts of the north, important linguistic variables
include the FOOT words and the BATH words, as discussed above
(4.4.2, 4.4.3). But in the continuum ranging from broadest Scouse
to RP there are several other variables of much more restricted
geographical range. Some are no doubt to be attributed to Irish
influence: the most obvious of these is the use by some speakers of
dental or alveolar stops for /θ, ð/, as in [t̪ɾ̪i] *three*, [tɹuːt̪] *truth*,
[mʊnt̪(θ)] *month*, [d̪at ~ dat] *that*. Knowles (1974: 323) found this to
be virtually restricted to working-class Catholics.

Voiceless stops sometimes lack complete closure in certain
syllable-final environments, so that varieties of fricatives, [ɸ, t̪, x]
result for /p, t, k/ in such words as [sneɪx] *snake*, [ʃɔːt̪] *short*, ['dɔːt̪ə]
daughter. The /t/ fricative, here written [t̪], is distinct from [s]: the
tongue tip, ungrooved, is the active articulator for [t̪], and the
duration of the friction is probably typically shorter than that of [s].
The /k/ fricative is sometimes uvular rather than velar, and may
have a degree of uvular scrape: [nɛχ] *neck*, [klɒχ] *clock*. Glottal stops
are noticeably rare. Voiced plosives, too, may on occasion lack

complete closure: *ti*[ɣ]*er* (all examples up to this point are from Knowles (1974)). This frication of plosives has its parallel in the [t̪] of Irish English (5.3.8 below); its extension to other places of articulation seems to be a local Scouse innovation. In syllable-initial environments, stops do have complete closure, but may be affricated: [kxɪŋg] *king*, [mi 'dᶻad] *my dad*. Affrication is also an alternative to frication in final position: [bakˣ ~ bax] *back*.

Words like *sing* tend to have final [ŋg] just as elsewhere in the north-west. Knowles points out (1978: 85–6) that in Liverpool, at least, it is oversimplifying to say that the pronunciation with [ŋg] is stigmatized, the one with plain [ŋ] (as in RP) prestigious. He considers that the only specifically Scouse and stigmatized form is [sɛːŋᵍ], with a lengthened vowel and a velar nasal with an offglide which 'sounds like a weak homorganic stop'; [sɪŋːg], on the other hand, 'is quite prestigious locally'.

Scouse /r/ may be an approximant, [ɹ], or a tap, [ɾ]. Even though the tap is traditionally regarded as an RP possibility (and indeed is one, though by no means the most usual kind of /r/), in Liverpool middle-class speakers tend to avoid it. Those who do use it use it particularly after /θ/ (*three, through*) and intervocalically (*ferry, hurry*); some speakers also use it after labials (*breathe, fresh*), after /g/ (*grass*) and after /sC/ (*sprout, scratch*).

Among the vowels, Liverpool is notable for the merger of the lexical sets NURSE and SQUARE, so that *spur* = *spare*, *curd* = *cared*, *fir-fur* = *fair-fare*. The quality of the merged vowel may be central, rounded [eː] or unrounded [ɜː], or centralized-front, [ëː ~ ëː]. The latter two are the characteristically Scouse qualities, [ëː] being the more conservative. Pronunciations such as [nëːs] are diagnostic for Merseyside; although NURSE and SQUARE are merged in some other parts of the north, e.g. in Wigan, the quality there is characteristically central, [nɜːs], [skwɜː], etc.

In final position FLEECE and GOOSE tend to be somewhat diphthongal, [ɪi ~ ɪi], [ʊu ~ ɪʊ]: *three, two*. This diphthong is also sometimes heard before /l/, as in *school* [skɪːʊl]. The FACE and GOAT vowels are diphthongal; GOAT exhibits a range of qualities including not only [oʊ] and [ɔʊ] but also [ëʊ], which to the outsider sounds incongruously 'posh' when in a broad-Scouse frame: ['ëʊl 'swɒn] *Old Swan* (a district). PRICE and MOUTH are generally of the type [aɪ, aʊ]. The CURE vowel is undergoing change, as elsewhere: the most conservative type, with /uːə ~ ʊə/, has Scouse variants of the type [ruə, ɪwə, uɛ], but these are being displaced by /ɔː/, thus *sure* [ʃruə ~ ʃuɛ ~ ʃɔː]. The FORCE diphthong, conservative [oə], is even more widely now merged with THOUGHT: of Knowles's subjects, [oə] was typical only of those born before 1918, those born since having [ɔː]. Hence *Shaw* has been acquiring new homophones: first *shore*, then *sure* (typically all three pronounced identically for those born since 1939) (Knowles 1978: 85).

One and *once* have /ɒ/; *book* popularly has /uː/. The *happy* vowel is [i]. In the first syllable of *eleven* and the last of *orange* a shift from older /ɪ/ to newer /ə/ is occurring; Knowles (1974: 299) also found /ɪ/ to be commoner among middle-class Protestants, /ə/ among working-class Catholics.

But it is perhaps its prosodic characteristics which most clearly mark out Scouse from other northern accents. This is one of the accents which uses a rise (with level tail) in some circumstances where RP would use a fall (historically, this is probably the rising onglide to a fall, spread out over a whole syllable or more). Example: Scouse *I don't ˈlike ˉit* (= RP etc *I ˈdon't ˈlike it/ˈlike it*). Conversely, a kind of fall is used where RP would tend to have a rise (and another very common, Near-RP or local, pattern is a fall-rise); example: Scouse *Are ˈyou from ˋLiverpool?* (= RP *Are ˈyou from ˌLiverpool?*, Near-RP *Are ˈyou from ˉLiverpool?*). Knowles argues for recognizing a 'skip'-fall in Scouse, intermediate between the fall and rise-fall types, and a skip-rise intermediate between rise and fall-rise: middle-class accents then lack the distinction between skip-fall and rise-fall, skip-rise and fall-rise (1978: 87).

Knowles has also attempted a detailed description of the articulatory setting responsible for the characteristic Scouse voice quality. It is a kind of velarization:

In Scouse, the centre of gravity of the tongue is brought backwards and upwards, the pillars of the fauces are narrowed, the pharynx is tightened, and the larynx is displaced upwards. The lower jaw is typically held close to the upper jaw, and this position is maintained even for 'open' vowels. The main auditory effect of this setting is the 'adenoidal' quality of Scouse, which is produced even if the speaker's nasal passages are unobstructed. (1978: 89)

4.4.11 Tyneside

The largest conurbation in what I have called the far north is conveniently referred to as Tyneside: more strictly Tyneside and Wearside, it comprises Newcastle-upon-Tyne itself together with the surrounding urban areas, formerly straddling the border between County Durham and Northumberland but now constituting the metropolitan county of Tyne and Wear. Its accent is known as **Geordie** ['dʒɔːdi] – a name applied also to its traditional-dialect, and also of course to anyone who comes from Tyneside. Geordie differs in several striking ways from other urban speech varieties of the north of England.

One of the most striking is a particular kind of glottalization of /p, t, k/, both in syllable-final position and also, sometimes, syllable-initially before a weak vowel. This may consist either in a purely glottal realization, [ʔ], or of a combined glottal and oral plosive. O'Connor (1947) writes the latter type [ʔp, ʔt, ʔk], commenting that the p, t, k symbols here stand for 'very weak [b̥, d̥, g̊]'. The auditory impression I receive is [pʔ, tʔ, kʔ], with glottal masking of the oral plosive burst. Examples: *paper* ['peəpʔa], *couple* ['kʊpʔəl]; *pity* ['pɪtʔi], *auntie* ['antʔi]; *local* ['loːkʔəl]; *represented* [ɹɛpʔɹəˈzɛnʔəd], *documents* ['dɒkʔjəmɪnʔs].

Uniquely among urban accents of England, Geordie has phonemic /h/ and no H Dropping. The cluster /hw/, however, is not used (except by one or two speech-conscious people): *when* [wɛn].

Of the liquids, /l/ is noticeably clear in all positions. (This does not necessarily apply throughout the social scale. I once succeeded in identifying a Near-RP hitchhiker as a Geordie by seizing on the fact that his /l/ was – hypercorrectly – dark in all environments.) Uvular /r/ is no longer usual on Tyneside (though also not quite extinct): /r/ is mostly [ɹ] or [ɾ]. These phonetic types can also arise through the T-to-R rule (4.4.9 above): *Has he go*[ɹ] *a job?*

Although uvular [ʁ] has virtually disappeared from Tyneside, it has left its influence on certain vowel qualities, notably those of the lexical sets NURSE and *lett*ER; also in the [iɑ], [uɑ]-type qualities of NEAR, CURE (though SQUARE is monophthongal [ɛː]).

In the broadest Geordie the lexical set NURSE is merged with NORTH, /ɔː/: *work* [wɔːk], *first* [fɔːst], *shirt* [ʃɔːt] (= *short*). What is elsewhere a central vowel has undergone backing through the influence of the /r/ [ʁ] which once followed. (*SED* records [ɔ˞ː] in such words in neighbouring parts of Northumberland: it is perhaps difficult to fix the moment at which uvular colouring in a vowel is attenuated to the point where it is no longer detectable.) In a less broad Newcastle accent, NURSE words have [ɜ:] or something similar, e.g. rounded centralized-front [øː]. It appears that no hyper-correction of the type *short* *[ʃøːt] occurs: either the merger of NURSE and NORTH was never categorical, or speakers are unusually successful in sorting the two sets out again.

Certain THOUGHT words (roughly, those spelt with *a*) have broad Geordie pronunciations with [aː] (phonetically just front of central) rather than [ɔː]. Examples are *all, talk, walk, war*; so also *know, cold*. Thus [wɔːk], which in most accents of English can only be *walk*, is *work* in broad Geordie, while *walk* has the unambiguous form [waːk]. This forms the basis of a well-known Geordie joke (transcribed phonetically in Viereck 1966: 95), in which a local man goes to see the doctor about his hurt knee; the doctor bandages it up and asks him, 'Do you think you can walk [wɔːk] now?', to which Geordie replies, 'What do you mean, can I work? I can hardly walk [waːk]!'

Long [aː] also regularly occurs in words of the lexical sets TRAP and BATH where there is a following final voiced consonant or final voiced consonant cluster, thus *lad* [laːd], *band* [baːnd] (but *slant, laugh* with [a]). Hence there is an opposition between [a] and [aː] only before voiceless consonants, and only if traditional-dialect forms are considered: *tack* [tak] vs. *talk* [taːk]. Those who do not use the traditional-dialect forms have [a] and [aː] in complementary distribution, as far as I can see. There is also a long back [ɑː], used in START words: *dark* [dɑːk], *starts* [stɑːʔs]; also *half* [hɑːf].

The FACE and GOAT vowels are either monophthongs or opening/centring diphthongs. Thus FACE may be [e(ː)] or [eə ~ ɪɐ], GOAT [o(ː) ~ e(ː)] or [ʊə ~ əə]. The diphthongs are nowadays perhaps rather old-fashioned; but the central rounded monophthong [ɵ(ː)] remains a very characteristic GOAT quality both for Tyneside itself and for all Northumberland: [a ˈdɵnt səˈpɵːz ɑ ˈnɒtʔɪst də ˌkɵːld] *I don't suppose I noticed the cold*.

The FLEECE vowel, /i/, has a strikingly diphthongal variant in final position: [nei] *knee*; [fɹeiz] *frees* (≠ [fɹiːz] *freeze*). Similarly, /u/ has an allophone [əʊ]. The MOUTH vowel may be of the [aʊ] or [ɛʊ] type, though traditional-dialect [u(ː)] is still very prevalent, as is a compromise [əu]: *down* [dun ~ dəun ~ daʊn]. There is variation in PRICE between an [ɛi] type and an [aɪ] type (the latter with an open central starting-point). I am not altogether clear what the conditions governing the choice between them are; Viereck (1966: 69–70) says that they are in free variation, and that there is also an [ɑɪ] type used after [ʁ] only; O'Connor writes [ɛi] everywhere. I suspect that some speakers, at least, have a Scottish-type distribution, with [aɪ] before a voiced fricative and finally, [ɛi] elsewhere. Examples: *Tyneside* ['tɛinsɛid], *like* [lɛik], *twice* [twɛis], *mind* [mɛind]; *five* [faɪv]; *in my time* [ɪn ˈmaɪ ˌtɛim].

The weak vowel of *lett*ER is particularly open in Geordie. Often it is very back: I write it [ɑ], although it is slightly less open than cardinal [ɑ]. This quality is presumed to be due historically to the influence of the [ʁ] which once followed it. Examples: *clever* ['klɛvɑ], *under* ['ʊndɑ]. The vowel is not necessarily as back as this; some speakers use a more or less front [ɛ]: ['klɛvɛ], ['ʊndɛ]. Words of the *comm*A set also have this [ɑ ~ ɛ]: *china* ['tʃɛinɑ]; according to McNeany (1971), though, they can also have final [ɪ].

Tyneside has /ə/, not the more usual /ɪ/, as the weak vowel in words such as *voices, ended*; on the other hand some Geordies have /ɪ/, not /ə/, in words such as *seven, almond, impression* [-ʃɪn]. There are unexpected vowel qualities in certain weak forms: McNeany (1971) mentions *at, of, as, can, us* with [ɪ]: ['lʊk ɪr 'ɪz] *look at us* (with restressed weak form of *us* 'me'). The items *from, but, could, that*, are among those with no distinct weak forms in Tyneside speech: *from* is always [frɒm].

The weak vowel in *happ*Y is close, [i]. The local form of address *hinny* is phonetically ['hɪni].

Tyneside has its characteristic local intonation patterns; Pellowe & Jones (1978) have made a start at describing them, though their treatment unfortunately excludes consideration of the meaning attached to particular patterns. They do, however, demonstrate the greater prevalence (compared with RP usage) of rise-fall and level nuclear tones. Impressionistically, I am struck by the tendency to use a low-to-high rise, with high level tail, in certain contexts where RP would have a high fall.

5

The Celtic countries

5.1 Wales

5.1.1 Introduction

There are places in Wales which have been English-speaking for centuries – the Pembroke area, for example, on the southern coast of Dyfed. But they are the exception rather than the rule. Although ordinary Welshmen have had some acquaintance with English since the Middle Ages, they have not had it as their mother tongue, as their first language, until quite recently – a matter of a century or two. In looking at the pattern of English in Wales today, one must remember that North America, for instance, has had a substantial body of native English speakers for longer than Wales has. Welsh English, as a native language, is mostly not much older than South African English.

Nowadays virtually everyone in Wales can speak English. But for a significant minority English is only a second language. These are the native speakers of Welsh, perhaps the most viable of the Celtic languages; in spite of the inroads made by English, particularly over the last hundred years, they still comprise something like 20 per cent of the Principality's total population of about two and three-quarter million. Many of the English-speaking majority, too, have some knowledge of Welsh. In many cases their parents, or at least their grandparents, spoke it. No one who lives in Wales can fail to notice the Welsh language around them, no matter whether they consider it a valuable element of their national and cultural heritage or a tiresome irrelevance rammed down their throats by chauvinist cranks. And there can be little doubt that the main influence on the pronunciation of English in Wales is the substratum presented by the phonological system of Welsh.

Geographically, Wales mostly consists of rugged mountainous

terrain. Most of the country is rather sparsely inhabited, with a mainly rural population. The exception to this is the industrial region of south Wales, the 'Valleys' of Glamorgan and Gwent. Since the Industrial Revolution this has been a region of densely populated mining and steel-making valleys separated by empty and desolate hill-tops. The largest towns in Wales are the seaports for the Valleys, namely Newport, Cardiff, and Swansea. They, too, owe their size to the Industrial Revolution: Cardiff, which today has a population of a quarter of a million, was in 1801 a village of under two thousand inhabitants.

The mountainous terrain has always meant that north–south communication within Wales is rather difficult. It has also tended to make south Wales fall under the anglicizing influence of the west of England (Gloucester, Bristol), mid Wales under that of the English midlands (Birmingham, Shrewsbury), and north Wales under that of the north of England (Liverpool, Chester).

The most immediately striking thing about a Welsh accent to many English ears is the intonation. It is perceived as 'sing-song' (which perhaps means no more than that it is different from that of English English); this impression is no doubt reinforced by differences in timing, with Welsh medial consonants in particular tending to be of longer duration than is usual in England. (See 5.1.6, 5.1.8 below.) The other striking characteristic is vowel quality: Welsh English tends to have more monophthongs and fewer diphthongs than most accents of English, while the diphthongs which are found tend to be narrow. This, together with the prevalence of clear [l] (particularly in the south) can be seen as characteristic of an area remote from the most recent metropolitan influences in English pronunciation.

5.1.2 Rhoticity

On the whole Welsh English is non-rhotic: *start* is [staːt], etc., and *north* is [nɔːθ]. Rhotic pronunciations are found, however, (i) in the old English-speaking areas of southernmost Dyfed (Pembroke, Tenby, Narberth) and the Gower peninsula; (ii) along the English border in easternmost Gwent and Powys, contiguous with the rhotic local accents of Gloucester, Hereford, and Salop; and (iii) to some extent in the second-language English of those who have Welsh as their first language.

Group (iii) can be recognized by the use of an alveolar roll [r] or tap [ɾ]. The words *farm* and *storm* have been borrowed into Welsh in the forms [farm] *ffarm* and [stɔrm] *storm* (also *ystorm, storom*), and these pronunciations may well be used in English also by Welsh speakers. English words borrowed into Welsh retain historical /r/ in all positions. Spelling pronunciation no doubt has a rôle to play here, too: Welsh itself is in all cases fully rhotic, so that the reading rule applies of pronouncing [r ~ ɾ] for every letter *r*. Anglicization, the loss of a particularly 'Welshy' accent, involves among other things the cutting out of /r/ in non-prevocalic positions.

The local accents referred to in (i) and (ii) above may strike the outsider as west-of-England rather than Welsh. As far as I am aware, there is as yet no published dialectological research into the rhotic accents of southernmost Dyfed: the area in question is that part of the former county of Pembrokeshire which lies to the south of the *landsker*, the traditional Welsh–English language boundary. The Gower, together with the rest of Glamorgan, southern Powys, and Gwent, fall within the area reported on by the *Survey of Anglo-Welsh dialects* (Parry 1972, 1977). This records /r/ in *harvest* and *forks* as almost entirely lost except along the English border; in *hearse* and *birch* it is slightly less restricted geographically, and may involve either a rounded [œ꞉] or an unrounded west-of-England type [ɜ꞉].

There are other ways, too, in which the accent of these areas is quite different from what is heard elsewhere in Wales. In the Gower, the characteristically west-of-England traditional-dialect feature of Initial Fricative Voicing (4.3.6 above) has been reported, with sporadic [v] in *farmer* and *feet*, and [z] in *seven, silver, south*, etc. (Parry 1972: 145; 1977: 115–20, which shows [v] in *fellies* and *furrow*, though not in other words, rather more widely). In Pembroke MOUTH words seem to be commonly pronounced with an [ɛʊ]-type diphthong, something which would be unremarkable in the south of England but which differs strikingly from the [au ~ əu] which prevails elsewhere in Wales.

I shall have no more to say on areas (i) and (ii) above. The rest of this chapter deals with the more typically Welsh accents of English.

Returning to the question of the phonotactics of /r/, it must be said that the non-rhoticity of the great majority of Welsh accents of English is a little surprising. After all, the pronunciation model offered both by the pockets of long-indigenous English in Wales and by the local forms of English along almost the whole stretch of the English border (from Gloucester nearly to Chester) is rhotic. The Welsh language itself readily tolerates preconsonantal and final /r/, with no tendency to vocalization. Why, then, is Welsh English usually non-rhotic? The answer presumably lies in the fact that Welsh English is from a historical point of view very largely the English imposed by schoolteachers. Whether themselves Welsh or English, they would certainly strive, as always, to present a type of English in conformity with current views of good speech – not only in grammar but also in pronunciation. By the nineteenth century, which is when English became really thoroughly established in Wales, non-rhoticity was already the polite norm in England: non-prevocalic /r/ had already come to be associated, as it is now, with forms of English which were either provincial or else distant from the metropolis, or both, and the appropriate model for Wales was therefore a non-rhotic one.

5.1.3 A typical vowel system

The vowel system typical of south-east Wales is shown in (195). (See 5.1.4 below for possible additions.) Incidence is as shown in (196).

(195)

ɪ	ʊ	iː		uː			
ɛ ə ɒ		ei əi ɔi	əu ou		ɛː 3ː ɔː		
a					aː		

(196)

KIT	ɪ	FLEECE	iː	NEAR	jɜː ~ iːə	
DRESS	ɛ	FACE	ei	SQUARE	ɛː	
TRAP	a	PALM	aː	START	aː	
LOT	ɒ	THOUGHT	ɔː	NORTH	ɔː	
STRUT	ə	GOAT	ou	FORCE	ɔː	
FOOT	ʊ	GOOSE	uː	CURE	uːə	
BATH	a ~ aː	PRICE	əi	*happ*Y	[i] = /iː/	
CLOTH	ɒ ~ ɔː	CHOICE	ɔi	*lett*ER	ə	
NURSE	3ː	MOUTH	əu	*comm*A	ə	

Systemically, the principal differences vis-à-vis RP are the STRUT–Schwa Merger and the absence of phonemes corresponding to RP /ɪə/ and /ʊə/. In STRUT words the vowel used is typically mid, unrounded, and central or somewhat back of central, [ə ~ ʌ̈].

It does not contrast with the /ə/ of unstressed syllables, so that *a large untidy room* and *a large and tidy room* tend to be homophonous, and so do *unorthodoxy* and *an orthodoxy*, while *seagull* tends to rhyme with *eagle*. In NEAR words there is usually /jɜː/, so that *beer* /bjɜː/ can be said to rhyme with *fur* /fɜː/ as well as with *fear* /fjɜː/, while *year*, *ear*, and (/h/-dropped) *here* are all identical as /jɜː/. Some speakers, though, use a disyllabic sequence /iːə/, thus *beer* /'biːə/ etc., and in the environment __rV simple /iː/ is usual, thus *period* /'piːriːəd/ (RP /'pɪərɪəd/). Similarly, CURE words have a disyllabic sequence in monosyllables (*poor* /'puːə/), but not in the environment __rV (*fury* /'fjuːriː ~ 'fɪuriː/ – for /ɪu/ see 5.1.4 below).

As concerns phonetic realization of the vowels in the system, we may note particularly the long monophthongs. Unlike many English accents of English, Welsh accents typically have monophthongal realizations of the /iː/ of FLEECE, the /uː/ of GOOSE, and the /ɛː/ of SQUARE, as well as of the /aː/ of START–PALM and the /ɔː/ of NORTH–THOUGHT. The quality of /iː/ may sometimes be centralized and/or lowered, but it is usually of constant quality.

In many places the quality of /aː/ is socially sensitive, with a front [aː] being stigmatized as compared with a central to back RP-style [ɑ+ː]. In Cardiff a front vowel less than fully open is found in working-class speech, so that *start* may be [stæːt] or even [stɛːt]. A Cardiff accent is caricatured by calling the town ['kɛːdɪf]; and contrariwise the symbol of a very posh accent would be to call it ['kɑːdɪf]. It is reported that in Bangor in north Wales this sociolinguistic variable applies only in START words, while PALM words such as *tomato, bra, banana* keep front [aː] for everyone. If true, this would mean a marginal opposition between pairs such as *spa*, always [spaː], and *spar*, varying socially between [spaː] and [spɑ+ː].

Long mid central /ɜː/ is often rounded in south-east Wales, giving the effect of a centralized raised [œː] or lowered [øː], as *church* [tʃœːtʃ] etc.

Both long and short open back vowels, /ɒ/ and /ɔː/, tend to be rather open [ɒ(ː)] in Cardiff, and /ɒ/ may have little or no lip rounding. In all parts of Wales there seems to be a tendency for the pairs /ɛ, ɛː/, /a, aː/, /ɒ, ɔː/ to differ principally in length, rather than in quality; so that much the same vowel quality is often to be heard in the pairs *shed–shared, hat–heart, shot–short*.

In the PRICE and MOUTH words, mid central starting-points to the

diphthongs are very typical of Welsh English. That is why I have
thought it best to symbolize them /əi, əu/. The first element is
typically identical in quality with the STRUT vowel. Hence *life-time*
is ['ləiftəim], *out loud* ['əut 'ləud]. The final element tends always to
be close, and is noticeably resistant to Smoothing; if anything, a [j]
or [w] respectively tends to be inserted between these diphthongs
and a following vowel, thus *iron* ['əiən ~ 'əijən], *power* [pəuə ~
'pəuwə], etc. It is said that it is impossible for the Welsh and the
English to sing the round *London's Burning* together, owing to the
inevitable clash in the line *Fire! Fire!* between ['fəijə 'fəijə] and ['faː
'faː].

   In FACE and GOAT words, many Welsh people use long monophthongs, [eː] and [oː], rather than the diphthongs implied by the
notation /ei, ou/ used above. In the more anglicized places such as
Cardiff and Newport the norm is diphthongal, so that a monophthongal realization [feːs, goːt] is associated with particularly old-
fashioned speech. Further away from English influence it is the
monophthongs which are still the norm. The quality commonly
used in south Wales is about cardinal 2 and 7; in north Wales a
rather opener quality is used, [ẹː, ọː]. There are, furthermore, areas
where a phonemic opposition exists between diphthong and monophthong in FACE and GOAT words, as discussed in the next section.

   With this reservation, and with the possible addition of a diphthong /ɪu/, also discussed in the next section, it appears that the
vowel system presented above applies to all Welsh accents of
English. The same is true of the table of lexical incidence, except
that FORCE words quite widely have /oː/ (= /ou/) or /oːə/; in many
parts of Wales one can find homophony in pairs such as *coat–court*,
poke–pork.

   Assuming a monophthong rather than a diphthong in the FACE
and GOAT words, we can rearrange the monophthongs of a Welsh
accent of English into the pattern shown in (197).

(197)   *short*   *long*

ɪ		ʊ		iː		uː
	ə			eː	ɜː	oː
ɛ		ɔ		ɛː		ɔː
	a			aː		

The monophthongs of Welsh itself are shown in (198). (The brack-
eted items are found only in north Wales, being merged with /ɪ/ and
/iː/ respectively in the south.)

(198)   *short*   *long*

ɪ	(ɨ)	ʊ	iː	(ɨː)	uː
	ə		eː		oː
ɛ		ɔ			
	a			aː	

Comparison of the two systems shows that the only English vowels
which do not correspond to vowels of Welsh are those of SQUARE,
NORTH–THOUGHT, and NURSE: /ɛː, ɔː, ɜː/. Otherwise, the vowels of
KIT, DRESS, TRAP, LOT, FOOT, STRUT correspond exactly to those of
the Welsh words *dim, pen, pan, ton, trwm* and *yn* respectively; those
of FLEECE, FACE, START–PALM, GOAT, and GOOSE to those of *ci, lle,
tad, bod,* and *drwg* respectively. Long /ɛː/ and /ɔː/ must have been
easy for Welsh speakers confronted with learning English to add to
the Welsh system, since they were merely a matter of adding length
to the already known qualities of short /ɛ, ɔ/. (Note, too, that at least
two dialects of Welsh have been described as including in their
vowel systems an /ɔː/ used only in English loan-words such as *lawn,
brawn*: Pilch 1958, Thomas 1958). Long /ɜː/ presented more of a
problem, since Welsh short /ə/ in any case has a restricted phonotactic distribution, usually occurring only in clitics and non-final
syllables. This is perhaps the explanation of the auditorily unusual
quality of /ɜː/ in many Welsh accents; I think it would not be unfair
to say that to an Englishman it is often reminiscent of the slightly
inaccurate attempts at this vowel made by learners of English as a
foreign language. (English NURSE words borrowed into Welsh are
pronounced in that language with /ər/, as *nyrs* itself, /nərs/.)

Welsh has rather a large number of diphthongs, including both
/əi, əu/ and /ai, au/ (as in *cei, rhowch, llai, llaw* respectively). Thus it
is at first sight surprising that it is on the whole the /əi, əu/ types
which have been selected as the equivalents for English PRICE and
MOUTH words, rather than the apparently more appropriate /ai, au/.
The explanation presumably lies in the fact that English PRICE and
MOUTH had still not acquired fully open starting-points in RP
(etc.) at the crucial period when Welsh English pronunciation was

becoming fixed. And the relatively recent borrowings into Welsh of English words reflect the same equivalence: *nice* becomes *neis* [nəis], *line* becomes *lein* [ləin], and *round* becomes *rownd* [rəund].

5.1.4 Five possible extra contrasts

In certain Welsh accents of English there is a contrast between such items as *pane* and *pain*, *daze* vs. *days*, *made* vs. *maid*, *Dane* vs. *deign*. The first in each pair has a monophthongal [eː], while the second has a closing diphthong, [ei ~ ɛi] etc. Thus *pane* and *pain* may be distinct as [peːn], [pɛin]. The effect is as if the Long Mid Mergers (vol. 1, 3.1.5) had failed to apply.

The same phenomenon is to be observed with the back vowels, though there it is perhaps slightly rarer. But there are Welsh accents in which *toe* [toː] is distinct from *tow* [tou ~ təu], and likewise *nose* from *knows*, *doe* from *dough*, and *throne* from *thrown*.

This pair of contrasts first came to my attention in the speech of a student from Clydach, West Glamorgan, and I duly reported it (Wells 1970: 238) as belonging to the Swansea Valley. Later research confirms it for various localities in Glamorgan, southern Powys, and eastern Dyfed, including Merthyr Tydfil, the Rhondda, and Carmarthen. It is not known in Cardiff or Newport or, as far as I know, in mid or north Wales.

It is possible that these /eː — ɛi/ and /oː — ɔu/ oppositions in south Wales are to be seen not as historical survivals but rather as spelling pronunciations dating from a time when English was very definitely a second language. For those who have the opposition, /ɛi/ is used whenever the spelling includes an *i* or a *y* (thus *pain*, *day*), but a monophthong otherwise (*pane*). (Limited observations suggest that the names of letters of the alphabet may constitute an exception, with *J* being /dʒɛi/ rather than the /dʒeː/ one might expect.) In GOAT words, a diphthong is used where the spelling includes a *u* or a *w* (*dough*, *know*), but a monophthong otherwise (*doe*, *no*). Against the spelling-pronunciation hypothesis one must admit the fact of many Welsh-speaking localities where these oppositions are not found in the local accent of English.

One might be forgiven for assuming that /ɛi/ and /ɔu/, like /eː/ and /oː/, are taken straight from the sound system of Welsh. Surprisingly, though, this is not the case. Welsh, as spoken in the

Swansea Valley, has no such diphthongs; words such as *cei, neu,* which do have [ɛi] in some areas, have the /əi/ used locally for English PRICE words, while *rhowch, tywyll* have the /əu/ used for MOUTH. It can be argued, though, that /ɛi/ and /ɔu/ are implicitly made available by Welsh phonology: all Welsh diphthongs can readily be analysed as consisting of one of the monophthongs plus a semi-vowel (an analysis that cannot readily be made for English RP diphthongs). So the diphthongs in question here are, within a Welsh-language framework, more correctly written /ɛj, ɔw/, and include simple /ɛ, ɔ/ in the same way as /aj, əj, ɔj, ʊj/ (*llai, cei, rhoi, mwy*) include simple /a, ə, ɔ, ʊ/ and /ɪw, ɛw, aw, əw/ (*rhiw, llew, taw, rhowch*) simple /ɪ, ɛ, a, ə/. It is thus a matter of a slightly extended range of phonotactic possibilities rather than the adoption of a new sound type. This explanation may also account for the resistance of Welsh English diphthongs to Smoothing (5.1.3 above). It does not, however, shed any light on the question why the /eː − ɛi/ and /oː − ɔu/ oppositions should have been preserved/introduced in some areas of south Wales but not in others.

The same areas which have the /eː − ɛi/ and /oː − ɔu/ oppositions may also have the opposition /əi − ai/, as exemplified in the minimal pair *eye* /əi/ vs. *aye* /ai/. But the functional load of this opposition is vanishingly small. The same is true of a possible opposition /əu/ vs. /au/, as in *cow* etc. vs. the interjection *ow!*.

The fifth possible extra contrast is a good deal more widespread. It involves a diphthong /ɪu/ in opposition to /uː/. (This /ɪu/ corresponds to the Welsh diphthong spelt *iw*.) The GOOSE words spelt with *o, oo,* or *ou* have monophthongal [uː]-type pronunciations everywhere in Wales, thus *lose* /luːz/, *moon* /muːn/, *soup* /suːp/. But those spelt *u, ue, eu,* or *ew* are often found with a diminuendo diphthong [ɪŭ] rather than with the /uː/ or /juː/ found in standard accents, thus *include* [ɪnˈklɪud], *new* [ˈnɪu]. The difference between the diphthong [ɪu] and the semivowel-plus-vowel sequence [juː] is a minor one phonetically, involving a switching of the feature [syllabic] from [−, +] to [+, −]; but it does have phonological implications. It means that *suit* /sɪut/ does not rhyme with *boot* /buːt/ (compare the RP rhymes /s(j)uːt/, /buːt/). It can lead to the use of prevocalic sandhi forms before words beginning /ɪu/, as *an union, an uvular R* /ən ˈɪuvɪulər ˈaː/. And it furnishes one or two additional minimal pairs such as *through* /θruː/ vs. *threw* /θrɪu/. (See vol. 1,

3.1.10.) This /ɪu/ is readily found in the environment __rV, as *plural* /'plɪurəl/, and in CURE words such as *pure* /'pɪuə/, *sure* /'ʃɪuə/.

Currently, a process of lexical diffusion seems to be eliminating /ɪu/ from those words where it does not correspond to RP /juː/. Thus for *rude*, /rɪud/ is giving ground to /ruːd/, and for *flu* and *flew* /flɪu/ is giving ground to /fluː/. In Bangor, Gwynedd, a correspondent reports a minimal pair *blue* [bluː] vs. *blew* [blɪu] (past tense of *blow*), which implies a lexical distribution which no longer corresponds to history or to spelling but is typical of the situation halfway through a lexically diffused change.

The sequence /juː/ is foreign to the sound system of Welsh, whereas /ɪu/ (or /ɪw/), as we have seen, is not. English *use* (n.) is borrowed into Welsh as *iws*, and *uniform* as *iwnifform*. Accordingly, it is easy for /ɪu/ to be perceived as a typically Welsh diphthong, and someone anxious to lose his local accent may overdo the switch from /ɪu/ to /uː/. It is presumably hypercorrection of this kind which is responsible for pronunciations such as [sɪtuː'eɪʃn̩] *situation*, ['aktuːəli] *actually*, [spɛkuː'leːʃn̩] *speculation* sometimes to be heard in the Near-RP of some educated Welshmen. Actually, though, [sɪtuː'eɪʃn̩] may strike the ear as further from RP ['sɪtjʊ'eɪʃn ~ 'sɪtʃʊ'eɪʃn̩] than is the local-accent [sɪtɪu'eːʃən].

After non-coronal consonants Welsh people seem to weaken what may be seen as an underlying /juː ~ ɪu/ to [ə] more readily than the English: thus *particular* /pə'tɪkələ/, *regularly* /'rɛgələliː/, *vocabulary* /vou'kabələriː/, all heard from educated speakers.

5.1.5 Further remarks on vowels

The phonetic quality of /ɪ/ seems to be rather opener in Cardiff than elsewhere, while all Cardiff short vowels are usually unrounded (including /ʊ/ and /ɒ/). Elsewhere more mainstream realizations are found. The vowel of DRESS is everywhere rather open – about cardinal 3, [ɛ]. The /a/ of TRAP is generally fully open, [a ~ a–], though in Cardiff it ranges to [æ].

In the Welsh-speaking areas of north Wales, and also quite widely in the south, including most of anglicized Gwent, LOT words spelt with *a*, such as *wash*, *wasp*, *quarry* are quite often pronounced with /a/ rather than the standard /ɒ/, thus /waʃ/ etc. (Parry (1977: 33, 85) shows /a/ as common in *wasps*, occasional in *quarry*, and absent from *wash*.) Rather than an archaism preserving a Middle English vowel quality, this is likely to have originated as a spelling pronunciation (particularly since in Welsh orthography *wa* always stands for /wa(:)/).

The situation in the BATH words is not altogether clear. In general the short vowel predominates, so that the situation in most of Wales is like that in the north of England, with a local-accent /a/ (= TRAP) confronting an RP-style /aː/ (= START–PALM). In the south-east of the country, however, including Cardiff, the long vowel is established in some at least of the BATH words, e.g. *class, grass* /klaːs, graːs/, while in others there is sociolinguistic variation between long and short, e.g. *chance, fast* /tʃa(ː)ns, fa(ː)st/. An informant from Rhondda insisted that he made a distinction between *fast* 'rapid', which was [fast], and *fast* 'abstention from food'. [faːst]. The records of the Survey of Anglo-Welsh dialects show a geographically rather random pattern of variation between /a/ and /aː/ in *grass*; and for Undy (Gwent), [aɬː] is reported (Parry 1977: 30). In *chaff* the *Survey* records show /a/ as predominating. In Cardiff, long /aː/ is reported in *bag* (Lediard 1977: 264).

The opposition between /oː/ and /ɔː/ (GOAT vs. THOUGHT–NORTH) is perhaps sometimes missing in north Wales, though the matter has not yet been properly investigated. At the very least, north Wales *coat* and *caught* may have very similar qualities.

Welsh English has a definite tendency to avoid /ə/ in final checked syllables, with typical pronunciations such as ['moːmɛnt] *moment*, ['wɛlʃmɛn] *Welshmen* (RP [-mənt, -mən]). Suffixal *-ed* and *-est*, too, may often be heard with /ɛ/, as ['landɛd] *landed*, ['brəitɛst] *brightest*. Uncertainty about vowel reduction also leads, conversely, to apparent hypercorrections such as ['proːgrəm] *programme* (RP [-græm]). In Welsh itself /ə/ never occurs in the final syllable of a polysyllabic word.

Unusual variants of lexical incidence, common in Wales, include /tʊθ/ *tooth* (RP /tuːθ/); /ðėiə/ *their*, distinguished from /ðɛː/ *there* (adverb) (RP both /ðɛə/); and *whole*, in south Wales sometimes pronounced /huːl/.

5.1.6 Consonants

One respect in which the consonants of a strong Welsh accent clearly differ from those of an English accent is that of duration. Welsh medial consonants, in particular, tend to be rather long.

This is most obvious in the environment 'V—V. It applies, for instance, to the /d/ in *ready* or the /v/ in *ever*; but it is most obvious with voiceless consonants, as /p/ in *chapel*, /t/ in *matter*, /θ/ in *nothing*, /s/ in *missing*. This phenomenon, frequent in the less anglicized areas, seems not to occur in the speech of Gwent or Cardiff. It has potentially important phonological consequences in that it may lead to the loss of the opposition between single and double consonants, so that for instance *meeting* may be pronounced identically with *meat-tin* ['miːtːɪn]. It also means that the alveolar stop in a phrase such as *brought together*, geminated in RP (/-tt-/ = [tː]), may well have a **shorter** duration in Welsh English than in RP.

In Welsh the consonants /t, d, n/ are often dental rather than alveolar; this sometimes applies to Welsh English, though not to that of the cities of south Wales.

The voiceless plosives /p, t, k/ are strongly aspirated in most positions; so often are the voiceless fricatives, at least in Welsh-speaking areas, as [sʰiː] *see*. In /s/-plus-stop clusters, as in other accents, there is no aspiration; it is striking, though, that Welsh people quite often feel that words such as *spin, steam, score* are phonemically /sb-, sd-, sg-/ rather than /sp-, st-, sk-/. This may just be the effect of Welsh spelling (which gives the borrowed English words *spite* and *scope* the written forms *sbeit* and *sgôp*); or it may reflect a reliance on presence vs. absence of aspiration as the principal feature distinguishing /p, t, k/ from /b, d, g/.

There are two other respects in which typically Welsh accents differ in their realization of plosives from typically English accents: the absence of glottalized allophones, and the absence of 'overlapping' in adjacent plosives. Thus *cup* is typically [kʰəpʰ], not [kʰəʔp], *fat* [fatʰ] not [faʔ], and *thick* [θɪkʰ] not [θɪʔk]. And one can usually hear the release of the /p/ in *captain*, of the /k/ in *actor*, and of the /b/ in *abdicate*; compare the inaudible release of the first of each cluster of adjacent plosives in most other accents, e.g. *actor* (Welsh English ['akʰtʰə], RP ['æk̚tə]).

Cardiff and Newport are exceptions in this regard, as in several others. In these cities one can find Glottalling of /t/ before syllabic [l], thus *little* ['lɪʔl̩]. In the environment 'V—V, Cardiff /t/ is often voiced or tapped, thus ['maɾə] *matter*. Also in Cardiff, allophonic devoicing of /b, d, g/ may be taken to such an extreme that the fortis/lenis opposition may be variably neutralized in certain environments: thus *catarrh* and *guitar* may be homophonous, and *found* in the phrase *found him* sound identical with *fount*. The same may apply with fricatives, too, giving running-speech versions of *plays* sounding identical with *place*. (The examples are taken from Mees 1977.)

In its standard form the Welsh language has no /tʃ/ or /dʒ/ except as loan phonemes. It is for this reason that Welsh speakers from north Wales sometimes have rather [ts]-like versions of these affricates, as [starts] etc. *starch*. Northern Welsh, furthermore, has no /z/ or /ʒ/, which leads to the well-known Welshism of saying 'iss' for *is* (i.e. [ɪs] in place of [ɪz]), and of making *prison* rhyme with *listen* and *vision* ['vɪʃɒn, 'vɪʃən], with *fission*. The systemic oppositions /s/ vs. /z/, /ʃ/ vs. /ʒ/, may be wholly lacking in unsophisticated accents of Welsh-speaking north Wales.

On the other hand there are various other consonant-types used in Welsh but quite foreign to the English of England. In particular, Welsh has a voiceless uvular fricative, /x/ (spelt *ch*), and a voiceless alveolar lateral fricative, /ɬ/ (spelt *ll*). These are sometimes retained when Welsh people use place-names, personal names, or occasional Welsh words containing them when speaking English. Examples are ['amlʊx] *Amlwch*, [ɬan'vənɪð] *Llanfynydd*, [ɬɛ(ː)u] *Llew*, and the interjection of disgust [axə'viː] *ach-y-fi*. North Welsh dialects, and educated Welsh everywhere, also have a voiceless alveolar roll, /ɾ̥/ (spelt *rh*), as ['ɾ̥ɪdjan] *Rhidian*. More commonly, though, non-Welsh speakers replace these by English-type consonants, as shown in (199).

(199)   Welsh /x/ is replaced by English /k/, as *Pentyrch* /pɛn'tɜːk/.
        Welsh /ɬ/ is replaced by English /l/ or /θl/ or /fl/ or /kl/, as *Llanedyrn* /lan'ɛdɪn/, *Llangollen* /lan'gɒθlən/, *Llanelli* /lə'nɛθliː/, /klan'ɛfliː/ etc.; also by a pseudo-Welsh cluster /xl/, as /xlan'ɛxliː/.
        Welsh /ɾ̥/ is replaced by English /r/, as *Rhyl* /rɪl/.

It might seem difficult to anglicize a place-name such as *Rhosllanerchrugog* (Welsh /'ɾ̥oːs'ɬanɛrx'riːgɔg/); it comes out as /'rouslanə'kriːɡɒɡ/.

Even /ð/ (in Welsh spelt *dd*), a thoroughly English consonant, is felt to be foreign when in syllable-initial position, and is replaced by /d/: thus *Ynysddu* is usually called /ənɪs'diː/, and *Llanddewi*

/lən'djuːiː/. And of course ignorance of Welsh spelling conventions leads to un-Welsh pronunciations of names which phonetically ought to offer no problems in English, as when *Dafydd* /'davɪð/ is called /'dafɪd/. Then it must also be pointed out that there are several place-names in anglicized areas which have Welsh-looking spelling but an established un-Welsh pronunciation, e.g. *Rhiwbina* /ruː'bəinə/ (not, as one might suppose, /ruː'biːnə/).

The absence of [x] corresponding to Middle English [x] (vol. 1, 3.1.3) reflects the relatively recent arrival of English in Wales. If a word such as *trough* had come into use in Wales at a time when it still had final [x] in England, a trace at least of such a pronunciation would be likely to have persisted in Wales, where [x] is a familiar sound type. But for this word Parry (1977: 122–3) records only final [f], [ɣ], or zero consonant. (Earlier English borrowings into Welsh do have [x], as *dracht* 'draught'.)

The realization of the liquids in Welsh English calls for some comment. Only in Cardiff and parts of the anglicized south-east does /l/ have complementarily distributed clear and dark allophones, as in RP. In other parts of the south, e.g. Merthyr, Rhondda, Neath, /l/ tends to be relatively clear in all positions. In north Wales there is a general tendency towards pharyngalization which makes /l/ often rather dark in all environments. The realization of /r/ ranges from rolled [r] or [ɾ], particularly in Welsh-speaking areas, to approximant [ɹ]. Even in Cardiff, though, Mees (1977) reports [ɾ] as very common for /r/ when intervocalic or after certain consonants (/b, v, θ/), as ['dɪnəɾ ən] *dinner and*, ['ɛvɾi] *every*. Uvular [ʁ] is not unknown in Wales: correspondents tell me it is to be heard in parts of both Gwynedd and Dyfed as a social/geographical characteristic, not just as a personal idiosyncrasy. In Welsh uvular /r/ is known as *tafod tew* ('thick tongue').

The residualism of a final [g] in *sing, hang, wrong*, etc. (thus [sɪŋg], [haŋg], etc.) spills over into Clwyd from adjacent parts of the north of England (4.4.6 above).

In Welsh the semi-vowels /j, w/ are excluded from the environment of a following /iː, ɪ/ or /uː, ʊ/ respectively. This constraint also applies in some Welsh English. Parry (1977: 90–4) records *yeast* and *yield* with no initial /j/ as the predominating forms, and *woman* and *wool* with no initial /w/ as widespread. But the types [iːst] *yeast* and ['ʊmən] *woman* are quite common in the rural speech of the west of England, too, so that this does not necessarily have to be attributed to interference from the phonology of Welsh.

South Wales shares with most of England the tendency to H Dropping. As elsewhere, this is phonologically variable: [h] is more likely to be present in middle-class or careful speech, less likely to be present in working-class or casual speech. Hypercorrect [h], as [hɛg] *egg*, is also found. In north Wales (at least in the Welsh-speaking areas) there is no H Dropping prevocalically. *Wh-* words have plain /w/ everywhere.

5.1.7 Connected-speech variants

Mees's study of the speech of Cardiff schoolchildren (1977) shows that processes of assimilation and elision appear to be commoner and more varied there than in RP. As well as Yod Coalescence and dealveolar Place Assimilation, there are some less common types. One is assimilation of the fortis/lenis feature (which, as we have seen, is the feature responsible for the distinctions /p–b, t–d, f–v/ etc. in Welsh English): by this optional rule, any obstruent becomes fortis before a following fortis consonant. Thus *his sister's teacher* may become [ɪs ˈsɪstəs ˈtiːtʃə]. Other types are illustrated by the examples [ˈwɒdn̩] *wasn't*, [ɔːllat] *all that*, [ˈwɒssə] *what's the*. Elisions include [bə wiː] *but we*, [ɐʊnd] *round*, [ɪ wəs] *it was*. The elision of initial /ð/ in *the, this, then*, etc., is particularly frequent.

A well-known phonological characteristic of the Welsh language is the existence of mutations. One of them, Soft Mutation, which is triggered by a variety of morphological and syntactic environments, involves the voicing of underlyingly voiceless plosives and the switching of underlying voiced plosives and /m/ into fricatives. One observer (Parry 1971) reports the extension of this process into rapidly spoken English, giving the example [ɒn ˈdɒpʰ əðə ˈvəs] *on top of the bus* (i.e. with the /t/ of *top* becoming [d] and the /b/ of *bus* becoming [v] in accordance with the rule of Soft Mutation). I cannot say I have ever observed this myself.

5.1.8 Prosodic features

Welsh accents have one unusual stressing characteristic. This relates to longer words and compounds, and consists in the avoi-

dance, in many instances, of secondary stresses in the word –
stresses other than the main word stress – together with resyllabi-
cation. Thus *Bridgend* is pronounced /brɪ'dʒɛnd/: compare its RP
form /'brɪdʒ'ɛnd/, optionally reducible, depending on rhythmic
factors, to /brɪdʒ'ɛnd/ or /'brɪdʒɛnd/. So also *Port Talbot* /pə 't-/.

Popular English views about Welsh accents include the claim
that they have a 'sing-song' or 'lilting' intonation. This is felt
particularly to be the case for the industrial valleys of south Wales
which have only rather recently abandoned Welsh as first language.
Certainly rhythm and intonation are among the diagnostic characteristics for recognizing an accent as Welsh. In the absence of a
proper investigation of the intonation of Welsh English, I can
suggest only that one striking usage is that of a rise-fall tone in cases
where standard accents would have a simple fall, e.g. *It's ˈno longer
ˇvalid* (= RP *It's ˈno ˈlonger ˇvalid*). This gives the impression of
throwing into inexplicable prominence the syllable after the one
bearing the intonation nucleus. The width of this rise-fall is more
striking in the Valleys than in Cardiff: thus *It's a nice day, isn't it?*,
[. . . ˆɪnɪt], (200).

(200)

Rhondda   Cardiff   RP [-ɪzn̩tɪt]

There is also something noticeable about the high-rise tone in
Welsh English. Where there is a tail, the nuclear syllable is low and
level, the tail steadily rising, and the whole thing rather more rapid
than in RP; and it is used in yes–no questions where RP might well
prefer a low-rise. For example, (201).

(201)   Welsh   RP

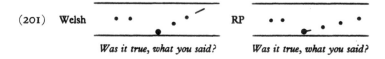

Was it true, what you said?   *Was it true, what you said?*

5.1.9 Sociolinguistics in Cardiff

In her study of the speech habits of Cardiff schoolchildren, Mees
(1977) analysed six phonological variables: the consonant in *-ing*,
the quality of /aː/ in START words, the possibility of H Dropping,
the quality of /əi/ in PRICE words, that of /əu/ in MOUTH words, and
that of /ou/ in GOAT words. The findings for *-ing* and /h/ are very

much what might be expected in most parts of England; the others are summarized here. The sample was a small one, a mere fifteen children; they were divided by father's occupation into three equally sized socio-economic classes. The figures in (202) relate to reading-passage style.

(202)

		Upper middle	Lower middle	Working
/aː/ START	000 = all [ɑ+ː] 400 = all [æː ~ ɛː]	032	068	316
/əi/ PRICE	000 = all [äɪ] 200 = all [əi]	110	142	163
/əu/ MOUTH	000 = all [äʊ] 200 = all [əu]	060	110	170
/ou/ GOAT	000 = all [əʊ] 100 = all [ou ~ oː]	007	063	096

This shows that non-RP realizations of the vowels of PRICE and MOUTH are general, even in the more formal styles of speech; the quality of the START vowel is clearly a more powerful social marker.

5.2 Scotland

5.2.1 Introduction

Scotland has always had a linguistic tradition rather different from that of England. This is partly for political reasons: until 1707 Scotland was an independent state, and in the 1970s we have seen a resurgence of national consciousness, an awareness of distinctness. Linguistically this is reflected in the fact that RP does not enjoy the same tacit status in Scotland as it does in England and Wales; a Scottish accent can be prestigious in a way that a local English accent is not. It is also reflected in the modest degree of literary recognition accorded not only to Scottish Gaelic (the Celtic language closely related to Irish) but also to **Scots**. Scots, according to one's point of view, can be considered either a group of dialects of English, or a distinct language.

Anglo-Saxons captured Edinburgh in the seventh century, and ever since then at least part of Scotland has spoken a Germanic language, although at least until the Reformation Gaelic was spoken by a majority of the population and over a wider geographical area than Scots. The latter, nevertheless, was the language of court and government under the Stewart monarchy. The use of English as a spoken language – Standard English with a Scottish accent, that is, rather than Scots – began only in the eighteenth century, and did not become general until later still.

The Anglo-Saxons in Lothian spoke a northern ('Northumbrian') dialect of Old English. Its linear descendant, with Scandinavian and Norman-French elements added, gradually came to be used throughout southern and north-eastern Scotland. Up to the fifteenth century it was known, rather confusingly, as Inglis; by then it had become the official language of the Kingdom of Scotland, and was renamed Scottis or Scots. This was the language of the poets Henryson, Dunbar, and Douglas, who flourished around 1500.

Since the sixteenth century the status of Scots has steadily declined. In the absence of a Scots translation, the language of the English Bible became the language of religion and serious thought. The Union of the Crowns of England and Scotland in 1603, and then the Union of Parliaments in 1707, meant that the official written language of the whole country came to be the English of England. By 1761 we hear of Scottish Members of the British Parliament taking lessons in elocution so that the English might understand them better. Scots was downgraded to the rôle of domestic dialect. This trend was not overturned by sporadic literary revivals, even from such talented poets as Burns and, in our own day, MacDiarmid. The official and usual literary language of Scotland has for three centuries been Standard English – pronounced, though, with a Scottish accent and retaining a few scotticisms in vocabulary. This Scottish English co-exists with Scots in an accent and traditional-dialect set-up comparable with that found in the north of England (as discussed in volume 1, 1.1.2).

Meanwhile a quite distinct language was spoken throughout most of the more northerly and westerly parts of Scotland, in the Highlands and Islands. This was Scottish Gaelic. It is still spoken, particularly in the Hebrides, though by a decreasing number of people; a revivalist movement has recently made some headway. Like the other Celtic languages of the British Isles, it has been receding for centuries under the pressure of English – a pressure much accelerated in the Highlands of Scotland by the failure of the rebellion of 1745 and the population clearances and emigration which followed. Today Gaelic remains as the majority and community language only in the Outer Hebrides, in some of the Inner Hebrides, and in the two mainland parishes of Applecross and Ardnamurchan. Even there no monoglot speakers of Gaelic (except pre-school children) are to be found. However, Gaelic has left behind an identifiable phonetic influence on the English of the Highlands and Islands, even in areas where it has disappeared as a spoken language. This 'post-Gaelic' English is also noticeably 'correct', having as it does no Scots substratum. Hence the received wisdom that the purest English is spoken in Inverness; in Inverness, Scots has never been in general use, since there Gaelic was displaced directly by Standard English.

Before describing the phonetics of Scottish English we first give brief consideration to Scots.

5.2.2 Scots

The distinction between accent and dialect (i.e. traditional-dialect, discussed in volume 1, 1.1.2) is even more important in Scotland than in England. Many non-Gaelic-speaking Scottish people have at their command two forms of speech: one of them is Scottish English, i.e. Standard English spoken with a Scottish accent, as described in 5.2.3–5 below; the other is Scots, the traditional-dialect (some would say, the language) spoken in southern, central, and north-eastern Scotland. In rural areas the distinction between Scots and Scottish English may be quite sharp, so that it is very clear which is being spoken at any given moment. In urban areas, and particularly in the industrial cities, there is a continuum of variation such that one cannot make a clear-cut distinction. In Glasgow, for example, many would claim that authentic Scots, the traditional-dialect, has died out; yet working-class Glasgow speech includes many features which would normally be considered characteristic of Scots rather than of Standard English. Such features may be lexical (*gloaming* 'twilight', *greet* 'weep'), syntactic (*the woman that her dog got run over*), morphological ([dïzne] *does not*) and phonological (/u/ in MOUTH words). But even in the areas where Scots is spoken there are many middle-class Scottish people who natively speak only English.

395

Scots is unique among traditional-dialects of English in that it is
the only one to have a modern literary tradition distinct from that
of Standard English, a literary tradition of some importance. It
stretches in a somewhat fitful line from the *makaris* (poets) of the
fifteenth and sixteenth centuries, of which Dunbar is the best
known, to the eighteenth-century poets Ramsay, Fergusson and,
above all, Robert Burns, and down to the twentieth-century renaissance associated particularly with Hugh MacDiarmid. This latter
renaissance has involved a partly synthetic form of Scots known as
Lallans.

A glance at, say, Burns' best-known works reveals immediately
the sharp differences between Scots and Standard English:

> Ha! whaur ye gaun, ye crowlin ferlie?
> Your impudence protects you sairly;
> I canna say but ye strunt rarely,
>   Owre gauze and lace;
> Tho' faith! I fear ye dine but sparely
>   On sic a place.

Phonologically, Scots differs from (other forms of) English in
many ways. The consonant system includes the velar fricative /x/, a
consonant of frequent occurrence, as /dɔxtɪr/ *daughter*, /dɪxt/ *dicht*
'wipe', /pɛx/ *pech* 'be out of breath'; one or two words with /x/ are
found in Scottish English, where they can be considered as loan-
words from Scots, e.g. /drix/ *dreich* and the well-known /lɔx/ *loch*.
Phonotactically, Scots admits various un-English clusters such as
/kn-, vr-, -xt/. Most importantly, though, the lexical incidence of
phonemes differs radically from that found in English.

Thus the word for 'stone', in a Scottish accent of English
straightforwardly /ston/, takes the Scots form /sten/ *stane* or, in
Buchan, /stin/ *steen*. Corresponding to the [e ~ ɛ] of DRESS words in
other accents, Scots may have any of nine or more vowels: in the
Perthshire Scots described by Wilson (1915) they include /e/ in
dead, bread; /a/ in *wren, let*; /i/ in *well, friend* (though for most forms
of Scots /i/ in *deaf* and *head* would be more typical); /ʌi/ in *sweat*; /ɪ/
in *egg, chest* /kɪst/; /o/ in *any, many*; /ʌ/ in *web, cherry*; /ʏ/ in *bury*;
and of course straightforward /ɛ/ in *bed, bell*. In FOOT and GOOSE
words, where Scottish English has only /u/, Scots again exhibits a
range of possibilities, as in the data shown in data (203) from
Glenesk, Tayside (quoted from Catford 1957).

(203)

standard lexical set	Scots (Glenesk)	Scottish English
FOOT — book	u	u
bull	ʌ	
foot	ɪ	
GOOSE — boot	ø	
lose	o	
loose	ʌu	

Here the vowel of *book* betrays a loan from English; that of *bull* is the usual development from Middle English /u/; those of *foot* and *boot* represent developments of /ø/, the northern Middle English fronting of /o/; that of *loose* can be traced to Old Norse rather than to Old English.

The vowel system of Scots comprises a subset of the vowel system of Scottish English discussed below, namely a basic /i, e, ɛ, a, ɪ, u, o, ʌ/, to which certain local dialects add further items, giving anything from eight to twelve vowels in the system. To these must be added at least two, and commonly three, diphthongs. The vowel systems have been analysed and compared in a deservedly famous article by Catford (1958).

There are three main regional divisions within Scots: the central dialects of the Lowlands, including the densely populated industrial belt of Lothian and Strathclyde, and also covering the central, Fife, and Tayside regions; the southern dialects in parts of the Borders and Dumfries-and-Galloway regions; and the northern dialects spoken in the Grampian region from Stonehaven northwards, as well as in a few communities along the east coast of the Highland region.

Among the distinguishing phonological characteristics of the southern dialects is the use of [ʌu] rather than [u] in free-syllable MOUTH words, thus [kʌu] *cow* (although checked-syllable MOUTH words do have [u]); also [ɛɪ] in free-syllable FLEECE words, thus [mɛɪ] *me*.

A well-known northern characteristic is the use of a voiceless labial fricative, either [f] or [ɸ], in place of the [ʍ] found elsewhere in

397

5.2 *Scotland*

Fig. 11   Regional divisions within Scots (after Speitel & Mather 1968)
Note. The county boundaries shown are those prior to the local
government reorganization of the 1970s

when, where, what, and most other words with *wh* spelling. The
northern dialect of the Buchan area of the Grampian region, around
the towns of Fraserburgh and Peterhead, is known as 'Buchan
Doric': it featured in my own life story as the first dialect of English
I encountered which proved utterly opaque to my attempts to
understand it without first learning it. A sample utterance is ['fustɪ
kɑt], which means 'What is it called?' (literally, *How is't ye ca' it?*)
   Orkney and Shetland formerly spoke Norn, a dialect of Norse or

398

Norwegian. For some centuries now, though, they have spoken
Scots and English. Striking features of their Scots dialect include
the loss of the /t–θ, d–ð/ oppositions, with dental plosives for both
(*tin = thin* [ʈɪn]), and the use of /xw/ rather than /kw/ as an initial
cluster, thus /ˈxwɛstjən/ *question*. There is also the palatalizing in
certain circumstances of the consonants /d, l, n/, which has been
attributed to the Norse substratum.

A further description of Scots lies outside (or, as the Scots might
say, *outwith*) the scope of this book. In this chapter we restrict
ourselves from now on to consideration of Scottish English, i.e.
Standard English with a Scottish accent.

5.2.3 Monophthongs

The vowel system of a Scottish accent of English is typically as
shown in (204), type IV.

(204)	ɪ		i				u
	ɛ (ɛ̈) ʌ		e (ʌi)		(3)		o
		(ɒ)	ae (ɒɪ)		a	(ɑ)	ʌu ɔ

The parenthesized items may or may not be present. If /ɑ/ is
present in the system, then /a/ belongs in part-system A. Lexical
incidence is as shown in (205).

(205)	KIT	ɪ	FLEECE	i	NEAR	ir
	DRESS	ɛ[1]	FACE	e	SQUARE	er
	TRAP	a	PALM	a[3]	START	ar[7]
	LOT	ɔ[2]	THOUGHT	ɔ	NORTH	ɔr[8]
	STRUT	ʌ	GOAT	o	FORCE	or
	FOOT	u	GOOSE	u	CURE	ur
	BATH	a[3]	PRICE	ae, ʌi[5]	*happy*	e, ɪ, i[6]
	CLOTH	ɔ[2]	CHOICE	ɒɪ[6]	*lett*ER	ər[9]
	NURSE	3r[4]	MOUTH	ʌu	*comm*A	ʌ[10]

[1] or in some words /ɛ̈/, for those who have it.
[2] but /ɒ/ for those who have it.
[3] but /ɑ/ in some words for those who have it.
[4] but for those who lack /3/ there is a lexically determined choice between /ɛr/, /ʌr/,
/ɪr/ etc.; discussed below.
[5] possibly contrastive; discussed below.
[6] discussed below.
[7] but /ɑr/ for some who have /ɑ/.
[8] but /ɒr/ for some who have /ɒ/.
[9] but /ɪr/ or /ʌr/ for those who lack /ə/.
[10] or /ə/ for those who have this phoneme.

Realizationally, /i, e, ɛ, a, ɔ, o/ are typically monophthongs with qualities in the general areas implied by the corresponding cardinal vowels (though /ɛ/, in particular, may be rather closer than cardinal [ɛ] and /a/ less front than cardinal [a]); /u, ʌ, ɑ/ are also monophthongal, but somewhat advanced from cardinal values; /u/ may be [ʉ] or even fronter. The quality of the diphthongs is discussed below.

The Scottish vowel system is clearly distinct typologically from the vowel systems of all other accents of English (except the related Ulster), and constitutes our type IV (vol. 1, 2.3.6). It lacks any opposition of the kind /ʊ/ vs. /u/ (*pull* vs. *pool*, FOOT vs. GOOSE – though it must be noted that many FOOT words have Scots dialect forms with /ʌ/). It may also lack the oppositions /a/ vs. /ɑ/ (TRAP vs. PALM) and /ɒ/ vs. /ɔ/ (LOT vs. THOUGHT). There are no long–short oppositions of the kind found in other accents; on the other hand duration contrasts (without qualitative differences) may signal morphological boundaries in a way not found elsewhere.

In fact, vowel duration tends to vary sharply according to phonetic environment. The general rule, sometimes known after its discoverer as **Aitken's Law** (Aitken 1962; Lass 1974), is that a vowel is phonetically short unless it is followed by #, a voiced fricative, or /r/, in which case it is long (at least in a monosyllable).

Thus there is a short vowel in *bead*, for instance; it is pronounced [bid], and its vowel is durationally similar to those of *bid* [bɪd] and *bed* [bɛd]. Similarly, *mood* is [mud]; as we have seen, it rhymes with *good*, both words having short but close [u]. In the same way, the duration of the vowel in *lace* [les] is similar to that of *less* [lɛs], and that of *tote* [tot] to that of *pot* [pɔt ~ pɒt]. The Scottish pronunciation of a word such as *meter*, with a durationally short [i] in the first syllable, is rhythmically different from its pronunciation in other accents.

Vowels are long in morpheme-final position, or in the environment of following /v, ð, z, r/: this applies to all vowels except /ɪ/ and /ʌ/ (which are always short). Thus we have long vowels in *key* [kiː], *two* [tuː], *stay* [steː], *know* [noː], etc.; and in words such as *sleeve* [sliːv], *smooth* [smuːð], *maze* [meːz], *pour* [poːr], *Kerr* [kɛːr], *Oz* [ɔːz].

This long duration is also retained if a morpheme-final vowel is followed by a suffixal /d/, as in *agree#d* [əˈgriːd]. As we have seen, though, a vowel before a final /d/ belonging to the same morpheme is short, as *greed* [grid]. Hence there is a phonetic contrast between the two types of word with final /d/, those which are morphologically simple and those which contain a word-internal #. So there is a phonetic distinction between *need* [nid] and *knee#d* [niːd], *brood* [brud] and *brew#ed* [bruːd]. Not all speakers have the distinction in vowels other than /i/ and /u/, but those who have also distinguish between pairs such as *staid* [sted] and *stay#ed* [steːd], *toad* [tod] and *tow#ed–toe#d* [toːd], *bad* [bad] and *baa#d* [baːd], *nod* [nɔd] and *gnaw#ed* [nɔːd]. (There is also the possibility of a qualitative distinction, too, in the last two pairs, for those who have the extra phonemes /ɑ/ and /ɒ/.)

Some speakers also have instances of apparently autonomous length contrasts in other environments, e.g. *leek* [lik] vs. *leak* [liːk], *vane* [ven] vs. *vain* [veːn], *creek* [krik] vs. *creak* [kriːk], *choke* vs. *joke*, *made* vs. *maid*, *badge* vs. *cadge*.

Recent measurements by McClure (1977) confirm that the duration of vowels in the environment /__d/ also differs from that of those in the environment /__ #d/: the ratio ranges from 2.6 for /u/ (*could* vs. *coo#ed*) down to 1.3 for /a/ (*pad* vs. *baa#d*). Interestingly, this work also revealed a definite difference in duration between /__z/ and /__ #z/ (both 'long' environments in terms of Aitken's Law), though in this case it is a matter of a ratio of the order 1.2–1.3. The relevant measurements (in centiseconds) and ratios are set out in (206).

(206)	i	u	e	o	a	ɔ
__d	13	13	21.5	23	26	23.5
__ #d	28	34	31.5	31.5	35	33
__z	25.5	28	29	27.5	31.5	30
__ #z	30	34.5	35	37	39.5	36

Ratio between morphologically simple: morphologically complex words

	i	u	e	o	a	ɔ
__(#)d	1 : 2.2	1 : 2.6	1 : 1.5	1 : 1.4	1 : 1.3	1 : 1.4
__(#)z	1 : 1.2	1 : 1.2	1 : 1.2	1 : 1.3	1 : 1.3	1 : 1.2

These measurements relate only to one speaker (from Ayrshire), and represent the mean duration for two utterances of the word in isolation.

From a diagnostic point of view, the most important characteristic of the Scottish vowel system is its lack, as mentioned above, of a phoneme /ʊ/. The vowel of FOOT words is identical with that of

GOOSE words; I write it /u/ (although arguably it would be better written /ʉ/). Hence there are homophones such as *pull–pool, full–fool, look–Luke,* and rhymes such as *good–mood, foot–boot, puss–loose, pudding–brooding, wool–tool, woman–human.* This FOOT–GOOSE Merger is characteristic of all Scottish accents of all regional and social types; but of no others, except only those of Ulster and northernmost Northumberland, both of which have obvious linguistic links with Scotland. In the speech of anglicized Scots this is the one characteristic above all which seems virtually impervious to alteration, and it may accordingly be regarded as an infallible indicator of Scottish (or Ulster, etc.) origin. It is striking that McAllister (1938), the author of an influential Scottish-oriented speech training manual with decidedly prescriptive views, is obviously quite unaware of the possibility of having a phonemic opposition between /ʊ/ and /u/; she treats [ʊ] as an anglicizing optional variant of [u]. (In Scots dialects the incidence of vowels in words of the lexical sets FOOT and GOOSE may be quite different, e.g. [fɪt] *foot,* [gʏs] *goose;* the point remains that there is typically no phonemic contrast between vowels of the [ʊ] and [u] types.)

The phonetic quality of the /u/ of FOOT and GOOSE varies socio-linguistically. The elegant realization is fairly back, [u]; the usual quality, not back but central, [ʉ], or centralized front, [ʏ]. In the Glasgow area there may be only slight rounding. This was one of the variables studied by Macaulay & Trevelyan (1973; see also Macaulay 1974, 1977), who operated with a scale ranging from fronted back [u] to an unrounded lowered [ɪ]. (The latter type represents a further stage of the traditional-dialect development from [oː] via [øː] as discussed briefly in volume 1, 3.1.1.)

Many speakers of Scottish English have a single phoneme /ɔ/ common to LOT and THOUGHT (as well as to CLOTH, of course). This gives homophones of the type *cot–caught* /kɔt/, *knotty–naughty, don–dawn* (pairs always, I think, distinguished in England). Others have a contrast between two possible phonemes, at least in certain environments, with /ɔ/ in THOUGHT and some other vowel in LOT and CLOTH. This something else is indeed often /ɒ/, phonetically a back rounded vowel of the type [ɒ], so that LOT is opener than THOUGHT; sometimes, on the other hand, it seems to be closer (which reflects one of the possibilities in Scots, where LOT words may have /o/). Even those speakers who have the opposition between /ɔ/ and /ɒ/ (*dawn* ≠ *don*) may nevertheless use /ɔ/, not /ɒ/, in certain LOT words, e.g. *yacht, wash, watch, squad, squash, lorry.*

There are also several possibilities with the open vowel(s). Many Scottish people have just a single phoneme /a/ common to PALM and TRAP (as well as to BATH and, with following /r/, START); though its realization may vary both allophonically and socially. Others have two phonemes, /a/ in TRAP and /ɑ/ in PALM; often [a] and [ɑ] contrast only in a few environments, otherwise being in complementary distribution. Perhaps the environment in which an opposition is most readily found is that of a following nasal, with, for instance, *Sam* [sam] distinct from *psalm* [sɑm]. Studying a small group of members of Edinburgh University, Winston (1970) found that less than half had a phonemic contrast between the two vowels, although all used both phonetic qualities, [a] and [ɑ]. Back [ɑ], she found, typically occurred in the environments __#, __r#, and __rC (*bra, car, farm*); sometimes also before a fricative (*calf, path, mass, vast*). Before plosives, affricates, and medial /r/, [a] was regularly used (*cap, flat, back, tab, bad, bag, match, badge, marry*). I notice that the words *value, salmon,* and *gather* often seem to have [ɑ] rather than the [a] which one might expect on the basis of other accents; so sometimes do *alphabet* and *parallel.*

Where there is only a single open vowel, so that *psalm* and *Sam* are homophonous, I write it /a/, though obviously one could equally well write it /ɑ/. The quality varies not only allophonically but also socially. In Glasgow, for instance, Macaulay & Trevelyan (1973) demonstrated that a front quality, [æ ~ a], is associated with higher status than a backer [ɑ] type: in *hat* the pronunciation [hat] is associated with white-collar occupations, but [hɑt ~ hɑʔ] with unskilled manual occupations. Qualities of the type [æ], or even [ɛ], for this vowel are popularly believed to characterize the speech of the well-to-do suburbs of Morningside (Edinburgh) and Kelvinside (Glasgow) and widely considered 'affected'. The [æ] version is like that of RP, as [hæt]; the [ɛ] version may well be restricted to the environment of an adjacent velar and reflect the neutralization of the opposition /a ~ ɑ/ vs. /ɛ/ (TRAP vs. DRESS) in this environment, so that e.g. *cattle = kettle* ['kɛtl], *bag = beg* [bɛg].

Abercrombie (1979) claims that an implicational relationship holds between these three 'optional' vowel oppositions /u–ʊ, ɔ–ɒ, a–ɑ/: contrastive /ʊ/ implies the presence of contrastive /ɒ/, and contrastive /ɒ/ implies the presence of contrastive /ɑ/, but not the reverse.

The opposition between /ɛ/ and /ë/ is another one which applies only to some speakers: it is commonly found in the west of Scotland, in the Borders, in Perthshire, and sometimes in Edinburgh. (Winston (1970) reports that all her Edinburgh University subjects had contrastive /ë/, but there was no one word in which they all agreed in using it!) Where present, /ë/ is phonologically and phonetically distinct both from /ɪ/ and from /ɛ/, and in quality is typically somewhat less open than cardinal 3 and considerably centralized. The opposition can be tested by the triplet *river* vs. *never* vs. *sever*. If *never* rhymes neither with *river* (/ɪ/) nor with *sever* (/ɛ/), then it can be presumed to have /ë/. The lexical incidence of /ë/ varies somewhat with different speakers, but the following are further words in which it is commonly heard: *bury, devil, earth, clever, jerk, eleven, heaven, next, shepherd, twenty*. Other potential non-rhyming pairs for /ɛ/ vs. /ë/ therefore include *vexed* vs. *next*, *leopard* vs. *shepherd*. Kohler (1964) has offered a plausible explanation of its origin: in some dialects of Scots this [ë] is used in many or all words of the standard lexical set KIT; an [ɪ] was then acquired and used for KIT words in English; and the [ë] was retained in a handful of words which, although having the DRESS vowel in standard accents, belonged with KIT in Scots (compare the dialect spellings *niver* for *never*, etc.).

In Buchan English, as described by Wölck (1965), there is no fully front [ɛ] but only the centralized [ë] (which Wölck writes /ə/). This vowel is used not only in DRESS words but also in many unstressed syllables, where it corresponds to the /ə/ of standard accents.

In KIT words, the quality of /ɪ/ is – in an educated Scottish accent – much the same as in RP. In more popular accents it may be considerably opener and/or more retracted. In the north-east, it is often pretty open and [ɛ]-like, especially before /r/, and even among educated speakers. In Glasgow it ranges from [ɪ] to [ʌ], including various intermediate possible qualities. The back quality, of the type [ʌ], is particularly common after /w/ and /hw/, thus ['ʍʌsl̩] *whistle*; Fergusson (Edinburgh, 1750–74) has a joke-rhyme *windy–gloria mundi*! There may indeed be a neutralization of the opposition /ɪ/ vs. /ʌ/, so that *fin* may be identical to *fun* [fʌn] and *milk* rhyme with *bulk*.

The analysis of unstressed vowels, as often, presents problems. In many places where RP has /ə/, it seems correct to regard Scottish English as having /ɪ/ or /ɪr/, e.g. *pilot* /'paelɪt/, *letter* /'lɛtɪr/. It will be recalled that Scóttish /ɪ/ is in any case often very [ə]-like. Yet many speakers make a consistent distinction between *except* and *accept*, etc., so that we must phonemicize these as /ɪk-, ʌk-/ respectively. In final position, an opener vowel is usual; this *comm*A vowel may be analysed as /ʌ/, too (and this agrees with speakers' intuition). There is of course a consistent distinction between *comm*A and *lett*ER: *manner—manor* /'manɪr/ vs. *manna* /'manʌ/. The foregoing applies to most Scottish accents. In Edinburgh speech, however, it seems more realistic to recognize a phoneme /ə/ (as in the NURSE words discussed in 5.2.5 below), and analyse the words mentioned in this paragraph as /'paelət, 'lɛtər, 'kɒmə, 'manər, 'manə/.

The final vowel in *happ*Y words is perhaps most typically /e/ in Scotland, so that *lady* is /'lede/; *studied* /'stʌded/ differs from *studded* /'stʌdɪd/. Some Scottish people, though, use /ɪ/, while in the north-east /i/ is usual, thus /'ledi/.

5.2.4 Diphthongs

Many speakers of Scottish English have two perceptibly distinct diphthongs in PRICE words. One, phonetically, is approximately [aˑe], the other approximately [ʌi] (or, in working-class speech, [ëi]). There are several minimal pairs such as *tied* [taˑed] vs. *tide* [tʌid], *sighed* vs. *side, spider* vs. *wider*. As can be seen, these pairs are not identical in morphological structure: *tie#d, tide; sigh#ed, side*; in the third pair there is also a difference of syllabication, *spi$der* vs. *wide$#r*. This gives a clue to the explanation: basically we have here further instances of length variation in accordance with Aitken's Law. Unlike the monophthongs, though, this diphthong varies qualitatively as well as quantitatively; this seems to make speakers more aware of it and more disposed (if analysing their own speech) to regard /ae/ and /ʌi/ as distinct phonemes. Nevertheless, the two diphthongs are virtually in complementary distribution, provided that morphological and syllabic structure are taken into account. The first, [ae], is used in the environments which under Aitken's Law call for a long vowel, namely finally and before a voiced fricative or /r/, thus *buy, high, alive, prize, fire* [faer ~ fae.ɪr]. (In the north-east, for some reason, though, people say [fʌir] for *fire.*) It is also used in morpheme-final position before an ending or suffix, as *tried* (*try # ed*), *tries, high # er, shy # ly, shy # ness*; and in syllable-final position in words such as *diet* ['dae.ɪt], *pilot, tiger, py$thon, iron* ['ae.rŋ]. The other diphthong, [ʌi], is used elsewhere: namely, before a tautosyllabic consonant other than a voiced fricative or /r/, thus *wipe, tribe, light, wide, like, time, kind, mile, life, ice.* It can also occur before tautosyllabic /v/ in inflected noun plurals, by analogy with the singular form where [ʌi] is regular before /f/: thus sometimes *wives* [wʌivz], because of *wife* [wʌif]; *five knives* /faev nʌivz/. But it is very common in Scottish speech for the voiceless fricative to be retained in the plural, thus *knives* [nʌifs]. A medial consonant counts as tautosyllabic when it is immediately followed by a morpheme boundary, thus *shin # ing* (from *shine*) ['ʃʌinɪŋ], but *shy # ness* ['ʃaenɪs], *w*[ʌi]*p # er* but *v*[ae]*per, w*[ʌi]*d # er* but *sp*[ae]*der.*

To treat [ae] and [ʌi] as allophones of the same phoneme does thus involve the recognition of quite complicated rules for their distribution – rules dependent on morphology (*tied* vs. *tide*), on the consequences of morphology for syllabic structure (*spider* vs. *wider*), and on analogical regularization to reduce allomorphic variation (*fives* vs. *wives*), as well as on straightforward consideration of phonetic environment. It may well be felt that we are justified, then, in claiming that a phoneme split has occurred and that many kinds of Scottish English include distinct phonemes /ae/ and /ʌi/.

With the vowel of MOUTH things are rather different. Here there is no tendency to split into two phonemes; but there is considerable sociolinguistic variability, with qualities ranging from a high-status [au] or [ʌu] to a popular [u+]. Macaulay & Trevelyan have shown (1973) that in Glasgow this variation correlates clearly with social class. In those areas where Scots dialect is spoken alongside Scottish English, individual speakers usually have both possibilities in MOUTH words, /u/ for Scots and /ʌu/ for English. This /u/ in MOUTH is well-known as a Scotticism outside Scotland, and is familiar in such stereotyped Scottish pronunciations as 'hoose' for *house.*

In the case of CHOICE words, the usual pronunciation involves the diphthong here written /ɒɪ/, which ranges phonetically over [ɒɪ ~ ɔɪ]. Non-finally, some speakers use [ʌi] instead, thus merging pairs such as *vice–voice.* Another possibility, found particularly in the

Clyde valley, is to have instead of a diphthong a disyllabic sequence of /o/ plus /ɪ/, thus ['bo.ɪ] *boy*, ['vo.ɪs] *voice* (with the same sequence as *lowest*).

The FACE and GOAT vowels are generally monophthongal, and as such properly treated in 5.2.3 above rather than here. Diphthongal realizations are spreading, though, presumably due to English influence. In particular, [oʊ] for /o/ is now not uncommon.

5.2.5 Vowels before /r/

Scottish English is rhotic, and most or all vowels can occur before tautosyllabic /r/. In this respect it is strikingly conservative, having undergone neither Pre-R Breaking and Pre-Schwa Laxing (vol. I, 3.2.1) nor (in most cases) the NURSE Merger (vol. I, 3.1.8).

Some Scottish accents have undergone the NURSE Merger. In middle-class Edinburgh speech, for example, *dirt, pert*, and *hurt* are perfect rhymes, as are *bird, heard*, and *word*. All have an r-coloured [ɝ], which we analyse as /ɜr/. This, however, must be considered exceptional in Scotland. In working-class speech of the Glasgow area there is a partial merger, with the falling together of the vowels of *dirt* and *hurt, bird* and *word* (with /ʌr/), while *pert, heard*, etc., retain /ɛr/. In more prestigious west-of-Scotland accents the historical three-way contrast is typically preserved, with /ɪ/ (phonetically [ɪ ~ ə]) in *dirt* and *bird*, /ɛ/ in *pert* and *heard*, and /ʌ/ in *hurt* and *word*. Some speakers in fact have more than these three possible vowels in NURSE words: the /ë/ discussed above may occur before /r/ in *earth, jerk*, and *herd*, for instance; *shirt* [ʃərt] may not rhyme with any of *sk*[ɪ]*rt*, *p*[ɛ]*rt*, and *h*[ʌ]*rt*, nor *bird* [bərd] with any of *st*[ɪ]*rred*, *heard* [hɛrd], *herd* [hërd], *w*[ʌ]*rd*. It is unusual, however, to have as many as these five contrasting possibilities within the lexical set NURSE. We can tabulate the three most commonly encountered Scottish English arrangements as (207).

(207)	General	Popular Clydeside	Edinburgh
pert, heard . . .	ɛr	ɛr	
dirt, bird . . .	ɪr	ʌr	3r = [ɝ]
hurt, word . . .	ʌr		

The vowels /o/ and /ɔ/, too, remain in opposition before /r/: Scottish English has not in general undergone the FORCE Mergers (vol. 1, 3.2.7). Thus *short* /ʃɔrt/ does not rhyme with *sport* /sport/, nor *cork* /kɔrk/ with *pork* /pork/, while *horse* /hɔrs/ is distinct from *hoarse* /hors/. (In some cases, though, interference from Scots may muddy this general pattern; and some use /ɔ/, not /o/, after labials, thus /pɔrk/, /mɔrn/ *mourn* = *morn*.) Those who have contrastive /ɒ/ commonly use it, not /ɔ/, in NORTH words, thus rendering the distinction even more striking, as *horse* /hɒrs/ vs. *hoarse* /hors/ (Abercrombie 1979: 79).

Examples of contrasting vowels in the various pre-/r/ environments are set out in (208).

(208)	__r#	__rC	__rV
i	beer	fierce	weary
ɪ	stir	bird	spirit
e	air	scarce	fairy
ɛ	err	pert	ferry
a	bar	start	marry
ɔ	war	horse	sorry
o	wore	hoarse	story
ʌ	purr	word	hurry
u	poor	gourd	jury

There are some Scots who have /ɛr/ rather than /er/ in SQUARE: they will say *upst*[ɛː]*rs*, not *upst*[eː]*rs*. I have heard the claim that this pronunciation is used only by Roman Catholics in the Glasgow conurbation, and that it is due to Irish influence. I am not in a position to substantiate or disconfirm this claim.

5.2.6 Consonants

The consonant system of Scottish English has remained very conservative. It retains the velar fricative, /x/, as a member; although in English (as opposed to Scots) /x/ is really restricted to proper names (*Tulloch* /ˈtʌlʌx/, *Tough* /tux/, *Auchtermuchty* /ˈɔxtɪrˈmʌxte/) and sometimes to Greek- or Hebrew-derived words spelt with *ch* (*technical* /ˈtɛx-/, *patriarch* /-rx/, *epoch*, *parochial*). The consonant system also retains the item [ʍ], a voiceless labial-velar fricative, as in *where*, *whine*, etc.; I have chosen to phonemicize it as /hw/, though a case can also be made for treating it as a unit phoneme /ʍ/, or indeed – in some regional speech where the velar component is very prominent – as /xw/. As discussed in volume 1 (Glide Cluster Reduction, 3.2.4), /hw/ may also be found in occasional items where the spelling would not lead one to expect it, e.g. in south-east Scotland *weasel*; and conversely there are one or two items spelt *wh-* but nevertheless pronounced with plain /w/, e.g. *whelk*. (The pronunciations [w]*easel*, [ʍ]*elk* also occur, whether through spelling influence or otherwise.)

With many speakers, initial /p, t, k/ have little or no aspiration. We may thus have, for instance, [p⁼]*en*, [t⁼]*urn*, [k⁼]*ind* (compare RP [pʰ, tʰ, kʰ]). In the Gaelic-influenced speech of the Highlands and Islands, however, strong aspiration is the rule; and in this accent, indeed, not only are initial voiceless plosives in a stressed syllable post-aspirated, but final ones are pre-aspirated, so that we have for instance [luhk] *look*, [kʰaht] *cat*, [mɪl̪k] *milk*.

The place of articulation of /t/ and /d/ may be either alveolar or dental. It is not clear what are the social and geographical factors attaching to the dental place; it is found in Gaelic-influenced speech, but has also been reported in popular Edinburgh speech and sometimes in Aberdeen. Some Scots have alveolar /t, d/ but dental /l/; such speakers naturally also have dental allophones of /t, d/ in the environment of a preceding /l/, thus *belt* [bɛl̪t̪].

In the case of non-initial /t/, popular Scottish English shows a good deal of T Glottalling (vol. 1, 3.4.5), thus ['bʌʔɚ] *butter*, ['sɛnʔɪ'mɛnʔl] *sentimental*, ['mɪləʔn̩ʔ] *militant*. This usage seems particularly characteristic of the central lowlands of Scotland, less so of the southern regions (Borders; Dumfries and Galloway). In the Grampian region, Wölck (1965) characterizes it as particularly to be observed in coastal communities. In both Glasgow and Edinburgh it has been the subject of sociolinguistic investigation (Macaulay & Trevelyan 1973; Reid 1976); in both cities the use of [ʔ] as against [t] for /t/ in such environments (before an unstressed vowel or a word boundary) has been found to correlate clearly with social class and (where these were investigated) with social context and sex: [ʔ] is commoner with the lower-social-class groups, in group interaction, and with men, but [t] commoner with higher social class, in interviews, and with women. As a potential social marker, Glottalling evokes vehement castigation ('this degenerate tendency in modern speech', 'incorrect articulation', 'detracts from intelligibility', 'accounts in many cases for the dull pitching of the vowels which is also a characteristic of slovenly speech' – all from McAllister 1938).

Some speakers occasionally extend Glottalling to certain environments involving a following stressed vowel, as *guitar* [giʔ'ɑr], *pontoon* [pɔnʔ'un], *hotel* [hoʔ'ɛl]. (Data from Leslie 1976; it is not clear in such cases whether the [ʔ] should be regarded as belonging to the stressed syllable, thus [gi'ʔɑr], etc., or not.) Speakers who glottal /t/ may also optionally add masking glottal reinforcement to /p/ and /k/ in the same environments, thus ['hapʔe] *happy*, ['pʌrpʔl] *purple*, ['tʌrkʔe] *turkey* (data again from Leslie 1976; other Scots have queried whether these forms are correct, although Leslie is a native speaker of the Fife accent he is describing). In such cases the bilabial or velar articulation may be so masked by the [ʔ] that it is scarcely audible; but native speakers I have consulted insist that it must be present, and reject the possibility of complete Glottalling as in ʔ['teʔ ə 'siʔ] *take a seat* (reported as authentic by Lass 1976: 149).

In the dialects of Orkney and Shetland, as mentioned above, /θ/ and /ð/ are missing. Otherwise they are as in other accents, except for one or two differences of lexical incidence. Notably, *thither*, *thence*, *though* and *although* are generally pronounced with /θ/ in Scotland (as against the /ð/ used elsewhere); so also are *with* and *without*, although in this case the /θ/ pronunciation is also widely found outside Scotland. In some urban speech the initial cluster /θr/ has variants of the type [ʂɹ], [ɻ], so that *three* may be pronounced [ʂɹiː] or [ɻiː]; these variants are strongly stigmatized. Certain optional rules also affect /ð/. One makes it [r] initially in *the, this, that* (hence the dialect spelling *ra* for *the*); also sometimes in the environment 'V—V, thus ['bɹʌɾəɹ] *brother*. Another makes /θ/ [s] in final position, thus [bos] *both* (otherwise [boθ]).

Most Scottish speech is firmly rhotic, with /r/ retained in all positions where it occurred historically. Its occurrence after vowels has been discussed above; here we are concerned with the question of its realization. The popular stereotype is that Scotsmen 'roll their r's', which should mean that /r/ is realized as [r]. Reality is rather more complicated. (Elsewhere in this chapter I have used [r] to stand for various possible /r/ realizations indifferently. In this discussion of /r/, I shall use [r] to stand only for a voiced alveolar roll (trill), with other types of /r/ represented as [ɾ], [ɹ] etc.)

Writing in 1913, Grant claimed that the roll was indeed 'the most common form used in Scotland'. He went on, though, to say that

within recent years there has been a tendency to attenuate the force of the trill especially in final positions and before another consonant. [...] The trill may be reduced (finally and before consonants) to a single tap [ɾ], or even to a fricative consonant [ɹ], and in the latter case a change of quality in the preceding vowel is perceptible. The consonantal effect, in any case, is never lost in genuine Scottish speech, and the trill may still be said to be the characteristic Scottish sound corresponding to the letter *r*. (Grant 1913: §83).

Today, although [r] is still to be heard, particularly in the more northerly parts of the country, it is not really general. Even before the Second World War it was being reported (McAllister 1938: 94) that not more than three Scottish students out of ten used [r]; today the proportion would be still lower.

The most usual Scottish realizations of /r/ are an alveolar tap, [ɾ], and a post-alveolar or retroflex fricative or approximant, [ɹ ~ ɻ]. The first, [ɾ], seems to be particularly associated with the within-word environments V__V and C__V (*sorry, agree*); the second, with the environments V__C and V__# (*word, care*). In initial position (#__V) both are frequent. There is also stylistic variation dependent upon social context, so that – in the lowlands at least – the roll [r] tends to be virtually restricted to formal or declamatory-styles. In Edinburgh, Romaine (1978) reports a tendency for [ɹ] to be associated with girls, [ɾ] with boys; she also reports occasional zero realization of word-final /r/, particularly before a pause. (This could be the beginning of loss of rhoticity, which would bring Scotland into line with the general non-rhotic norm of England, although Romaine argues, on what seem to me rather tenuous grounds, that 'it is *not* being adopted in conscious imitation of a Southern English prestige model such as RP'.)

Uvular [ʁ] is surprisingly common as a personal idiosyncrasy in some parts of Scotland (e.g. Aberdeen); but it can hardly be regarded as a local-accent feature.

Scottish English does not exhibit the alternation of clear and dark /l/ found in, say, RP. Any given speaker tends to use much the same kind of /l/ in all phonetic contexts. Most commonly this is a velarized variety, [ɫ]. In the Glasgow area a pharyngealized variety (with a sort of [ɒ]-coloured resonance) is heard in popular speech; to avoid the social stigma associated with this, a neutral, [ə]-coloured [l] is recommended by the elocutionists. A clear variety, [l̪], is characteristic of the Gaelic and post-Gaelic areas: not only the Highlands and Islands, but also the south-west (Dumfries and Galloway – where it may be due rather to recent Irish influence).

Breaking of vowels before /l/ is reported in some urban varieties, thus [skuʌl] *school*, [koʌl] *coal*.

Yod Dropping (vol. 1, 3.1.10) is usual in Scotland after /l/ and, for most speakers, after /s/: [luːr] *lure*, [sut] *suit*. There seems to be less Yod Coalescence than in most accents: one hears pronunciations such as ['staʔju] *statue* in urban working-class speech, and higher up the social scale a form such as ['netçər] *nature* is not, as it would be in England, artificial.

It is well-known that in Scotland, unlike in England, there is no H Dropping (vol. 1, 3.4.1), except of course in unstressed pronouns and auxiliaries. Thus *heat* is always [hit], never *[it], even in the lowest-class urban casual speech; *half* is always [haf ~ hɑf]; but *him* has a weak form [ɪm] alongside its strong form [hɪm]. An exception to this generalization arises in those one or two north-eastern localities where the local Scots has H Dropping, notably in the Black Isle near Inverness.

One notices in Scottish English from time to time instances of Voicing Assimilation, thus ['moz 'valjəbl] *most valuable*. (The Elision of the /t/ of *most* before a following consonant is found in virtually all accents of English; but the change from [s] to [z] under the influence of the following voiced /v/ would not happen in most places – perhaps only in Scotland, Trinidad, and Guyana. It is commonplace in the foreigner's English of French people, and there counted an error.) I do not know what phonological, social, or stylistic constraints there may be on the operation of this process.

5.2.7 The Highlands and Islands

We have already noted certain phonetic characteristics of the English spoken in areas that are, or were, Gaelic-speaking, that is the Western Isles and the Highlands. These characteristics can be regarded as due to interference from Gaelic. For example, Gaelic /p, t, k/ are characterized by strong aspiration in initial position and pre-aspiration in final position. When we find the same thing in the

English of a Gaelic-speaking Hebridean community, it is clear that phonetic habits of Gaelic are being transferred to English as a second language. The same applies to the use of clear /l/ where most Scottish people use dark /l/; though in this case it appears that this putatively Gaelic characteristic can survive by several centuries the disappearance of spoken Gaelic, as perhaps in the south-west of Scotland.

Where the influence of Gaelic is very strong, there are many other instances of phonetic interference. Gaelic /b, d, g/ are typically voiceless (being distinguished from their congeners /p, t, k/ by virtue of their lenisness and non-aspiration). The use of such sound types for English /b, d, g/ may lead to their misidentification: they may be heard as /p, t, k/, particularly since in Scottish English these are usually unaspirated. Compton Mackenzie's novel *Whisky Galore* contains many examples of eye-dialect based on this, as *petter* for *better*, *inteet* for *indeed*, *clory* for *glory*. Furthermore, Gaelic has no voiced sibilants; hence English /z, ʒ, dʒ/ present difficulties and are liable to be pronounced as [s, ʃ, tʃ], with loss of the oppositions /s–z, ʃ–ʒ, tʃ–dʒ/, as in the eye-dialect forms *cowss* for *cows*, *pleshure* for *pleasure*, *enchoying* for *enjoying*. I have heard ['bɪsɪ] *busy*. Literary sources also imply confusion of /f/ and /v/ (*ferry good* for *very good* in the novel *Whisky Galore*); but Gaelic has a /v/, so this is comparable to confusing paired plosives.

Gaelic does lack, though, phonemes corresponding to English /θ/, /ð/, and /w/. A consistent use of nothing but Gaelic sounds therefore entails the use of [s] or [ts] for the two dental fricatives and [u] for /w/, with consequent loss of oppositions such as /θ/ vs. /s/. The resultant new homophones (*think* = *sink*, *mouth* = *mouse*) are not only foreign-sounding but also quite likely to engender serious misunderstandings or the breakdown of communication. So it is not surprising that with the increasing use of English and its eventual displacement of Gaelic such gross interference disappears. Pronunciations such as [sɪŋk] for *think* are not found in the post-Gaelic Highlands.

Another Gaelicism sometimes encountered is the use of a palatal nasal, [ɲ], for /ŋ/. J. D. McClure (personal communication) reports a speaker from Uist who invariably uses [ɪɲ] for *-ing*.

There is a phonological rule in Gaelic whereby the sequence /r/ plus /s/ coalesces into a retroflex fricative [ʂ]. Pronunciations such as

413

[foʂ]*force*, ['mɛʂe] *mercy*, ['paʂls] *parcels* reflect the persistence of this rule in Gaelic-influenced English. Unlike the previously mentioned Gaelicisms, this tendency is still widespread throughout the Highlands and is even sometimes encountered in the Lowlands. It can readily be observed to co-exist with the non-Gaelic /s/ vs. /z/ opposition, giving forms such as [kaʐ] *cars*, ['farmɘʐ]. Possibly it is not properly to be regarded as necessarily due to Gaelic influence at all.

5.2.8 Prosodic features

There is some evidence that syllabication operates in Scottish accents in a way somewhat different from that found in England. To English ears, at least, a consonant in the environment __# 'V often sounds in Scottish pronunciation to be syllabicated with the following vowel, thus [pu.'tʌp] *put up*, [sn̩.'tandru] *St Andrew*, [wi.'kɛnd] *weekend*. There is no distinction between *an aim* and *a name*: both are [ɘ.'nem] (Abercrombie 1979: 82–3).

Certain words are characteristically stressed in Scottish English differently from in RP: in particular verbs with the suffix *-ize*, as *organ'ize* (RP etc. '*organize*), and some with *-ate* as *adjudi'cate* (RP *ad'judicate*).

In popular Scottish speech there are certain weak forms sharply distinct phonetically from those found outside Scotland. Thus *to* may be [te] or [tɪ], as against the [tu ~ tʊ ~ tə] of English accents. This really represents an intrusion from Scots, where the corresponding word is conventionally spelt *tae*. In more prestigious varieties of Scottish English [te] and [tɪ] are firmly avoided. Somewhat similar considerations apply to [jɪ] for *you*, [ʌ] for *I*, and [fe] for *from*.

No comprehensive study of the intonation of Scottish English has yet been completed, although several very promising starts have been made. It is clear that there are considerable regional differences in intonation, but I am not at present in a position to describe them adequately.

Two patterns stand out in my mind as particularly Scottish. One is a nuclear tone which might be described as a narrow high to high-mid fall (mentioned by Jones 1956: §477). An example is given in

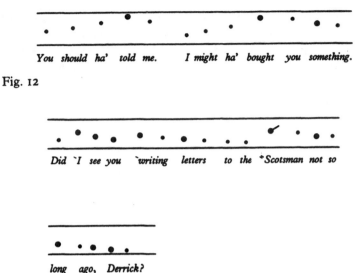

You should ha' told me.   I might ha' bought you something.

Fig. 12

Did `I see you `writing letters to the ⁺Scotsman not so

long ago, Derrick?

Fig. 13

fig. 12, in answer to *It's my birthday*. The other is a pattern involving a series of falls (or rise-falls), one on each accented syllable in the utterance, with a particularly wide fall on the first accented syllable (the onset of the head) and another on the last accented syllable (the nucleus). Analysing the conversational intonation of speakers from Ayr, Paisley, and West Kilbride (all in western Scotland), McClure (1980) pays particular attention to this pattern. He shows that for statements the two particularly salient such accented syllables have high fall and high fall, for *wh*-questions high fall and mid fall, and for yes–no questions mid fall and high fall. An example (from McClure 1980), is given in fig. 13.

5.2.9 Sociolinguistic studies

In their study of the speech habits of Glaswegians, Macaulay & Trevelyan (1973; see also Macaulay 1974, 1977, 1978) analysed five phonological variables: the vowels /u/ of GOOSE, /ɪ/ of KIT, /a/ of TRAP, and /ʌu/ of MOUTH, and T Glottalling. As well as children of ten and fifteen years, a judgement sample of sixteen adult informants was used, consisting of two men and two women from each of the occupational classes I (professional and managerial), IIa (white-collar, intermediate non-manual), IIb (skilled manual) and III (semi-skilled and unskilled manual). The findings for these adults can be summarized as in (209).

(209)		I	IIa	IIb	III
/u/ GOOSE	100 = all [u+] 400 = all [ɪ.]	145	212	284	321
/ɪ/ KIT	100 = all [ɪ] 500 = all [ʌ.]	174	238	287	283
/a/ TRAP	100 = all [æ ~ a] 400 = all [ɑ ~ ɒ]	133	201	261	260
/ʌu/ MOUTH	100 = all [au] 400 = all [u+]	152	247	334	362
/t/ → [ʔ]	000 = all [t] 100 = all [ʔ]	010	027	077	090

(syllable-finally, before V or #)

In almost all cases women scored lower (i.e. had fewer of the forms overtly stigmatized) than men in the same social class.

Reid (1976, 1978) carried out a smaller survey on eleven-year-old children in three Edinburgh schools: a fee-paying day school, a high-status Corporation school, and a low-status Corporation school. Scores for T Glottalling were as shown in (210).

(210)	Fee-paying school	High-status free school	Low-status free school
/t/ → [ʔ] 000 = all [t] 100 = all [ʔ]			
Reading-passage style	020	022	031
Interview style	037	068	098
Group-interaction style	058	085	100

It is clear that with these Edinburgh schoolchildren the degree of T Glottalling varies sharply not only with social class but also with contextual style.

Romaine (1978) investigated the realization of /r/ by twenty-four Edinburgh primary school children. She recognizes three possibilities: [ɾ], [ɹ], and zero. The percentage scores for these three types in the speech of ten-year-olds in two styles were as shown in (211) (Romaine 1978: table 4).

(211)	Single interview		Reading passage	
	Males	Females	Males	Females
[r]	57	45	43	38
[ɹ]	15	54	24	48
zero	28	1	33	16

5.3 Ireland

5.3.1 Introduction

The language situation in Ireland today has been shaped by three principal sources: the English language as introduced from England, and perhaps particularly from the west of England (Anglo-Irish); the Scots dialect, and the Scottish-type accent related to it, introduced into the northern part of the island from Scotland (Scotch-Irish); and the indigenous Irish language itself – also known as Gaelic, Irish Gaelic, and Erse – a member of the Celtic branch of the Indo-European family. It is estimated that at the beginning of the nineteenth century about half the population of Ireland spoke Irish; but by 1851 only a quarter did so, and only 5 per cent were monoglots with no knowledge of English. By now English is the ordinary vernacular language for most of the $4\frac{1}{4}$ million inhabitants of the island. There are, however, still several thousands of Irishmen whose everyday language is Irish; all of them know a little English, but some speak it very haltingly. Most of them live in the Gaeltacht areas, which receive extra economic aid from the government in an attempt to discourage migration away from these Irish-speaking areas, with consequent loss of the language. Even with those Irish people who have little or no knowledge of Irish, however, considerable traces of the phonetic influence of Irish remain in their English, just as happens with the Celtic languages in Britain. These traces may even be somewhat reinforced by the fact that Irish now enjoys official status in the Republic and is widely taught in schools.

There have been speakers of English in Ireland since about 1200. Nevertheless by 1600 English was almost extinct in Ireland, even in the Pale surrounding Dublin (which had been seized by a Norman earl in 1170 and colonized by settlers from Bristol). Only written documents survive to attest the old Anglo-Irish dialects of Fingal (north of Dublin) and Forth (south of Wexford). Present-day Irish English owes its characteristics overwhelmingly to the English spoken by the 'planters' installed as colonists in the seventeenth century.

Since then Irish English has proved remarkably conservative. With minor exceptions, neither the British innovations discussed in volume 1, 3.2 nor the American innovations of 3.3 are to be found in Ireland. The majority of the further innovations mentioned in 3.4 are equally unknown; indeed, even some of the older processes (Residualisms, 3.1) are incomplete as far as Irish speech is concerned. In particular, the NURSE Merger (3.1.8) does not apply in Ireland (*earn* ≠ *urn*), and in popular accents the FLEECE Merger (3.1.6) has not been entirely carried through (*meat* is a potential homophone of *mate*).

Neither RP nor popular accents of England exert much per-ceptible influence on Irish English. There are, it is true, some educated and cosmopolitan-minded Dubliners who have, con-sciously or unconsciously, adopted various RP characteristics. I have even heard pupils at a Protestant fee-paying secondary school on the outskirts of Dublin whose accents might almost be taken for those of Englishmen, were it not for the regular and effortless /hw/ in *why*, *where*, etc. (Glide Cluster Reduction, vol. 1, 3.2.4) and the sporadic clear or clearish allophones of /l/ in environments where the English use dark /l/. But such Irishmen are very exceptional. In Ireland RP is in no way taken as an unquestioned norm of good pronunciation. The ordinary educated Dubliner, for example, has an accent which is very firmly rhotic – a characteristic associated in England only with regional accents. (Although it could reasonably be said of an Englishman from the west that by cutting out his non-prevocalic /r/s he was rendering his speech more stylish, an Irishman would by doing so be introducing a quite foreign element.)

The description which follows relates first to the 'Anglo-Irish' accents of the Republic. A discussion of Ulster accents follows later.

5.3.2 The vowel system

A typical Irish accent of English has the vowel system shown in (212).

(212)

I	ʊ	iː			uː
ɛ	ʌ	eː			oː
æ	ɒ	aɪ (ɔɪ)	aː ɔː	aʊ	

The lexical incidence of these vowels is typically as shown in (213).

(213)

KIT	I	FLEECE	iː[1]	NEAR	iːr
DRESS	ɛ	FACE	eː	SQUARE	eːr
TRAP	æ	PALM	aː	START	aːr
LOT	ɒ	THOUGHT	ɔː	NORTH	ɔːr
STRUT	ʌ	GOAT	oː	FORCE	oːr[1]
FOOT	ʊ	GOOSE	uː	CURE	uːr
BATH	æ, aː[1]	PRICE	aɪ	*happ*Y	iː
CLOTH	ɒ, ɔː	CHOICE	ɔɪ[1]	*lett*ER	ər
NURSE	ʌr, ɛr[1]	MOUTH	aʊ	*comm*A	ə

[1] see below for discussion.

The vowels I write /ɒ, ɔː/ are in most Irish accents actually unrounded, of the type [ɑ, ɑː]. The question of a possible /ɔɪ/ is
discussed below. Bearing these two points in mind, it is clear that
this vowel system corresponds very closely to the range of phonetic
qualities associated with the vowel system of Irish – as spoken, for
example, in places as far apart as County Cork (Ó Cuív 1944) and
County Mayo (Mhac an Fhailigh 1968). (There are, however, some
vowel sounds which in Irish are mere allophonic variants, but
which in Irish English function as separate phonemes; scholars do
not always agree about the phonemics of Irish, but it seems clear
that [a] and [ɑ] are coallophones of one phoneme, as are [aː] and [ɑː];
possibly also [ɛ] and [ʌ], [ɪ] and [ʊ]. See Bliss 1972.) Thus the short
vowels /I, ɛ, æ, ɒ, ʌ, ʊ/ correspond to those of Irish *min, deich, fear,
mar, deoch, muc*, and the long monophthongs /iː, eː, aː, ɔː, oː, uː/ to
those of *mín, féin, meán, fáth, bó, rún*. Unstressed /ə/ is heard in the
first and last syllables of a word such as *galánta*, and the diphthongs
/aɪ, aʊ/ in *leigheas* and *leabhar* respectively.

So there is a measure of truth in the view that an Irish accent
consists in the sounds of Irish imposed upon English. Further
influence from the Irish substratum can be identified in the consonant system (see below). But it is far from the whole truth. For
example, the phonemes /z/ and /ʒ/ are thoroughly at home in Irish
English – yet they have no counterpart in Irish, except insofar as
they have been introduced in borrowed words. (There are some

people in the west, Irish speakers, who replace them in English by
/s/ and /ʃ/.)

5.3.3 Vowels before /r/

Unlike many rhotic accents, Irish English has a nearly complete
range of vowel oppositions in the environment of following /r/.
There are, it is true, a few neutralizations, particularly in Dublin
speech (where the influence of England is perhaps particularly
strong); but in general all or almost all the vowels remain in mutual
opposition in this environment. Examples are given in (214). Even
/ɒ/ and /ɔː/, not distinguished in the table, may sometimes be
distinct as *for* vs. *war*. (As in other accents where the FOOT–STRUT
Split has occurred (vol. 1, 3.1.7), there are virtually no words
containing /ʊ/ before /r/; but this is to be regarded as an accidental
gap rather than as a partial neutralization.)

(214)	__r#	__rC	__rV
iː	*beer*	*fierce*	*weary*
ɪ	(*myrrh*)	†	*spirit*
eː	*air*	*scarce*	*fairy*
ɛ	(*err*)	†	*ferry*
aː	*bar*	*barn*	(*Tara*)
æ	*Mar*[1]	†	*marry*
ɒ, ɔː	*for, war*	*horse*	*sorry, Laura*
ɔː	*wore*	*hoarse*	*story*
ʌ	*purr*	*nurse*	*hurry*
uː	*poor*	(*Swords*)[2]	*jury*
ʊ			(*hurry*)[3]
aɪ	*fire*	*iron*	*pirate*
aʊ	*flour*	†	*dowry*
ɔɪ	(*coir*)[4]		*Máire*
ə	*better*	*modern*	*operate*

†These gaps can be filled as __r#C, e.g. *myrrh's, errs*, etc.
[1] short for *Marion*.
[2] place-name; also pronounced /soːrdz/.
[3] alternatively with /ʌr/.
[4] also *employer* etc. (__ #r#)

Some of these oppositions must be considered marginal when
not prevocalic:
(i) /iːr/ vs. /ɪr/, as *mere* vs. *myrrh* (the latter more usually being
/mʌr/), *beer* vs. *fir* ('gentlemen' on public toilets);
(ii) /eːr/ vs. /ɛr/, as *care* vs. *Kerr*, *pair* vs. *per*, *scarce* vs. *hearse*:

neutralized in Dublin speech as /eːr/, or more elegantly as /ʌr/, phonetically [ɝː];
(iii) /aːr/ vs. /ær/, as *bar* vs. *Bar* (short for *Finbar*), *mar* vs. *Mar(ion)*;
(iv) /ɛr/ vs. /ʌr/ (or /ʊr/), as *earn* vs. *urn*, *kerb* vs. *curb*, *Hertz* vs. *hurts*, *Kerr* vs. *cur*, *prefer* vs. *fur*. In more sophisticated Dublin speech this opposition is sometimes neutralized as /ʌr/ [ɝː], although conservative speakers, along with most working-class and provincial Irish accents, retain the contrast.

A fifth potential opposition, /ɔːr/ vs. /oːr/, is often neutralized (to [ɔ̈ː]) in educated or progressive Dublin speech; in more popular or conservative Dublin accents, though, as in provincial ones, the contrast remains firm in pairs such as *horse* vs. *hoarse*, *born* vs. *borne*, *war* vs. *wore*, *for* vs. *four*. (See vol. 1, 3.2.7, First FORCE Merger.)

The interplay of points (ii) and (iv) above gives at least three sets of possibilities in various Irish accents, set out with RP for comparison as (215).

(215)

	Typical southern Irish provincial	Typical Dublin	Smart Dublin	RP	
care, pair	eːr	eːr	ʌr	ɛə	= SQUARE
Kerr, per	ɛr	eːr	ʌr	ɝː	=NURSE
cur, purr	ʌr ~ ʊr	ʌr ~ ʊr	ʌr	ɝː	

Thus the NURSE–SQUARE Merger, stigmatized in Liverpool, is perceived as elegant by (at least some) Dubliners. The reason, according to Bertz (1975: 142) is as follows: because of the Dublin merging of /ɛr/ and /eːr/, /ɛr/ does not occur in words such as *term*, *clergy*, *skirt*, while the /eːr/ which does occur there is considered 'uneducated'; and is therefore replaced by /ʌr/, which suffers from no such stigmatization; and then, by hypercorrection all cases of /eːr/ are replaced by /ʌr/ [ɝː]. In spite of its hypercorrect origin, this pronunciation has nevertheless won increasing prestige. Yet this development is still in progress, and most speakers seem to keep /eːr/ in at least some words.

5.3.4 Short vowels

Turning to the individual short vowels, we note that the quality of /ɪ, ɛ, ʊ/ corresponds on the whole to the phonetic quality implied by the symbol used. In Dublin, though, the first two are socially sensitive, with educated variants [ɪ, ę] alongside more popular variants [i̞, ɛ] (and also centring-diphthong allophones in the environment of a following /n/ or /l/).

The quality of /æ/ is commonly around cardinal [a], though educated Dubliners use [æ]. The realization of /ɒ/, as mentioned above, is typically an unrounded [ɑ], often somewhat advanced [ɑ+], thus *stop* /stɒp/ [stɑp]. In Dublin, according to Bertz, the [ɑ+] variant is restricted to 'progressive working-class women' and to the environment of a following /t/, as *not* [nɑ+t]; otherwise, Dublin /ɒ/ realizations range from [ɑ] through [ɒ] to [ɔ], with the more educated speakers sometimes using even closer qualities.

The quality of Irish English /ʌ/ is strikingly different from what is heard in most other accents. It is typically a mid centralized back somewhat rounded vowel which might best be symbolized [ɵ-] or [ɔ̈]. Unrounded back and central qualities, of the type [ɣ, ə], are also encountered, as well as a quality indistinguishable from conservative RP [ʌ] – the latter being associated with relatively high-status speech. There is, however, a complication with /ʌ/, namely the question of the extent to which the opposition between it and /ʊ/ is maintained. In his description of Dublin speech, Bertz says that in popular varieties the opposition is mostly neutralized as /ʊ/, i.e. [ʊ], but that in conservative middle-of-the-road accents ('General Dublin English') there is free variation between neutralization and opposition; and that in educated speech neutralization counts as informal. My impression of Irish accents as a whole is that most speakers have at least a potential /ʌ–ʊ/ opposition (much more so than in, say, Newcastle-upon-Tyne) – but that the lexical incidence of the two vowels differs considerably from that used in the standard accents. Thus Mac Éinrí, himself from a rural County Mayo background, includes among his minimal or near-minimal pairs for /ʌ/ vs. /ʊ/ not only *stud* vs. *stood* and *flood* vs. *good*, but also *pup* vs. *sup*, *pub* vs. *sub*, *tub* vs. *grub*, *nut* vs. *cut*, *blood* vs. *bud*, *judge* vs. *budge*, and *brother* vs. *mother* – all of which latter are perfect rhymes in the standard accents, belonging in every case to the lexical set STRUT. And Bertz reports that in a conservative Dublin accent, which preserves the opposition in other cases, there is no contrast before /l/, so that *dull* rhymes with *pull* [-ʊ·l]. Furthermore, among the list of homophones offered by Mac Éinrí (1975) are *could–cud*,

look–luck, put–putt, took–tuck, all with /ʊ/. Yet a further complication is that certain words which belong with FOOT in the standard
accents on the whole keep the historical /uː/ in Irish English.
Among them are *book, cook, crook, brook* and *rook*. (This pronunciation, as we have seen, also occurs in local accents of the north of
England.)

Returning to the front short vowels, we find that in some parts of
the west of Ireland *pin* and *pen* are homophonous as [pɪn], or
for some speakers [pɛn]. A *vet(erinary surgeon)* is frequently a
[vɪt]. This may reflect an earlier neutralization now subject to
hypercorrection.

A striking Irishism is the use of /æ/, not /ɛ/, in the words *many*
and *any*. In Dublin, Bertz reports, *any* is normally a homophone of
Annie; but *many* always has /ɛ/, as in RP, while *anything* fluctuates
between the two possibilities. Other lexical incidences differing
from standard accents, but not restricted to Ireland, are *carry,
catch,* and *drank* with /ɛ/, and *devil, engine* with /ɪ/.

The opposition /æ–aː/ carries a low functional load. The lexical
incidence of these vowels corresponds generally to standard accents
in that TRAP words have /æ/ and PALM words /aː/; thus there are
minimal pairs *cam* vs. *calm, Sam* vs. *psalm*, and non-rhyming pairs
such as *shadow* vs. *bravado, arrow* vs. *Tara, galley* vs. *gala*. The
names *Cahill* and *MacMahon* have more than one possible pronunciation; but the variants lacking medial [h] are /kaːl/,
/məˈmaːn/, which contrast with *pal* /pæl/, *man* /mæn/. But some
speakers seem regularly to lengthen the vowel before certain voiced
consonants, thus *bad* [baːd], *man* [maːn], which appears to endanger
the opposition in these environments. As far as the BATH words are
concerned, the situation is very far from clear. For 'General Dublin
English' Bertz (1975: 157) gives [æː] for *gas* as against [aː] for *glass*,
which suggests a phonetically tenuous distinction between, phonemically, the TRAP vowel in *gas* and the PALM vowel in BATH words
like *glass*, with a lexical incidence as in RP. But for 'Popular Dublin
English' he gives short [a] in *baths* itself. Nally (1971: 38) transcribes *blast, fasting, plaster* and *task* with /aː/, but *castle* with /æ/.
Some distinguish between a cobbler's *l*[æ]*st* and a final *l*[aː]*st*. From a
television newsreader I have noted [aː]*sk*, *p*[aː]*th*, and [aː]*fter* alongside *c*[æ]*stle* and *pl*[æ]*nt*. A group of twelve Irish candidates in a first-
year phonetics exam, asked to transcribe a passage from orthog-

raphy, were unanimous in writing *grasp* as /græsp/, and ten out of the twelve also put a short vowel in *aunt* (it is evidently only sophisticated middle-class Dubliners who distinguish in pronunciation between *aunt* /aːnt/ and *ant* /ænt/ – for most Irish people both are /ænt/). It may well be the case that the interplay of quality and length is more complicated than is allowed for by a simple opposition of /æ/ vs. /aː/. There is certainly a great deal of variation in this matter, and it has not yet been adequately described.

The CLOTH words pose a similar problem. The /ɒ/ vs. /ɔː/ opposition is well established in pairs such as *stock* vs. *stalk, knotty* vs. *naughty, clod* vs. *clawed* or *Claud, Moll* vs. *maul, collar* vs. *caller*. But *doll* and *was*, in Dublin at least, are reported as having /ɔː/ (cf. their /ɒ/ in RP). Among the CLOTH words, Bertz gives *cross, loss, lost, often*, and *cost* as varying freely between /ɒ/ and /ɔː/, as do also *swan* and *wrong*; but he gives *cough* with /ɒ/, a non-rhyme of *off* /ɔːf/. He also mentions *job, rob, dog*, and other similar words as having /ɔː/, and a context-sensitive alternation between /ɔː/ in *bog, rob, Ron* and /ɒ/ in *boggy, robber, Ronnie*; but these claims seem open to question.

5.3.5 Long vowels

The phonetic quality of the open long vowels varies socially and regionally. In provincial speech they have qualities similar to cardinals 4 and 5 respectively, /aː/ being [aː] and /ɔː/ [ɑː]. These qualities are also to be found in Dublin, but there more English-like realizations are more usual: /aː/ as [ɑ+ː], for example, and /ɔː/ as [ɔː] (or even closer). The [oː] quality used by some university-educated Dublin women is widely judged to be an affectation. The words *father, rather, drama* are quite commonly pronounced with [ɔː] in place of the expected [aː]; and the name of the letter *R* is /ɒr/ or /ɔːr/. Such pronunciations – ['fɔːɖɚ] *father*, ['ɒˈ'piː] *RP* – are very striking to the English ear. Bertz treats the vowel of *father* as phonologically /aː/, but with an unusual allophone virtually restricted to the lexical items mentioned; but there seems to be no reason to reject a simpler analysis, namely that it is a realizationally unremarkable /ɔː/ occurring in unexpected lexical incidence, which makes Irish *R* a homophone of *or* and gives *father* the same vowel as *author*.

The mid long vowels, /eː/ and /oː/, are typically realized as approximately cardinal monophthongs, [eː, oː]. There is some variation in the precise degree of vowel height used, relatively open qualities being perhaps a southern characteristic. In any case the development we have designated Long Mid Diphthonging (vol. 1, 3.1.12) has passed most Irish English by. However the speech of the capital city, Dublin, is distinguishable precisely by its having diphthongs for FACE and GOAT (except when followed by /r/). Thus Dublin /eː/ ranges from [ęɪ] to a popular [ɛɪ], /oː/ from [ou] to [ɔu]. Thus *face* is [feːs] in the provinces, [feɪs ~ fɛɪs] in Dublin; *goat* is provincial [goːt], Dublin [gout ~ gɔut]. In parts of Munster and northern Connacht there are also variants with an offglide [ə], thus [goˑət].

The phonetic quality of /iː/ and /uː/ is generally unremarkable, [iː ~ ɪi], [uː ~ ʊu]. Popular Dublin speech, though, includes some striking diphthongal variants of /uː/, thus [skɛʊl] *school*, [bĕuːk] *book*.

As discussed in volume 1, 3.1.6, the FLEECE Merger has not been entirely carried through in Ireland. Thus there occur sporadic rural or conservative working-class urban pronunciations such as /steːl/ *steal* (homophonous with *stale*, not with *steel*) and /meːt/ *meat* (= *mate*, ≠ *meet*). In old-fashioned popular Dublin speech, Bertz reports, this /eː/ for standard /iː/ is commonest in the items *leave*, *meat, eat, beat, cheat, tea, mean, easy, quay*, and *treat* ('buy a drink for'); also in *either* and, in oaths only, *Jesus* (hence the caricature spelling *Jaysus*). But the usage is recessive; people sometimes put it on as a joke or as a conscious Hibernicism. There are also what at first sight appear to be hypercorrections or confusions, such as /viːl/ *veil*, /peːk/ *peek*, /treː, θreː/ *tree* (standard forms: /veːl/, /piːk/, /triː/). Some of these may be archaisms surviving from the medieval Hiberno-English of Fingal, Forth and Bargy.

5.3.6 Diphthongs

The opposition /aɪ/ vs. /ɔɪ/ (PRICE vs. CHOICE) is not thoroughly established in some popular varieties of Irish English. And the associated phonetic qualities vary considerably, both regionally and socially. The Anglo-American stereotype is that the Irish say 'noice toime' in place of *nice time*; reality is rather more complicated. In rural Westmeath, Nally (1971: 34) describes two principal qualities, [ɛɪ] and [ʌɪ], which occur in a complicated more-or-less complementary distribution depending mainly on the preceding consonant: examples are [ɛɪ] *I* = *eye*, [dɛɪv] *dive*, [nɛɪn] *nine*, [sɛɪt] *sight*, [gɛɪd] *guide*, [ʃtɛɪl] *style*; [pʌɪ] *pie*, [bʌɪl] *bile* = *boil* = *Boyle*, [fʌɪt] *fight*, [vʌɪs] *vice* = *voice*, [lʌɪn] *line*, [ɹʌɪd] *ride*. Note the pair [ɛɪl] *I'll* vs. [ʌɪl] *aisle* = *isle* = *oil*. There is also a quality [ɑːj], which occurs only in final position and only in CHOICE words, as [bɑːj] *boy* (cf. [bʌɪ] *buy*). So here in general PRICE words are levelled with CHOICE words before a following consonant, but not in final position. Realizations of the [əɪ] type also seem quite common in provincial speech.

The absence of the PRICE–CHOICE opposition is now mainly a rural or southern characteristic, recessive in the face of an opposition made as in the standard accents. Because Irish has no diphthong resembling [ɔɪ], the seventeenth-century alternative pronunciation with the vowel of PRICE was in general adopted into the Irish English of that time, and now survives as an archaism. (On the other hand a preceding labial in Irish usually causes backing and rounding of the first element, producing a quality [ɒɪ] not too different from [ɔɪ].)

In the old-fashioned dialect of County Roscommon described by Henry (1957), the opposition is maintained by the fact that CHOICE words have [ɑ+ːɪ] while PRICE words have [ʌɪ] or [eɪ] allophonically distributed according to whether there is or is not a preceding labial.

In Dublin the neutralization of /aɪ/ vs. /ɔɪ/ is restricted to informal popular speech, particularly that of women, for whom *buy* and *boy* may be levelled as [bɑɪ]. Otherwise the opposition is maintained, the commonest Dublin realization for /aɪ/ being of the [ɑ+ɪ] type, with popular variants [ɐɪ, ǫɪ] and an educated variant [ɑɪ]. Bertz sees these rather back first elements as particularly characteristic of Dublin speech, as against the [aɪ] type, with a front first element, which he considers most usual in other kinds of Irish English. (On the other hand, it seems to me that a rounded centralized back first element, [ǒɪ], is also common in provincial Irish English, and it is this variant which is responsible for the stereotype of 'noice toime'.)

Dublin /ɔɪ/ is typically [ɔɪ], although it ranges anywhere from [ɑɪ] to [ʊɪ].

Many speakers who have a well-established PRICE vs. CHOICE opposition nevertheless use /ɔɪ/, the CHOICE vowel, in the words *violent, violet, violin,* where the spelling *io* is no doubt felt to give a kind of support to this pronunciation.

The MOUTH vowel, too, exhibits a fair range of phonetic variation. Commonest, perhaps, is the type [ʌʊ]; in Dublin there is a gamut of open starting-points from a popular [æʊ] through [aʊ] to educated [ɑʊ]. In popular Dublin speech there is also reportedly a potential neutralization of the opposition /aʊ/ vs. /ɔ:/ as [æʊ] in familiar style. Normally, though, they are in opposition: and there is one characteristically Irish oddity of lexical incidence whereby /aʊ/ rather than /o:/ occurs before /-ld/ in certain words, particularly *old* and *bold*. With *old* this may be restricted to jocular or non-literal use, as *the oul' fella* [aʊl]. In fact we can in effect recognize two distinct words *old*: one is vaguely self-deprecating, but otherwise virtually meaningless, and pronounced with the MOUTH vowel; the other is the ordinary word, pronounced with the GOAT vowel. *Where's my* [aʊl] *coat?* may thus mean something different from *Where's my* [o:ld] *coat?*.

In familiar styles of popular Dublin speech the opposition /u:/ vs. /aʊ/ is sometimes neutralized before /r/, so that *poor* becomes a homophone of *power*, both [pæʊ¹].

5.3.7 Weak vowels

In weak checked syllables the merger of KIT and schwa is well advanced; phonologically there is only one reduction vowel. Thus *abbot* and *rabbit* rhyme perfectly, both with one another and, usually, with *grab it*, all /-æbət/. *Starlet* and *starlit* are normally homophonous, /'sta:rlət/, and so are *roses–Rose's* and *addition–edition*. The town on the main road from Dublin to Port Laoise is sometimes spelt *Monasterevin,* sometimes *Monasterevan,* and this does not give rise to rival spelling pronunciations as it would tend to do in England. The suffix *-ing* is popularly /ən/, making *lyin'* and *lion* homophones. The first syllables of *prefer, tremendous, peculiar, secure, hilarious, specific* all have [ə] (compare RP [ɪ]).

There are certain differences vis-à-vis RP in the extent of vowel weakening. Thus for example the first syllables of *opinion* and *official* have /o:/ in Irish English (compare RP /ə/). *Saint* has no weak form. Pairs such as *except–accept, effect–affect* tend to remain distinct in that *accept* and *affect* may have /æ/. There is at least a potential contrast between the first syllables of *anon, inert,* and *unarmed,* with /ə/, /ɪ/, and /ʌ ~ ʊ/ respectively. On the other hand there are various words with weak forms not used in RP: examples are *when* /hwən/, *I* /æ/, *what* /hwət/, *sure* /ʃər/. The *my* weak form [mi] extends much further up the social scale than in England. So does the weakening of /juː/, as in *nephew* /ˈnɛvjə/; likewise Yod Dropping, with forms such as *speculate* /ˈspɛkəleːt/, *Portugal* /ˈpɔːrtəgəl/, and even *ruffian* /ˈrʌfən/ (homophonous with *roughen* and *roughin'*). Conversely, *villain* may be /ˈvɪljən/.

The final vowel in *happ*Y is /iː/, phonetically [i] or [ị]. A few speakers susceptible to RP influence use an opener [ɪ]. Rural dialect forms have hardly been investigated, but include [əi] and [ə] in Connacht, according to Henry (1958: 141).

Nouns and adjectives like *window, yellow* have popular variants with /ə/ in the final syllable (Weak GOAT, vol. 1, 2.2.25) alongside the formal or middle-class /oː/ form. But verbs of this shape, such as *follow, swallow* have popular variants with /iː/, not /ə/. A. J. Bliss suggests (private communication) that this is because verbs need to be able to add *-ing*, and [ˈfɑliən] *following* does not involve the awkwardness of *[ˈfɑləən].

5.3.8 Alveolar and dental stops

Turning to the consonant system, we find the most striking charac-teristics of an Irish accent in two areas: that of the dentals /θ/ and /ð/ and that of the liquids /r/ and /l/.

The English stereotype of an Irish accent ('brogue') includes the use of /t, d/ instead of /θ, ð/ and/or vice versa. This is reflected in eye-dialect spellings such as 'tink, tirty' and, conversely, 'afther, betther, dhrink, murdher'. It has some basis in fact. But several distinct issues must be disentangled: the possible general absence of the opposition, the neutralization in particular environments of an opposition which is otherwise in operation, and the phonetic quality (in particular, plosive or fricative) of phonemic /θ, ð/.

The oppositions /t/ vs. /θ/ and /d/ vs. /ð/ seem to exist, at least potentially, in all forms of Irish English. The sporadic absence of these oppositions, under what I think is a variable rule which levels them as alveolar plosives, seems to be primarily an urban pheno-menon associated with Cork and parts of Dublin. Context-sensitive neutralization, however, involving the use of exclusively dental plosives in the environment of a following /r/, is found all over Ireland.

The only part of Ireland where /θ/ and /ð/ are consistently realized as fricatives is Ulster (including Donegal, which politically is in the Republic). Elsewhere phonetic [θ] and [ð] are on the whole restricted to the speech of sophisticates or of those making a conscious effort at elegance. For most Irish people the phonemes /θ/ and /ð/ are realized as dental plosives, [t̪] and [d̪] respectively. Sometimes there may be some affrication, giving variant realizations [t̪θ], [d̪ð]. The distinction between pairs such as *tin* and *thin*, *fate* and *faith*, *den* and *then*, *breed* and *breathe* thus depends on place of articulation rather than on manner. The difference between [tʰɪn] *tin* and [t̪ʰɪn] *thin*, [feːt] *fate* and [feːt̪] *faith*, [doː] *dough* and [d̪oː] *though* is not always obvious to a non-Irish ear. Speakers of other accents of English may react more strongly to the plosiveness of [t̪] and [d̪] than to their dentality, so that the sounds are categorized as /t/ and /d/. Hence an Irishman who, as far as his own phonological system is concerned, is pronouncing *thin* (/θɪn/, i.e. [t̪ʰɪn]), may nevertheless be imagined by the average Englishman to be saying *tin* /tɪn/.

We could of course choose to symbolize the Irish English dental phonemes as /t̪/ and /d̪/ rather than as the phonetically inaccurate /θ/ and /ð/. But this would raise other difficulties, particularly when making a phonemic transcription of the many middle-class southern Irish who fluctuate between plosive and fricative realizations.

In postvocalic position, and even sometimes prevocalically, the /t−θ/ opposition is reinforced by the use of special allophones of /t/. Foremost among these is a kind of voiceless alveolar slit fricative, for which the appropriate IPA symbol would appear to be [t̞]. It is one of the most conspicuous features of Irish English, and common at all social levels and perhaps in all parts of the country (always excluding Ulster); though Henry (1958: 123) regards it as most typical of South Leinster and the midlands. Examples are *bottom* ['bɑt̞əm], *jetty* ['dʒɛt̞i], *ditto* ['dɪt̞oː], and *hit* [hɪt̞] (distinguished from *hiss* [hɪs] largely by being a slit fricative as against a groove fricative). This allophone does not, however, occur in preconsonantal position, either within or across words. Hence in final position there arises an alternation which Bertz illustrates by the example *mea*[t̞] *exports*, but *mea*[t] *sales*.

The use of this [t̞] as an allophone of /t/ can be seen as a kind of lenition (a process common and productive in all Celtic languages). A further stage in this process yields [h], which is actually the phonologically lenited form of /t/ in Irish. This further stage sometimes occurs in Irish English, too; Henry gives the examples *rat* [ɹah], *not at all* [nɒhə'ʈɒːl]. *Saturday* is often pronounced with ['sahə-]. Similar lenitions are sometimes encountered with other plosives: from a locality in County Laois Henry (1958: 125) quotes instances such as [ə'xlɑx] *o'clock*, [ɣoːt] *goat*.

Other important allophones of /t/, in Dublin at least, are [ʈ] and [ʔ]. Both have the effect of reinforcing the distinctiveness of /t/ vis-à-vis /θ/, since in principle they are not possible realizations of the latter. T Voicing (compare vol. 1, 3.3.4) is very typical of Dublin working-class accents, particularly with men: *daugh*[t]*er*, *co*[t]*age*, *ge*[t]*ing*, *trai*[t]*or* (≠ *trader*), *wha*[t] *is wrong*, *eigh*[t]*een*. It is mostly restricted to intervocalic position. The further development to [ɾ], with possible neutralization of the opposition /t–r/, is also found, being common – and increasingly so – with younger speakers. It is restricted to the environment V__# #V, as *turn it off*, *eight o'clock*, [hwaɾ aɪ 'miːn] *what I mean*. *Cut it* may even be ['kʊɾə], homophonous with *Curragh*. Whereas T Opening is widespread in Ireland and T Tapping, as we have seen, on the increase, T Glottalling is found only in the casual speech of younger working-class Dubliners (for whom it may conceivably be an import from Cockney or Glaswegian). It, too, is mainly intervocalic, as in *started* ['staˑʔəd], *scooter*, *bottle*, [a 'hɛɪʔ ɪʔ] *I hate it*.

Hence in a word such as *atom* there are a whole range of possible realizations of the intervocalic /t/. Alongside plain ['ætəm], which is perhaps largely restricted to sophisticated speakers influenced by RP, we find also ['æʈəm] and, in Dublin at least, ['æʈəm] and ['æʔəm]. It is also reported (Bertz 1975: 275) that an unaspirated dental [ʈ] can occur here.

Absence of the /t/ vs. /θ/ and /d/ vs. /ð/ oppositions, as mentioned above, is mainly urban. In Cork it is the alveolars which are generalized, with [tʰɪn] for both *tin* and *thin*, [doː] for both *dough* and *though*. In popular Dublin speech, though, Bertz reports generalization of the dentals as a possibility in running speech (1975: 273), so that *tin* and *thin* can both be [ʈʰɪn], *dough* and *though* both [ɖoː]. According to Henry (1958: 123) this is also found in County Sligo.

Otherwise, though, the neutralization of these oppositions is context-sensitive, involving typically the generalization of dentals in the environment of a following /r/, as shown in (216).

(216) $\begin{bmatrix} \text{alveolar} \\ \text{stop} \end{bmatrix}$ → [dental] / — (ə)r.

Thus someone who consistently distinguishes *tin* from *thin* may nevertheless very likely pronounce *try* and *better* with [t̪], *dream* and *thunder* with [d̪]. Then *tree* and *three* are homophonous, [t̪ɹiː], as are *breeder* and *breather* ['bɹiːd̪ə]. Sometimes this process is inhibited by an intervening morpheme boundary (Nally 1971: 36), giving possible contrasts such as *bol*[d]*er* vs. *boul*[d̪]*er*, *wi*[d]*er* vs. *spi*[d̪]*er*, *prin*[t]*er* vs. *win*[t̪]*er*.

Neutralization in the direction of the alveolar plosives may be found in two possible environments: before /l/ and before /s/. The first, when found, gives forms such as ['atliːt] *athlete*; someone who pronounces *faith* as [feːt̪] may nevertheless say *faithless* as ['feːtləs]. Much more widespread is the rule making dentals alveolar before /s/; this makes *faiths* and *fates* homophonously [feːts] even for those who regularly distinguish between *faith* and *fate*.

The typically plosive quality of /θ, ð/ makes clusters such as /θt, ðd, tθ, dθ/ awkward. With *breathed*, for example (RP /briːðd/), the obvious way out for an Irish accent is to use the syllabic allomorph of the -ed suffix, making *breathed* disyllabic just as *seeded* is. *Breadth* (RP /brɛdθ/) is usually homophonous with *breath* in Irish English, /brɛθ/ (i.e. [brɛt̪] for many speakers); similarly *width* = *with*, and *eighth* [eːt̪ ~ eɪθ], rhyming with *faith*.

5.3.9 The liquids

Irish English /l/ is in general strikingly clear in all environments: [fiːl̪] *feel*, [mɪl̪k] *milk* (compare RP [fiːɫ], [mɪɫk]). Even in Dublin, where a certain amount of clear vs. dark alternation on the RP pattern is found, the 'dark' allophone is usually only moderately velarized. (Under the influence of the accents of Britain and America, though, things may be beginning to change: F. Mac Éinrí informs me (private communication) that to his surprise he finds quite a number of his 18–20-year-old students using [ɫ].)

The typical /r/, by contrast, has a strikingly 'dark' resonance in Irish English, particularly in final and preconsonantal environments. Before a stressed vowel, /r/ is usually realized as a post-alveolar approximant, as in RP, with fricative variants after /t, d/; in other environments, a retroflex approximant is general. Thus we have [ɹɛd] *red*, [əˈɹaɪv] *arrive*, [bɹɪŋ] *bring*; but [ˈsɒɻi] *sorry*, [faːɻm] *farm*, [hweːɻ] *where*. In the latter cases the retroflexion typically colours some or all of the preceding vowel, too; indeed, V plus /r/ may be coalesced in realization as an r-coloured vowel. The usual auditory impression, though, is one of steadily increasing r-colouring (retroflexion) as the realization of /Vr/ progresses: [faˤːɻ] *far*. The degree of retroflexion seems to vary regionally, socially, and stylistically to some extent: Bertz found it stronger in Ringsend and the southern Docklands than in other parts of Dublin. Working-class Dublin children, though, he continues (1975: 152), may even lose it altogether in some environments, pronouncing [hɪɐ] *here* – presumably an innovation imported from England.

With this very minor exception it is clear that Irish English is firmly rhotic, something that has always struck English ears rather forcefully. Hence eye-dialect representations such as *sorr* 'sir', i.e. /sʌr/ [söˤːɻ]. However, as in some American accents, there is a tendency in popular Dublin speech to drop /r/ after /ə/ in a pretonic syllable, making *surprise* for example start just like *suppose*, /səˈpraɪz/ (as against the more elegant /sərˈpraɪz/). The word *Saturday*, too, is usually pronounced without any /r/.

There is some suggestion that /r/ may have velar or uvular variants in County Louth and County Tipperary/County Limerick.

5.3.10 Other consonants

There is no H Dropping in Irish English: *harm* is consistently distinguished from *arm*, etc., at all social levels. The letter *H* itself, though, is called /heːtʃ/, at least by Catholics. (This is in fact widely considered a sectarian shibboleth, with the Protestants calling it /eːtʃ/, cf. RP /eɪtʃ/.) The clusters /hj, hw/ are regular in words such as *human*, *where*; they may optionally be realized as single-segment voiced fricatives, [ç] and [ʍ] respectively. Exceptionally, the word *humour* is usually /ˈjuːmər/. Although most Irishmen keep /h/ in the environment of a following /w/ (*where* etc.), Glide Cluster

Reduction does occur sporadically (a) when the word in question is unstressed, and (b) in popular Dublin speech.

The phonological distribution of /h/ is not restricted in Irish English – unlike most accents of English, where it can only occur syllable-initially. In particular, /h/ is found in the environments 'V＿V and 'V＿#, though perhaps only in geographical and personal names: /bə'læhiː/ *Bellahy*, /'hɒhiː/ *Haughey*, /'fæhiː/ *Fahy*, /ˌkɪltʃɪ'mɒh/ *Kiltimagh*, /mə'græh/ *McGrath* (I have noticed this final /h/ particularly clearly in the phrase *the McGrath boys*). The surname *O'Shaughnessy* exemplifies /h/ in the environment of a following consonant.

The wider distribution of [h] is, of course, a carry-over from Irish. So is the occasional use of [x], although the relationship between [h] and [x] is not always clear. The *Taoiseach* may be ['tiːʃə], ['ʈiːʃə], ['ʈiːʃək(x)], or (most sophisticated) ['ʈiːʃəx].

Other unusual possibilities of phonological distribution – unusual, that is, from the point of view of other accents of English – are exemplified in the place-name *Bweeng* (County Cork) /bwiːŋ/ and the surname *Keogh* /kjoː/.

Irish is a language which, like Russian, makes a systemic phonological distinction between 'broad' (velarized or velar) and 'slender' (palatalized or palatal) consonants, auditorily signalled largely by transitional glides onto or off the consonant in question. Not surprisingly, such effects are still to be found in some Irish English, particularly in remote rural areas. Among the many examples collected by Henry (1958) are ['kˠɑːvz] *calves*, ['dïɑkʈəɹ] *doctor*, [bʷəiɳɖəɹ] *binder*, ['bɹɪmʷɪŋ] *brimming* (all from the south-west); ['kʲabɪdʒ] *cabbage*, [gʲiːs] *geese*, ['ɒːgʷəʃt] *August* (from County Meath in the east). Further examples, perhaps more typical of Irish English in general, involve palatal(ized) consonants following front vowels: [bɑːɹc] *bark*, (with lenition) [kɪç] *kick*. From popular Dublin speech Bertz quotes, as occasional variants, [ʈuː] *two*, ['b̥uːzər] *boozer*, [ʈɔːk] *talk*. But perhaps the most striking such effect involves the use of [ʃ, ʒ] rather than their 'broad' counterparts [s, z] in preconsonantal position, as [ʃtaːɹ] *star*, [fɪʃt] *fist*, [moːʃt] *most*, ['caʃl] *castle*, ['bɪʃcət] *biscuit*, ['wɪʒdəm] *wisdom*, ['pʊʒl] *puzzle*, ['lɪʃn̩] *listen*. This is part of the general-Irish stereotype of an accent from the west (that is, [də 'wɛʃt]). Perhaps rather more widespread is the

use of retroflex fricatives for /rs, rz/, as [kʌˈʂ] *curse*, [ˈkɑblə̢z] *cobblers*.
There are one or two further complications. In some parts of the
south the 'slender' consonants of Irish were (or are) merely non-
velarized in quality, rather than actually palatal(ized). When such
qualities are used as realizations of English /Cj/, as can happen, the
impression results of a generalized Yod Dropping (vol. 1, 3.1.10), as
[ˈtaŋkuː] *thank you*. In the midlands a rather different development
has occurred. Here the Irish 'slender' /t̡, d̡/ were phonetically
affricated, and thus similar to English /tʃ, dʒ/, with which they were
accordingly identified. This led to the use of Irish /k̡, g̡/ as replace-
ments of English /tj, dj/ in words such as *tune*, *dew*. These palatalized velars are interpreted within an English frame of reference as
/kj, gj/. Hence there is a popular rural midland pronunciation of
tune as /kjuːn/ and *dew* as /gjuː/. Indeed, *tube* and *cube* are homophones in this kind of accent: both are pronounced /kjuːb/.

Yet another traditional characteristic of the 'brogue' (that is, an
Irish accent or the exaggerated stereotype of such an accent) is the
use of bilabial fricatives for /f/ and /v/, thus [ɸɑɹ] *for*, [loːɸ] *loaf*,
[leːβ] *leave*. These may still be heard in the west. A bilabial fricative
can also be used for /hw/, involving a loss of the opposition between
/hw/ and /f/, thus [ɸeːɹ] *where* (potentially homophonous with *fair*).
A trace of this remains in the fact that the Irish surname *Ó Faoláin*
has two competing anglicizations, *Phelan* and *Whelan*: in the first
Irish [ɸ] becomes English /f/, in the second English /hw/.

5.3.11 Processes

Several phonological processes found in Irish accents merit particular mention: Schwa Absorption, certain special types of
Epenthesis, and Yod Coalescence. We take them in order.

As an optional rule in Irish accents, Schwa Absorption takes the
characteristic form ə → Ø / 'V__X, where X is a liquid or a nasal.
Thus we have potential rhymes such as *owl–vowel*, *reel–real*,
mile–trial (these as in many parts of England); *silent–violent*;
fair–player, *roar–slower*; *fine–Brian*; *seem–museum*; and potential
homophones such as *pear–payer* /peːr/, *more–mower* /moːr/,
line–lion /laɪn/, *runes–ruins* /ruːnz/. As we have seen above, Irish
English often has /ə/ where RP (in this respect more conservative)
generally retains /ɪ/. Hence the number of words available as candi-

dates for the operation of Schwa Absorption is higher than it would otherwise be: not only *lion* but also popular *lyin'* is /laɪən/ and thus reducible by Schwa Absorption to /laɪn/, which makes them homophones of *line*. Similarly *seein'* /'siːən/ can become homophonous with *seen* = *scene*, and *throwin'* with *thrown* = *throne*. With a different phonological environment, *quite* and *quiet* may level as /kwaɪt/. All of these levellings would tend to be avoided in more educated accents, at least in careful speech. The same applies to *-ing* /ən/ as the input to Syllabic Consonant Formation, as *waiting* ['weːtn̩], *rotting* = *rotten* ['rɒtn̩].

As well as the familiar Plosive Epenthesis which makes *false* and *sense* homophones of *faults* and *scents* respectively, Irish English exhibits striking Epenthesis processes inserting [ə] and [d]. Schwa Epenthesis is restricted to popular speech: it involves the insertion of [ə] between a plosive (including /θ/, i.e. [t̪]) and a liquid or nasal, as *petrol* ['pɛt̪əɹəl], *Dublin* ['dʊbəlɪn], *Kathleen* ['kæt̪əliːn]; or between two consonants, each of which is a liquid or nasal, as *film* ['fɪləm], *form* ['fɔɹəm], *Drimnagh* ['dɹɪmənə], *tavern* ['tævəɹən]. It can be viewed as the inverse of Schwa Absorption. The two processes together result in metatheses such as *apron* /'eːpərn/. An item which does not exactly fit into this pattern is /'tʃaːrləs/ *Charles* (apparently regularly disyllabic in Ireland, with the alternative form /'tʃaːrəlz/ [-ɹlz]; compare RP monosyllabic /'tʃɑːlz/).

D Epenthesis can come into operation in two environments. One of them is between a preceding /l/ or /n/ and a following /z/, which yields homophones such as *bills* = *builds* /bɪldz/, *holes* = *holds*, *mines* = *minds* /maɪndz/. The other is between a preceding /r/ and a following [n] or [l], whether syllabic or not; the intrusive [d] here has a nasal or lateral release respectively. Examples are *turned* [tʌɪdn̩d], *girls* [gɛɹdlz], *snoring* [snɔːɹdn̩]. This D Epenthesis may make the following sonorant syllabic, so that for example *aren't* becomes a homophone of *ardent* [aːɹdn̩t]. The details have been documented by Bertz for popular Dublin speech, but their geographical and social spread have not yet been investigated.

Yod Coalescence in stressed syllables is common in Dublin not only in popular accents but also in conservative educated speech: *dew* = *due* = *Jew* [dʒuː]; *tune* [tʃuːn] (otherwise [tjuːn, djuː]). (After /n/, Yod Dropping seems on the whole commoner: *nude* [nuːd].) Eye-dialect representations such as *projuce* (for *produce*) reflect this tendency. In unstressed syllables, however, Yod Dropping is strikingly frequent: see above 5.3.10 and note eye-dialect representations such as *eddication*. The very widespread pronunciation *tremen*[dʒ]*ous* results perhaps from a morphological rather than a phonological process, like *griev(i)ous* and *mischiev(i)ous*.

5.3.12 Prosodic features

Word stress seems to be rather more flexible in Irish accents than in RP: *af'fluence* alongside *'affluence*, *dis'cipline* or *'discipline*, *or'chestra* or *'orchestra*, *muni'cipal* or *'municipal* (RP *mu'nicipal*). One type of stress variability can perhaps be captured by saying that the Alternating Stress Rule of *SPE* is optional in Irish English: hence the prevalence of stressings such as *concen'trate, edu'cate, exagge'rated, recog'nize, specia'lized, subse'quently* (all alongside RP-type initial stressed alternatives). Some alternate *'educate* with *He edu'cated her, 'recognize* with *He recog'nized her*, where adding an unstressed pronoun triggers a stress shift.

The intonation of (southern) Irish English has been little studied: but it is not strikingly different from that of RP. One apparently valid difference of some importance is that in an Irish accent yes–no questions are normally said with a low-fall nuclear tone (as against the low-rise of RP). A neutral kind of intonation for the question *Would you like some tea?* might be

(217):

as against RP

(218):

5.3.13 The north: introduction

The northernmost part of Ireland stands apart from the rest of the island not only politically but also linguistically. The Plantation of Ulster in 1609 meant the introduction of two kinds of English into the surrounding Irish-Gaelic speaking areas: one, Scots dialects stemming from south-west Scotland, and the other, English speech mostly from the north and west midlands. These English-speaking

areas of Ulster remained for some time cut off from the English of
Dublin and its surroundings by a belt of Irish Gaelic stretching
across Louth, Monaghan, and Cavan.

The (historical) province of Ulster is rather larger than the present Northern Ireland (i.e. that part of Ireland which is politically a
part of the United Kingdom rather than of the Republic of Ireland).
Three counties now in the Republic belonged historically to Ulster:
Donegal, Monaghan, and Cavan. In speech all of these (but particularly the first) are similar to Northern Ireland rather than to the
south. Western Donegal remains partly Irish-speaking; there were
pockets of Irish Gaelic elsewhere in Ulster until well into this
century. Hence three main sources of influence are to be traced in
Ulster English: Scotch-Irish, Ulster Anglo-Irish, and Irish Gaelic.

Even the Irish of Ulster differs rather noticeably from that of the
rest of the island. It, too, has been subject to considerable Scottish
influence, dating from well before the Plantation. Western
Scotland was the home of the Galloglasses ('foreign soldiers'),
formidable warriors of Norse descent and Gaelic speech, tens of
thousands of whom came to fight in Ulster as mercenaries in the
thirteenth century. Other Scottish mercenaries and settlers made
their home in Ulster in the sixteenth century. (Some scholars would
argue that the influence was even stronger in the other direction.)
The upshot is that contemporary Donegal Irish (the only Ulster
Irish still extant) has a number of points in common with Scottish
Gaelic and at odds with the Irish of further south, including
important differences in the vowel system.

Ulster English, too, differs from other Irish English in its vowel
system. Most importantly, the opposition between the FOOT and
GOOSE vowels is missing: as in Scotland, these are merged into a
single phoneme /u/. Vowel length, too, is generally similar to that of
Scottish English, being dependent mainly upon phonetic environment (e.g. [bɛːl] *bell*, [bʉt] *boot*, although in accents of England the
first is short, the second half-long). The dental fricatives /θ/ and /ð/
are used as in the standard accents, without the [t̪, d̪] variants found
in southern Ireland and without the tendency to lose the /t-θ, d-ð/
oppositions. Phonetic [t̪, d̪] do occur, though, as positional variants
of /t, d/ in the environment of a following /r/.

The last-mentioned is not the only point on which Ulster English
agrees with other kinds of Irish English. It also shares full rhoticity,

with /r/ realized as a post-alveolar or retroflex approximant (with which one may compare the more usual fricative, tap, or roll of Scottish accents). On the whole it shares the 'clear' realization of /l/ in all environments (but see below).

Scots, Gaelic, and seventeenth-century English have all contributed to Ulster English. Though rural dialects are still distinguishably either Scots or Hiberno-English in type (in the north and south of Ulster respectively), urban speech – and particularly that of the capital, Belfast – represents an amalgam which can no longer be unscrambled.

5.3.14 The north: vowel system and vowel length

It is the vowel system that is the most characteristic thing about an Ulster accent. The most typical system seems to be as shown in (219). (As discussed below, it is not a clear-cut matter to decide which phonemic vowels are restricted to checked syllables and which can occur free; a case can be made out for interchanging /ε/ and /e/ in the table below.)

(219)

ɪ		i				u	
ε	ʌ	e					o
	(ɒ)	aɪ	ɔɪ	a	ɔ	au	

The lexical incidence of these vowels is shown in (220).

(220)

KIT	ɪ	FLEECE	i[1]	NEAR	ir
DRESS	ε	FACE	e	SQUARE	εr[1]
TRAP	a	PALM	a	START	ar
LOT	ɒ, ɔ	THOUGHT	ɔ	NORTH	ɔr
STRUT	ʌ	GOAT	o	FORCE	or
FOOT	u[1]	GOOSE	u	CURE	ur
BATH	a	PRICE	aɪ	*happy*	e, ɪ
CLOTH	ɔ	CHOICE	ɔɪ	*lett*ER	ər = [ɚ]
NURSE	ʌr[1]	MOUTH	au	*comm*A	ə

[1] see below for discussion.

In Ulster, as in Scotland, there has been a near-complete loss of phonemic vowel-length distinctions. The merger in /u/ of the FOOT and GOOSE vowels, historically short and long respectively, has already been mentioned (but see below on the possibility of /ʌ/ in

FOOT words). The sets TRAP and PALM are also merged, in /a/, as are
LOT and THOUGHT, in /ɔ/ (with certain reservations discussed
below).

The distribution of phonetic length in vowels is broadly as follows: (i) All vowels are short before a following /p, t, tʃ, k/; thus [fit]
feet, [bʉt] *boot*, [met] *mate*, [bot] *boat*, [bɪt] *bit*, [kʌt] *cut*, [sɛt] *set*, [pat]
pat, [pɔt] *pot* (or [pɒt], etc.; the vowel transcriptions in this paragraph are narrowed only in respect of length, not in respect of
quality). (ii) All vowels except /ɪ/ and /ʌ/ are long before a following
final /v, ð, z, r/ or # ; thus [griːv] *grieve*, [lʉːz] *lose*, [seːv] *save*, [loːð]
loathe, [fɛːr] *fair*, [haːv] *have* = *halve*, [kɔːz] *cause*. So far, we have no
more than the outcome of the operation of Aitken's Law (5.2.3
above). But a peculiarly Ulster development has then resulted in
(iii), the use of long allophones of /e, ɛ, a, ɔ/ in any monosyllable
closed by a consonant **other** than /p, t, tʃ, k/. We might refer to this
extra development as Ulster Lengthening (though of course in the
case of /e/ the net result is rather the restoration of a historically long
vowel). Examples are [reːd] *raid*, [bɛːd] *bed*, [paːd] *pad*, [pɔːd] *pod*.

The foregoing paragraph can be summarized in tabular form,
(221).

(221) in monosyllables	i, u, o	ɪ, ʌ	e, ɛ, a, ɔ
—{p, t, tʃ, k}#	short	short	short
—{f, θ, s, ʃ, b, d, dʒ, g, m, n, ŋ, l}#	short	short	long
—{v, ð, z, r, zero}#	long	short	long

A sonorant (i.e. nasal or lateral) before the final consonant is
ignored for purposes of determining vowel length: e.g. *lamp* has
short [a], like *lap*, and *belt* has short [ɛ], like *bet*. There is, however, a
degree of social and regional variability in vowel length. In Larne,
for example, as described by Gregg (1964), stressed /e/ is always
long, even before voiceless plosives as in *cape* [keːp]; so usually is /o/,
as *wrote* [ɹoːt], *rogue* [ɹoːg]; /ɛ/ 'varies unsystematically in length, but
tends to be fully long especially in monosyllables', as *neck* [nɛːk],
step [stɛːp]. In Belfast, James Milroy has observed (1976a) that
lengthening in the environment of a following sonorant plus voiceless plosive, contrary to the rule given above, is increasingly found
in the speech of younger women in the linguistically more innova-
tive areas: thus *rent* [ɹɛːnt] (otherwise [ɹɛnt]). But in Larne speech

Gregg regards a short vowel in this environment as evidence of Belfast influence, the traditional Larne vowel being long.

Vowels in polysyllabic words are most commonly short. Thus in Belfast one finds *mess* [mɛːs] but *message* ['mɛsɪdʒ]. In many cases, however, internal morpheme boundaries condition the occurrence of long vowels in polysyllables. Thus the verb *can* has a long vowel in accordance with the rule given above, [kaːn]; and this long vowel is preserved in its *ing* form, *canning* ['kaːnɪŋ] (morphologically [kaːn#ɪŋ]). But the surname *Canning*, being morphologically simple, has a short vowel, ['kanɪŋ]. Similar minimal pairs are *tanner* (who tans) ['taːnər] vs. *tanner* ('sixpence', 'shoemaker') ['tanər], *tenner* vs. *tenor*, *wedding* (act of wedding) vs. *wedding* (ceremony). Other minimal pairs dependent upon vowel length conditioned by a morpheme boundary may arise in the case of /i, u, o/ followed by /d/, as in Scotland: *a greed* [ə'grid] vs. *agreed* [ə'griːd], *brood* vs. *brewed*, *rode* vs. *rowed*. The Scotch-Irish areas may also have pairs such as *spoke* (noun) [spok] vs. *spoke* (verb) [spoːk] (Gregg 1964: 170). For /a/, in more southerly country areas at least, there are also certain pairs which appear to evidence an autonomous length contrast in polysyllables, e.g. *gather* with [a] vs. *father*, *rather* with [aː]. But throughout Ulster the oppositions associated in other accents with TRAP vs. PALM or TRAP vs. BATH are unknown in monosyllables: thus *cam* = *calm* [kaːm], *ant* = *aunt* [ant]. This, combined with the allophonic length rules described above, leads to one or two pronunciations which seem quite unexpected from the point of view of RP: e.g. the strong form of *can* has a long vowel, [kaːn], while *can't* has a short one, [kant] (conversely in RP: /kæn, kɑːnt/).

5.3.15 The north: vowel quality

The phonetic qualities of the vowels vary within Ulster both regionally and socially, as well as allophonically. We look in turn at /e/, at /u/, at /ɪ, ʌ/, at /ɛ, a, ɔ/, and at the remaining vowels.

In most of Ulster /e/ is monophthongal and half-close or slightly opener. But in Belfast two very different types of realization are to be encountered: in open syllables a long monophthong almost as open as cardinal 3, but in closed syllables a centring diphthong, perhaps most typically [eə], but ranging from [ɛə] to [iə] (all short or long). Thus we have on the one hand [wɛː] *way*, [dɛː] *day*, etc., and on the other hand [seːəm] *same*, [seːəv] *save*, or (with a shorter diphthong) [steət] *state*, [feəs] *face*. The monophthongal variant is also found before a morpheme boundary, e.g. [dɛːz] *days*, which in consequence differs phonetically from [deːəz] *daze* (and similarly in *brayed* vs. *braid*, *lays* vs. *laze*, *stayed* vs. *staid*, etc.). It is not altogether clear whether this necessarily involves the phonetic identity of, for example, *brayed* and *bread*, *Fay's* and *fez*. If, as seems likely, it does, then it would seem reasonable to regard [ɛː], even in FACE words, as realizing /ɛ/ rather than /e/; and we should have to say that in a typical Belfast accent /ɛ/ is permitted in open syllables and /e/ excluded from them – the precise converse of the situation in nearly all other accents of English.

As in other parts of Ireland, the FLEECE Merger is not altogether complete. Pronunciations such as [beːt] for *beat* persist in unselfconscious popular speech, potentially distinct both from *beet* [bit] and from *bait* [beət]. In East Belfast street gangs are known as [teːmz] *teams*; they may [beːt] up their enemies (Maclaran 1976: 61). But 'tay' (i.e. [teː]) for *tea* is reported to be now only jocular in Belfast, though it persists in rural areas.

Ulster /u/ usually has rather little lip rounding: it may sound almost like [ɨ] in quality. In the 'short' environments (i.e. when followed by a consonant other than /v, ð, z, r/) it is less than fully close and central, [ʉ], as *doom* [dʉm], *soot* = *suit* [sʉt]. In the 'long' environments it is close and central or centralized-front [ʉː], as *who* [hʉː], *choose* = *chews* [tʃʉːz]. Both short and long variants are much fronter after /j/, as *mule* [mjʏl], *few* [fjʏː]. Before /r/ an opener allophone is used, a centralized [øː] or [ɵː], as *cure* [kjøːr], *poor* [pɵːr].

The vowels /ɪ/ and /ʌ/, as we have seen, are always short. The usual realization of /ɪ/ is [ɪ], opener and more centralized than in the standard accents, thus *sit* [sɪt], *big* [bɪg]. In the urban speech of Belfast it is often even opener, reaching an almost open [ɛ̈] quality – particularly before /l/, thus *fill* [fɛ̈l], also *thing* [θɛ̈ŋ] (otherwise [θɪŋ]). This quality is also used in many KIT words in Scotch-Irish traditional-dialect (see 5.3.19 below), where it is phonemically opposed to ordinary /ɪ/. Unstressed /ɪ/ may be qualitatively like the stressed vowel, or – if followed by a velar or palato-alveolar – less open and centralized, [ɪ], as ['fɪzɪks] *physics*. The *happY* vowel is /ɪ/ in Belfast, so that *happy* is phonetically ['hapɪ ~ 'hapɛ̈]. In the Scots areas it may instead be /e/, thus ['hape].

The quality of /ʌ/ varies regionally, with a near-cardinal [ʌ], half-open back unrounded, in the Scotch-Irish area, but a rather closer centralized slightly rounded [ɔ̈] (similar to southern Irish /ʌ/) in the Anglo-Irish area. Rounding is variable in Belfast; some Belfast people have a centralized [ɐ̈] much as in RP.

In the Scotch-Irish area and in Belfast /ε/ and /a/ are frequently neutralized in most environments involving an adjacent velar: thus *peck = pack, beg = bag*, and sometimes *kettle = cattle*. The result of neutralization is phonetically like /ε/, as [pε(ː)k, bεːg, kε(ː)tl]. As far as Belfast is concerned, this neutralization is believed to be recessive when the velar precedes (*cattle*) and when a voiced velar follows (*bag*), but is firmly established in the environment of a following /k/ (*knack = neck* /nεk/).

In popular Belfast speech the vowels /ε, ɑ, ɔ/ all tend to be fully open front or central, if short, but closer and/or backer and diphthongized, if long. In the short environments, in fact, one has the impression of a complete three-way neutralization of sets such as *pet–pat–pot* as [pa–t]. A careful study by James Milroy has, however, led to the conclusion that 'although short /ɔ/ and /a/ tokens may in certain circumstances merge in short [ä], and although short /a/ undoubtedly merges with short /ε/ before /k/, [...] it is clearly not the case that all three have merged completely. Thus, while *pot* and *pat* may often be indistinguishable, *pet* is slightly higher, and it is possible to differentiate *pot* and *pat* by lengthening and backing the /a/ token.' (J. Milroy 1976a: 85). So, paradoxically from the point of view of the standard accents, we have the possibility of distinguishing TRAP words from LOT words by making them phonetically backer, thus *pat* [pɑːt] vs. *pot* [pa–t].

The popular Belfast tendency towards diphthongization of the lengthened allophones of /ε, a, ɔ/ gives phonetic realizations such as [bεˑəd] *bed*, [lεˑig] *leg*; [hɑːv ~ hɔːv ~ hɔˑəv] *have*, [mɑːn ~ mɔˑən] *man*; [kɔːd ~ kɔˑəd] *cod*, [dɔːl ~ dɔˑəl] *doll*. Initial /k/ and /g/ may receive a palatal onglide before /ε, a/, thus [kjεːb ~ kjɑːb] *cab*; in Belfast this is now restricted to older speakers, particularly Catholic males.

Middle-class Belfast people avoid the centring glides, saying for instance [bεːd] *bed* rather than [bεˑəd]. They also avoid the backest realizations of /a/ and the openest realizations of /ε/.

Outside Belfast, Ulster English has consistent monophthongs for

/ɛ, a, ɔ/. The first two are consistently opener than in RP, being around cardinal [ɛ], [a] respectively (or, in the latter case, rather more central). The LOT vowel differs noticeably as between the Scots area to the north and the Anglo-Irish area to the south, being of the type [ɔ] in the former and [ɑ] in the latter. Systemically it is merged with the THOUGHT vowel in the former, but distinct (at least to some extent) in the latter. Thus in Larne *stock* = *stalk* [stɔːk], phonemically both /stɔk/, and *collar* = *caller* /'kɔlər/. But in Belfast and in mid and south Ulster *stock* [stɒk ~ stɑk ~ sta‑k] is distinct from *stalk* [stɔ(ː)k], so that we must recognize two distinct phonemes, though their opposition is restricted to a small set of environments (e.g. that of a following voiceless plosive). There is a complication in that certain words belonging to the standard lexical set THOUGHT have /ɒ/ rather than the expected /ɔ/. These typically include *draw, fall, walk,* and *caught. Water* often has /a/.

The MOUTH words have a diphthong of the [əʉ] type, short or long, in the local accents of both the Scots and the Anglo-Irish areas. In Belfast the diphthong is extremely variable and a sensitive social marker. A relatively front first element, [ë] or fronter, is working-class; middle-class speakers prefer back [ɑ] or even [ɔ]. The second element is [ʉ ~ y ~ ɨ], often with little or no rounding. The result can suggest PRICE rather than MOUTH to an English ear. One or two common words (*how, now*) may receive special treatment in working-class Belfast speech, with an open first element [a ~ ɑ] and a second element ranging over [i ~ ʉ], a retroflex approximant [ɻ], and zero.

The PRICE words are distributed into two distinct phonemic categories in the Scotch-Irish area (as in Scotland), with [əi(ː)] in some words and [a(ː)e] in others. The choice between these two diphthong types is partly conditioned by phonetic environment, e.g. [əi] before voiceless consonants, [ae] before vowels, thus [ləik] *like,* ['raeət] *riot;* but in many environments both are possible. There are minimal pairs such as [ləiː] *lie* (fib) vs. [laːe] *lie* (recline), [məiːn] *mine* (noun) vs. [maːen] *mine* (adjective). (These examples are taken from the description of Larne speech by Gregg 1964: 173, where copious lists are presented.) Hence we must undoubtedly recognize two distinct phonemes for this type of accent. In the remainder of Ulster, however, there is only a single phoneme in all PRICE words, which I write /æi/. Phonetically it ranges from [æˑɪ] to

[eɪ]; the latter sounds just like RP /eɪ/, but is used in Belfast vernacular for /aɪ/ in closed syllables, as [weɪn] *wine* (compare [weˑən] etc.
wane).

Both MOUTH and PRICE diphthongs are usually realized as monophthongs in the environment of a following /r/. Thus *power* is
[ˈpɑːəɹ] and *fire* [ˈfɛːəɹ ~ fʌːɹ] (compare, however, [ˈtɹəʉəl] *trowel*,
[ˈtɹæiəl] *trial*, where no monophthonging occurs).

Vowels before /r/ call for some comment. In the Anglo-Irish area
the NURSE Merger (vol. 1, 3.1.8) has applied, but it is not clear
whether the resultant [ɜː] (often with some lip rounding) can be
regarded as an allophone of /ʌ/ (which would account for the
rounding) or as realizing /ə/ (which would then occur in stressed
syllables only when followed by /r/). In many rural areas the pre-
NURSE-Merger situation is preserved: /ɛr/ is used in words with the
spelling *er*, and in some with *ear* or *ir*, while /ʌr/ is used in those with
the spelling *ur* and some with *ir*. Thus we may have [sɛɹv] *serve* but
[kɜɹv ~ kəɹv] *curve*, [ɛɹn] *earn* but [əɹn] *urn*, [pɹəˈfɛːɹ] *prefer* but [fɔɹ
~ fəɹ] *fir, fur*. In Belfast the vowels are on the whole merged. The
SQUARE words generally seem to have /ɛ/ in Ulster, as [fɛːɹ] *fair*; but
in Belfast they may fall in with NURSE so that *fair* is homophonous
with *fir, fur* (as in Dublin and Liverpool). According to James
Milroy (private communication), *her* and *hair* are usually merged in
minimal pair lists read aloud by informants, but nevertheless often
distinct in casual speech: [hʌɹ ~ hɔ̈ɹ] vs. [hɛːɹ].

Except in Belfast, the opposition between NORTH words, with
/ɔr/, and FORCE words, with /or/, seems well preserved in Ulster:
thus in Larne *horse* contrasts with *hoarse* as [hɔːɹs] vs. [hoːɹs]; in
Belfast both are usually [hoːɹs].

There is one characteristic of Belfast working-class speech that
could be termed 'dialectal' in the sense discussed in volume 1, 1.1.2.
This is the pronunciation of certain FOOT words with /ʌ/ rather than
the usual /u/, as *butcher* /ˈbʌtʃər/, *bull* /bʌl/, *look* /lʌk/ etc. (alongside
/ˈbutʃər, bul, luk/). An investigation of this characteristic by
Maclaran (1976) shows that although /u/ is not only the middle-
class form but also the one explicitly regarded as 'correct' by
everyone in Belfast, nevertheless /ʌ/ is used – inconsistently
and sporadically – by an actually increasing number of younger
working-class speakers. One boy is reported as saying that he was

beaten up at the shipyard for using [wʉd] rather than [wʌd] as the pronunciation of *would* (strong form), even though he otherwise had a broad local accent (Maclaran 1976: 53). But although peer-group pressure for /ʌ/ in FOOT is strong among young men, they often switch to the 'correct' /u/ as they get older.

Assorted Northern Ireland pronunciation variants involving non-standard lexical incidence of vowels include the following: /i/ in *king, brick, finish*; /a/ in words with the spelling *wa-*, as *watch, wall, water*; /ʌ/ in *want, what*; /ɒ ~ ɔ/ in *oven* and *does* (but *doesn't* with the expected /ʌ/). Many of these forms are predominantly rural and derive from Scots traditional-dialect.

5.3.16 The north: consonants

The most striking consonantal difference between northern and southern Irish accents concerns /θ/ and /ð/, which in the north are dental fricatives, [θ̪] and [ð̪] (compare the southern [t̪], [d̪]). Thus *think* is [θɪŋk], *breathe* [bɹiːð̪].

Dental plosives do, however, occur in the north as allophones of /t/ and /d/. They are found not only adjacent to /θ, ð/ (*width* [wɪd̪θ]) but also to some extent in the vicinity of /r/, as *tree* [t̪ɹiː], *ladder* ['lad̪ə] (as they are indeed throughout Ireland). But in Ulster these are nowadays predominantly rural pronunciations: in Belfast it is only the older speakers who use dental plosives conditioned by a neighbouring /r/. In words such as *butter* and *water*, where rural speakers have [t̪], Belfast prefers an alveolar tap (T Voicing). Those who do use dentals typically do so only if the conditioning /r/ is in the same morpheme, so that there are minimal pairs such as *flatter* (*v.*) with [t̪] vs. *flatter* 'more flat' with alveolar [t], *bou*[ld]*er* vs. *bo*[ld]*er*.

T Voicing is common in other intervocalic environments, too, and may lead to neutralization of the /t/ vs. /d/ opposition, thus ['pɑɹde] *party*, rhyming with *hardy*. It is presumably for this reason that Protestants are known colloquially as *Prods* (rather than as *Prots). Examples of [ɾ] from Adams (1948) include [pʉɾ'ɒːn] *put on* and ['hwɒɾde'dʉː] *what did he do?*.

Preglottalization of intervocalic /p/ and /t/ is common in Ulster, as *pe*[ʔ]*pper, bu*[ʔ]*tter*. (According to Milroy, Londonderry city has this for both /p/ and /t/, but Belfast commonly only for /p/.) Straight intervocalic T Glottalling (/t/ realized as simple [ʔ]) is associated with County Antrim, where it alternates with [ʔt]. Before syllabic [n̩], and sometimes before syllabic [l̩], it is more widespread: forms such as ['bʌʔn̩] *button* and ['laʔn̩] *Latin* are usual in Belfast, and ['bɑʔl̩] *bottle* not uncommon (alternatively ['bɑt̩l̩]).

Palatal realizations of /k/ and /g/ are widespread in Ulster, particularly word-initially before a front or open vowel. In Belfast speech it is most noticeable in pronunciations such as *cab, can, car* [caːɹ]. It seems to be untypical of the firmly Scots areas, and variable elsewhere in respect of the details of the conditioning environment. It has been claimed that in one Donegal locality the pair *back* and *baulk* can be distinguished not by their vowels but by their final consonants, as [baːc] vs. [baːk].

Ulster /ʃ, ʒ, tʃ, dʒ/ have a stronger palatal component in their realization than their counterparts in England, tending towards [ɕ, ʑ, tɕ, dʑ]. This may be attributable to Irish Gaelic influence, [ɕ] being the phonetic quality of the 'slender' /s̡/ of Ulster Irish. In the Scots-Irish area palatalized [n̡] and [l̡] are also encountered, generally as realizations of /nj, lj/: ['jʉn̡ən] *union*, ['mɪl̡ən] *million* (but note also ['n̡eːɹle] *nearly*, [gə'l̡oːɹ] *galore*).

The extension of NG Coalescence (vol. 1, 3.1.2) to all environments yields pronunciations such as ['fɪŋɚ] *finger* – stigmatized and now becoming rarer in the Belfast working-class accent; *language* with [-ŋw-] is usual.

Of the liquids, /r/ is usually a retroflex approximant. A roll or trill [r, ɾ] is still used in rural Ulster, particularly after /t/, as *train, string* [st̠ɾ-]. In Ulster, as elsewhere in Ireland, /l/ is typically clear in all environments; dark [ɫ] is, however, very common in Belfast (and probably in some country areas to the north and west) in intervocalic and final positions after central vowels and centring diphthongs, as *fill* [fëɫ], *fail* [fɪ̈·əɫ]; also initially before the back variants of /a/, as *lad* [ɫɑːd ~ ɫɔːd]. Polite speakers correct vowel quality and [ɫ] together; *pull* thus varies between a broader form [pʌɫ] and a less broad [pʉl].

Initial /hw/ remains (as phonetic [ʍ]) in the more rural areas, with simple /w/ now usual in Belfast and some other urban parts (Glide Cluster Reduction, vol. 1, 3.2.4).

5.3.17 The north: processes

Some interesting varieties of optional Elision are attested in working-class Belfast speech. One involves the deletion of /r/, sporadically in initial position in allegro speech, as *he 'an down the 'oad* (Milroy 1976b: 115), and more regularly between /θ/ and a close vowel, as [θiː] *three*. The fricative /θ/ itself may become [h] in *nothing, anything* (as in RP), and in fast speech initially (*thick*).

Another Ulster type of Elision involves initial or medial /ð/. The word *mother*, for example, may be pronounced either as ['mʌðɚ] or as ['mɔːɚ] (deletion of medial /ð/ seems necessarily to entail compensatory lengthening of the vowel). A study of this variable by L. Milroy (1976) shows it to be very much commoner in men's than in women's speech. Deletion of initial /ð/ gives *'em 'ere* for *them there* and makes *in the house* differ from *in a house* (if at all) only in the length of [n].

The possibility of /r/ insertion at the end of *how, now*, and occasionally in checked syllables (*down*) was mentioned above in the discussion of MOUTH.

Weakening of vowels in unstressed syllables is restricted in comparison to that of RP: a word such as *postman* keeps a strong vowel in its second syllable in Northern Ireland, thus ['postmaˑn]. So also *Oxford* /-ford/; and names like *Birmingham* and *Cunningham* have /-ham/.

5.3.18 The north: intonation

Belfast intonation (and probably that of Ulster English in general) is strikingly different both from that of RP and from that of southern Irish English. In a very high proportion of tone groups the nuclear tone is rising rather than falling; a rise is the unmarked tone not only for questions but also for statements and commands. A fall is used only for echo questions and for exclamations, or as part of a compound fall + rise tone on statements. Both rises and falls also differ in realizational detail from those of standard accents. The rises are abrupt, a following tail being on a plateau (compare RP rises, which are spread over any tail). The falling tone moves only down to mid level (compare RP falls, which usually reach quite a

Unmarked statement plus rhetorical tag question:

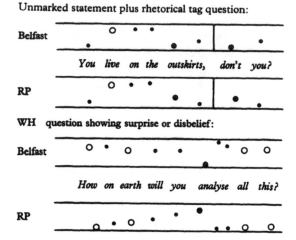

Fig. 14

low pitch). In fig. 14 we see typical Belfast intonation patterns, set against their RP semantic equivalents (from Jarman & Cruttenden 1976).

5.3.19 The north: accent and dialect

In discussing Ulster accents we must look finally at regional differences within Ulster and at the accent/dialect situation. As mentioned above, we can distinguish a northern Ulster Scots (Scotch-Irish) area from a southern Ulster English (Anglo-Irish) area. Belfast itself is situated on the border between them, and represents an amalgam of the two, with its own particular developments.

The Scotch-Irish area forms a nearly continuous belt across the north of the island: it includes the towns of Letterkenny, Coleraine, Ballymena, Larne, and Newtownards, together with their surrounding countryside. Here there is a traditional-dialect vs. accent situation similar to that found in Scotland, with a rural Scotch-Irish traditional-dialect (perhaps better termed Hiberno-Scots, since it is a variety of Scots) in use alongside an urban more-or-less standard English spoken with a local accent (which Gregg, on whose lucid description this paragraph is based, calls 'Scotch-Irish Urban'). Thus for example *dead* is [did] in the rural traditional-dialect, but [dɛ:d] in the urban accent. Some other typical examples are given in (222).

(222)		Rural Scotch-Irish dialect	Scotch-Irish urban accent
more		mɛ:r	mo:r
cinders		'ɐʌɲərz	'sɪndərz
bright		bræxt	brəit
blaze		bli:z	ble:z
make		mɑ:k	me:k
cow		kʉ:	kəʉ

A phonetically identical [spɪn] means *spoon* in the rural Scotch-Irish dialect, but *spin* in the Scotch-Irish urban accent; similarly [wʌn] can represent *wind* or *one*, [rɑ:n] *wren* or *ran*.

   The transition to the 'Ulster Anglo-Irish' area is marked by differences of grammar and vocabulary and minor differences in phonetic detail – but above all by the absence of the characteristically Scots dialect/accent situation and the kind of Scotch-Irish lexical incidence just outlined. Here *more* loses its [mɛ:r] form, appearing only as [mo:r]; *bright* is [brəit]; *cow* is [kəʉ]. Thus the Ulster Anglo-Irish forms very largely coincide with the local-accent non-dialect variants of the Hiberno-Scots area. Indeed, as Gregg says (1972: 113), the Scotch-Irish speakers know that the Ulster Anglo-Irish speech of their neighbours generally approximates much more closely to Standard English than their own Scottish type of dialect. Nevertheless there are certain Ulster Anglo-Irish dialect forms incidentially distinct from local-accent Standard forms: examples are [jo:] *ewe*, rhyming with *snow*, as against the [jʉ:] which is the local-accent version of the standard pronunciation (compare Scotch-Irish [jəʉ]), and [θo:] *thaw* (as against standard [θɔ:] and Scotch-Irish [θəʉ]).

5.3.20 Summary

We can summarize the principal differences between Irish accents in general and RP as follows. Systemically, there are no phonemically distinct centring diphthongs (RP /ɪə, ɛə, ʊə/). Nor, often, is there any /ɜ:/, NURSE words being divided into /e:r ~ ɛr/ and /ʌr ~ ər/ sets. In the south the opposition of /ʌ/ vs. /ʊ/ is neutralizable or has low functional load. There is not everywhere a clear /aɪ/ vs. /ɔɪ/ distinction (PRICE vs. CHOICE), though where there is there may be further phonemic distinctions among these sets. In Ulster the collapse of vowel length distinctions followed by new lengthenings has meant the disappearance of /æ/ and /ʊ/ as distinct phonemes, and partly also of /ɒ/. In certain circumstances the opposition between /t, d/ on the one hand and /θ, ð/ on the other may be neutralized; this varies geographically and socially. Phonemic /h/ is firmly preserved everywhere.

Irish English is rhotic, with a high proportion of vowel oppositions operating also before /r/. In weak syllables the opposition between /ɪ/ and /ə/ is largely lost. In *wh-*, /h/ is often lost in Dublin and Belfast, but otherwise retained.

In lexical incidence there is some measure of retention of [eː] in words like *meat*; this may or may not be the phoneme of FACE words. The lexical incidence of /ʌ/ and /ʊ/ does not always correspond to membership of the standard lexical sets STRUT and FOOT respectively; *cook* and certain other FOOT words go with GOOSE everywhere.

Realizationally, the most striking characteristics are the generally monophthongal vowels in FACE and GOAT; in the south, unrounded vowels in LOT and THOUGHT, but rounded in STRUT; in the north, fronted and possibly unrounded vowels in FOOT – GOOSE and MOUTH, along with idiosyncratic vowel qualities in KIT, DRESS, TRAP, and LOT; in the south, the realization of /θ, ð/ as plosives [t̪, d̪]; everywhere, the predominantly clear /l/ and dark (retroflex) /r/.

Sources and further reading

Other works which attempt a similar geographical coverage to the three volumes of *Accents of English* include Bähr 1974; Blunt 1976; and Wise 1957. The only one of these on which I have drawn is Bähr, and that very sparingly.

4.1 RP is well documented; the standard works are *EPD* and Gimson 1980; other important texts are Jones 1956, 1975. See also Abercrombie 1953; Brown 1977; Elyan *et al.* 1978; Eustace 1967; Giles 1970; Gimson 1970; Spencer 1957; Trim 1961; Ward 1948; Wells & Colson 1971; Windsor Lewis 1969, 1972.

4.2 There are references to Cockney in Gimson 1980; Jones 1956; O'Connor 1948: 56–9; Ward 1948. Sivertsen 1960 is a comprehensive description. More popular treatments: Barltrop & Wolveridge 1980, Franklyn 1953; Matthews 1938. I have drawn extensively on Beaken 1971; Bowyer 1973; Hudson & Holloway 1977; Hurford 1967; see also Bowyer 1971; Hurford 1968, 1968–70. Literary: Matthews 1938; Page 1970; Sivertsen 1960: 157–64.

4.3 General: *LAE*; *SED*; Hughes & Trudgill 1979: 44–50; Wakelin 1972a,b. The present treatment supersedes Wells 1970. East Anglia, Norwich: Trudgill 1972, 1973, 1974; Trudgill & Foxcroft 1978. Suffolk: Kökeritz 1932. The west country: Bristol: Weissmann 1970; comic treatment: Robinson, 1970, 1971; Cornwall: Wakelin 1975; Devon: Kingdon 1939a,b,c; open vowels: Fudge 1977; initial fricative voicing: Wakelin & Barry 1969.

4.4 General: *LAE*; *SED*; Hughes & Trudgill 1979: 54–69; Kolb 1966; Wakelin 1972a. The present treatment supersedes Wells 1970. Midlands: Fox 1967; Heath 1980; Painter 1963; Wilson 1970. Middle north: Lodge 1966, 1973, 1978; Hedevind 1967; Knowles 1974, 1978; Petyt 1977, 1978; comic treatment: Shaw 1966. Far north: Hughes & Trudgill 1979; McNeany 1971; O'Connor 1947; Pellowe *et al.* 1972a,b; Pellowe & Jones 1978; Viereck 1966; comic treatment: S. Dobson 1968. Uvular /r/: Påhlsson 1972.

5.1 Welsh and English in general: Fishlock 1972 (particularly chs 4–5); Pilch 1957; Stevens 1973. Welsh English: Fowkes 1966; Parry 1964, 1971, 1972, 1977. The present treatment supersedes Wells 1970. Cardiff: Lediard 1977; Mees 1977; Windsor Lewis 1964. Dialects of Welsh: A. R. Thomas 1967, 1973; Watkins 1962. Intonation:

C. Thomas 1967. Bangor: I am indebted to H. S. Chapman for making available the results of interviews he carried out with two dozen informants there.

5.2 Aitken & McArthur 1979 is highly recommended; it appeared after I had drafted this chapter. Scottish English and the language situation in Scotland: Catford 1957; Grant 1931; McClure 1974, 1975; McIntosh 1952; Mather 1974; Wood 1979; Woolley 1954. Phonetics of Scottish English: Abercrombie 1979; also Abercrombie 1954; Grant 1913; Jones 1956: §§180–1; McClure 1970. Gaelic interference: Bähr 1974: 147–72. Scots: McClure 1979; McClure *et al.* 1980; Murison 1977; see also Grant & Dixon 1921; Taylor 1974. Dialectology: Catford 1958; Grant 1911; McIntosh 1952; Mather 1964; Mather & Speitel 1975; Speitel 1968; Speitel & Mather 1968; Wilson 1923, 1926; Wölck 1965.

5.3 English in Ireland: Bliss 1976; Henry 1958; also Hogan 1927, 1934; Joyce 1910. Bibliography: Aldus 1969. Irish language: Ó Cuív 1969; O'Rahilly 1972; Wagner 1958. Influence of Irish on English: Adams 1967; Bliss 1972; Hughes 1966 [1973]. Irish accents in general: Bliss n.d. (ms.); Henry 1958; Mac Éinrí 1975 (ms.). Dublin: Bertz 1975. Other southern localities: Henry 1957; Nally 1971. Ulster: Adams 1948, 1964; Gregg 1958, 1964, 1972, 1975 (ms.); Jarman & Cruttenden 1976; J. Milroy 1975, 1976a and b; L. Milroy 1976, 1977; J. & L. Milroy 1978; L. & J. Milroy 1977. Eye-dialect: Taniguchi 1972 (phonetics unreliable because of 'inaccessibility to opportunity of hearing Irish dialect as it is actually spoken'). Stage Irish: Truninger 1976. As this book was in proof there appeared J. Milroy 1981: *Regional accents of English: Belfast* (Belfast: Blackstaff).

References

Abercrombie, D. 1953. English accents. *English Language Teaching*. 7.113–23
Abercrombie, D. 1954. A Scottish vowel. *Maître Phonétique* 102.23–4. Reprinted in Abercrombie 1965: 137–8
Abercrombie, D. 1965. *Studies in phonetics and linguistics*. London: Longman
Abercrombie, D. 1979. The accents of Standard English in Scotland. In Aitken & McArthur 1979: 68–84. Also, 1977, in *Work in Progress*, Department of Linguistics, Edinburgh University, 21–32
Adams, G. B. 1948. An introduction to the study of Ulster dialects. *Proceedings of the Royal Irish Academy* 52.C.1–26
Adams, G. B. (*ed.*) 1964. *Ulster dialects*. Includes chapters by the editor 'Ulster dialects', 'The last language census in Northern Ireland', and 'A register of phonological research on Ulster dialects'. Holywood, Co. Down: Ulster Folk Museum
Adams, G. B. 1967. Phonemic systems in collision in Ulster English. *Verhandlungen des zweiten int. Dialektologenkongresses*, 1965, 1.1–6 (*Zeitschrift für Mundartforschung*)
Aitken, A. J. 1962. Vowel length in modern Scots. Mimeo, University of Edinburgh
Aitken, A. J. & McArthur, T. 1979. *Languages of Scotland*. The Association for Scottish Literary Studies, Occasional Paper no. 4. Edinburgh: Chambers
Aldus, J. D. 1969. Anglo-Irish dialects: a bibliography. *Regional Language Studies* 2.1–17. Memorial University of Newfoundland
Anderson, J. M. & Jones, C. (*eds*) 1974. *Historical linguistics*. Amsterdam: North-Holland
Bähr, D. 1974. *Standard English und seine geographischen Varianten*. Munich: Wilhelm Fink
Barltrop, R. & Wolveridge, J. 1980. *The muvver tongue*. London and West Nyack, NY: Journeyman Press
Beaken, M. A. 1971. A study of phonological development in a primary school population of East London. PhD thesis, University of London
Berlin, B. & Kay, P. 1969. *Basic color terms: their universality and evolution*. Berkeley: University of California Press

References

Bertz, S. 1975. Der Dubliner Stadtdialekt. Eine synchronische Beschreibung der Struktur und Variabilität des heutigen Dubliner Englischen. I. Phonologie. Doctoral dissertation, University of Freiburg i.Br.

Bliss, A. J. 1972. Languages in contact: some problems of Hiberno-English. *Proceedings of the Royal Irish Academy* 72.C.3.63–82

Bliss, A. J. 1976. The development of the English language in early modern Ireland. In T. W. Moody, F. X. Martin, & F. J. Byrne (*eds*), *A new history of Ireland*, vol. III.546–60. Oxford: Clarendon Press

Bliss, A. J. n.d. The English language in Ireland. Mimeo

Blunt, J. 1967. *Stage dialects.* San Francisco: Chandler Pub. Co.

Bowyer, R. 1971. The living dialect of Bermondsey, London SE. BS dissertation, University of Leeds

Bowyer, R. 1973. A study of social accents in a South London suburb. MPhil dissertation, University of Leeds

Brown, G. 1977. *Listening to spoken English.* London: Longman

Catford, J. C. 1957. The Linguistic Survey of Scotland. *Orbis* 6.1.105–21

Catford, J. C. 1958. Vowel-systems of Scots dialects. *Transactions of the Philological Society* 1957.107–17

Chambers, J. K. & Trudgill, P. 1980. *Dialectology.* Cambridge University Press

Chambers twentieth century dictionary. 1972. Ed. A. M. Macdonald. Edinburgh and London: Chambers

Chomsky, N. & Halle, M. 1968. *The sound pattern of English (SPE).* New York: Harper & Row

Cooper, J. 1978. Jilly Cooper finds comfort in Radio Four. *Sunday Times* (London), 13 August 1978

Dobson, E. J. 1968. *English pronunciation 1500–1700.* Vol. 2, *Phonology.* Oxford University Press (First edn 1957)

Dobson, S. 1968. *Larn yersel Geordie.* Newcastle-upon-Tyne: F. Graham

Ellis, S. 1969. *Studies in honour of Harold Orton.* Leeds Studies in English. Leeds: School of English, University of Leeds

Elyan, O., Smith, P., Giles, H., & Bourhis, R. 1978. RP-accented female speech: the voice of perceived androgyny? In Trudgill 1978: 123–31

EPD: Jones 1963; Gimson 1977

Eustace, S. S. 1967. Present changes in English pronunciation. *Proceedings of the 6th International Congress of Phonetic Sciences.* Prague: Academia

Fishlock, T. 1972. *Wales and the Welsh.* London: Cassell

Fowkes, R. A. 1966. English, French, and German phonetics and the substratum theory. *Linguistics* 21.45–53

Fox, A. T. C. 1967. Systemic variation in North Staffordshire speech. *Work in Progress*, Dept of Phonetics, University of Edinburgh, no. 1

Franklyn, J. 1953. *The Cockney. A survey of London life and language.*
London: Deutsch

Fudge, E. 1977. Long and short [æ] in one Southern British speaker's
English. *Journal of the International Phonetic Association* 7.2.55–65

Giles, H. 1970. Evaluative reaction to accents. *Educational Review* 23

Gimson, A. C. 1970. British English pronunciation – standards and
evolution. *Praxis* 17

Gimson, A. C. 1977. *English pronouncing dictionary (EPD).* Originally
compiled by Daniel Jones. Fourteenth edn. London: Dent
(Twelfth edn: see Jones 1963)

Gimson, A. C. 1980. *An introduction to the pronunciation of English.*
Third edn. London: Edward Arnold (First edn 1962; second edn
1970)

Grant, W. 1911. Introduction, and dialect map of Scotland. In Warrack
1911

Grant, W. 1913. *The pronunciation of English in Scotland.* Cambridge
University Press

Grant, W. 1931. *The Scottish national dictionary.* Edinburgh: Riverside
Press

Grant, W. & Dixon, J. M. 1921. *A manual of modern Scots.* Cambridge
University Press

Gregg, R. J. 1958. Notes on the phonology of a Co. Antrim Scotch-Irish
dialect. *Orbis* 7.2.392–406, 8.2.400–24

Gregg, R. J. 1964. Scotch-Irish urban speech in Ulster. In Adams 1964

Gregg, R. J. 1972. The Scotch-Irish dialect boundaries in Ulster. In
Wakelin 1972b

Gregg, R. J. 1973. The diphthongs əi and ɑi in Scottish, Scotch-Irish
and Canadian English. *Canadian Journal of Linguistics* 18.2.136–45

Gregg, R. J. 1975. The feature 'dentality' as a sociolinguistic marker in
Anglo-Irish dialects. Paper read at the 8th International Congress
of Phonetic Sciences, Leeds 1975

Heath, C. D. 1980. *The pronunciation of English in Cannock,
Staffordshire.* Publications of the Philological Society no. 29.
Oxford: Blackwell

Hedevind, B. 1967. *The dialect of Dentdale in the West Riding of
Yorkshire.* Uppsala: Universitetsbiblioteket

Henry, P. L. 1957. An Anglo-Irish dialect of North Roscommon.
Doctoral dissertation, University of Zurich

Henry, P. L. 1958. A linguistic survey of Ireland: preliminary report.
Lochlann 1.49–208 (= supplement 5 of *Norsk Tidskrift for
Sprogvidenskap*)

Hogan, J. J. 1927. *The English language in Ireland.* Dublin: Educational
Co. of Ireland. Reprinted 1970 College Park, Maryland: McGrath

Hogan, J. J. 1934. *Outline of English philology, chiefly for Irish students.*
Dublin: Educational Co. of Ireland

Hudson, R. A. & Holloway, A. F. 1977. Variation in London English.

Mimeo, Dept of Phonetics and Linguistics, University College London

Hughes, A. & Trudgill, P. 1979. *English accents and dialects*. London: Edward Arnold

Hughes, J. P., 1966 [i.e. 1973]. The Irish language and the 'brogue'. A study in substratum. *Word* 22.259–75

Hurford, J. R. 1967. The speech of one family: a phonetic comparison of the three generations in a family of East Londoners. PhD thesis, University of London

Hurford, J. R. 1968. The range of contoidal articulations in a dialect. *Orbis* 17.2.389–95

Hurford, J. R. 1968–70. Specimens of English: Cockney. *Maître Phonétique* 130.32–4, 132.41–3, 134.38–9

Jarman, E. & Cruttenden, A. 1976. Belfast intonation and the myth of the fall. *Journal of the International Phonetic Association* 6.1.4–12

Jones, D. 1956. *The pronunciation of English*. Fourth edn. Cambridge University Press

Jones, D. 1963. *English pronouncing dictionary (EPD)*. Twelfth edn. London: Dent (First edn 1917)

Jones, D. 1975. *An outline of English phonetics*. Ninth edn. Cambridge University Press (Previous edns: Cambridge: Heffer)

Joyce, P. W. 1910. *English as we speak it in Ireland*. London and Dublin: Longman

Kingdon, R. 1939a. General South West English. *Maître Phonétique* 65.9

Kingdon, R. 1939b. South Hams dialect. *Maître Phonétique* 65.9–10

Kingdon, R. 1939c. East Devon dialect. *Maître Phonétique* 67.5

Knowles, G. O. 1974. Scouse: the urban dialect of Liverpool. PhD thesis, University of Leeds

Knowles, G. O. 1978. The nature of phonological variables in Scouse. In Trudgill 1978: 80–90

Kohler, K. 1964. Aspects of the history of English pronunciation in Scotland. PhD thesis, University of Edinburgh

Kökeritz, H. 1932. The phonology of the Suffolk dialect. Uppsala: Uppsala Universitetets Årsskrift

Kolb, E. 1966. *Linguistic atlas of England. Phonological atlas of the Northern region*. Bern: Francke

LAE = Orton *et al.* 1978

Lass, R. 1974. Linguistic orthogenesis? Scots vowel quantity and the English length conspiracy. In Anderson & Jones 1974: 2.311–52

Lass, R. 1976. *English phonology and phonological theory*. Cambridge University Press

Lediard, J. 1977. The sounds of the dialect of Canton, a suburb of Cardiff. Appendix A in Parry 1977

Leslie, D. 1976. Ambisyllabic conditioning of phonological rules. Ms.

Lodge, K. R. 1966. The Stockport dialect. *Maître Phonétique* 126.26–30

Lodge, K. R. 1973. Stockport revisited. *Journal of the International Phonetic Association* 3.81–7

Lodge, K. R. 1978. A Stockport teenager. *Journal of the International Phonetic Association* 8.56–71

McAllister, A. H. 1938. *A year's course in speech training.* University of London Press

Macaulay, R. K. S. & Trevelyan, G. D. 1973. Language, education and employment in Glasgow. SSRC report

Macaulay, R. K. S. 1974. Social class and language in Glasgow. *Language in Society* 2.173–88

Macaulay, R. K. S. 1977. *Language, social class and education: a Glasgow study.* Edinburgh University Press

Macaulay, R. K. S. 1978. Variation and consistency in Glaswegian English. In Trudgill 1978: 132–43

McClure, J. D. 1970. Some features of Standard English as spoken in South-West Scotland. MLitt dissertation, University of Edinburgh

McClure, J. D. (ed.) 1974. *The Scots language in education.* Aberdeen: Association for Scottish Literary Studies Occasional Papers no. 3

McClure, J. D. 1975. The English speech of Scotland. *Aberdeen University Review* 46.173–89

McClure, J. D. 1977. Vowel duration in a Scottish accent. *Journal of the International Phonetic Association* 7.1

McClure, J. D. 1979. Scots: its range of uses. In Aitken & McArthur 1979

McClure, J. D. 1980. Western Scottish intonation: a preliminary study. In Waugh & van Schooneveld 1980

McClure, J. D. n.d. Two sociolinguistic variables in Scottish English. Mimeo

McClure, J. D., Aitken, A. J., & Low, J. T. 1980. *The Scots Language. Planning for modern usage.* Edinburgh: Ramsay Head Press

Mac Éinrí, F. 1975. An Irish English vowel system. Paper read at the 8th International Congress of Phonetic Sciences, Leeds 1975

McIntosh, A. 1952. *An introduction to a survey of Scottish dialects.* Edinburgh: Nelson

Maclaran, R. 1976. The variable (ʌ), a relic form with social correlates. *Belfast Working Papers in Language and Linguistics* 1.45–68

McNeany, V. 1971. Vowel-reduction in localized Tyneside and RP speech. Mimeo, Dept of English Language, School of English, University of Newcastle-upon-Tyne

Martinet, A. 1957. *Miscelánea homenaje a André Martinet.* Universidad de La Laguna

Mather, J. Y. 1964. Dialect research in Orkney and Shetland after Jakobson. *Fróðskaparrit* 13.33–43

Mather, J. Y. 1974. Social variation in present-day Scots speech. In McClure 1974

Mather, J. Y. & Speitel, H. -H. 1975. *The linguistic atlas of Scotland.*

Scots section. London: Croom Helm

Matthews, W. 1938. *Cockney past and present*. Reprinted 1972 with new preface. London: Routledge & Kegan Paul

Mees, I. 1977. Language and social class in Cardiff. Thesis, University of Leiden

Mhac an Fhailigh, E. 1968. *The Irish of Erris, Co. Mayo*. Dublin: Institute for Advanced Studies

Milroy, J. 1975. Preliminary notes on Belfast vowel phonology. Mimeo, Dept of English, Queen's University of Belfast

Milroy, J. 1976a. Length and height variations in the vowels of Belfast vernacular. *Belfast Working Papers on Language and Linguistics* (= *BWPLL*) 1.69–110

Milroy, J. 1976b. Synopsis of Belfast vowels. *BWPLL* 1.111–16

Milroy, J. & Milroy, L. 1978. Belfast: change and variation in an urban vernacular. In Trudgill 1978: 19–36

Milroy, L. 1976. Phonological correlates to community structure in Belfast. *BWPLL* 1.1–44

Milroy, L. 1977. Guide to phonemic transcription of educated Ulster speech. Mimeo, Northern Ireland Polytechnic

Milroy, L. & Milroy, J. 1977. Speech and context in an urban setting. *BWPLL* 2.1

Mitford, N. (ed.) 1956. *Noblesse oblige*. London: Hamish Hamilton

Murison, D. 1977. *The guid Scots tongue*. Edinburgh: Blackwood

Nally, E. V. 1971. Notes on a Westneath dialect. *Journal of the International Phonetic Association* 1.1.31–8

Nicolson, H. 1927. *Some people*. London: Constable

O'Connor, J. D. 1947. The phonetic system of a dialect of Newcastle-upon-Tyne. *Maître Phonétique* 87.6

O'Connor, J. D. 1948. *New phonetic readings from modern English literature*. Berne: Francke

Ó Cuív, B. 1944. *The Irish of West Muskerry, Co. Cork*. A phonetic study. Dublin: Institute for Advanced Studies

Ó Cuív, B. (ed.) 1969. *A view of the Irish language*. Dublin: Stationery Office

O'Rahilly, T. 1972. *Irish dialects past and present*. Dublin: Institute for Advanced Studies

Orton, H. 1933. *The phonology of a South Durham dialect*. London: Kegan Paul, Trench, Trubner & Co

Orton, H. 1939. Retroflex consonants in English. *Maître Phonétique* 67.40–1

Orton, H., et al. (ed.) 1962–71. *Survey of English dialects (SED)*. Introduction; Basic material (four volumes). Leeds: Arnold

Orton, H., Sanderson, S., & Widdowson, J. 1978. *The linguistic atlas of England (LAE)*. London: Croom Helm (American edn 1977, Atlantic Highlands, NJ: Humanities Press)

Page, N. 1970. Convention and consistency in Dickens's Cockney dialect. *English studies* 51.4.339–44

Påhlsson, C. 1972. *The Northumbrian burr.* Lund Studies in English 41. Lund: CWK Gleerup

Painter, C. 1963. Black Country speech. *Maître Phonétique* 120.30–3

Parry, D. R. 1964. Studies in the linguistic geography of Radnorshire, Breconshire, Monmouthshire and Glamorganshire. MA thesis, University of Leeds

Parry, D. 1971. Newport English. *Anglo-Welsh Review* 19.44.228–33

Parry, D. 1972. Anglo-Welsh dialects in South-East Wales. In Wakelin 1972b: 140–63

Parry, D. (ed.) 1977. *The survey of Anglo-Welsh dialects.* Vol. 1. The South-East. Swansea: David Parry, University College

Pellowe, J. & Jones, V. 1978. On intonational variability in Tyneside speech. In Trudgill 1978: 101–21

Pellowe, J., Nixon, G., & McNeany, V. 1972a. Defining the dimensionality of a linguistic variety space. Mimeo prepared for Colloquium on Urban Speech Surveying, Newcastle-upon-Tyne, April 1972

Pellowe, J., Nixon, G., Strang, B., & McNeany, V. 1972b. A dynamic modelling of linguistic variation: the urban (Tyneside) linguistic survey. *Lingua* 30.1–30

Petyt, K. M., 1977. 'Dialect' and 'accent' in the industrial West Riding. A study of the changing speech of an urban area. PhD thesis, University of Reading

Petyt, K. M. 1978. Secondary contractions in West Yorkshire negatives. In Trudgill 1978: 91–100

Pilch, H. 1957. Le bilinguisme au Pays de Galles. In Martinet 1957: 1.223–41

Pilch, H. 1958. Das kymrische Lautsystem. *Zeitschrift für vergleichende Sprachforschung* 75. 24–57

Ramsaran, S. M. 1978. Phonetic and phonological correlates of style in English: a preliminary investigation. PhD thesis, University of London

Reid, E. 1976. Social and stylistic variation in the speech of some Edinburgh schoolchildren. MLitt thesis, University of Edinburgh

Reid, E. 1978. Social and stylistic variation in the speech of children: some evidence from Edinburgh. In Trudgill 1978: 158–71

Robinson, D. ['Dirk Robson'] 1970. *Krek waiter's peak Bristle. A guide to what the natives say and mean in the heart of the Wess Vinglun.* Bristol: Abson Press

Robinson, D. ['Dirk Robson'] 1971. *Son of Bristle.* Bristol: Abson Books

Romaine, S. 1978. Postvocalic /r/ in Scottish English: sound change in progress? In Trudgill 1978: 144–57

Ross, A. S. C. 1954. Linguistic class-indicators in present-day English. *Neuphilologische Mitteilungen* 55.20–56

Schmitt, L. E. (ed.) 1968. *Germanistische Dialektologie.* Festschrift für

References

Walther Mitzke zum 80. Geburtstag. *Zeitschrift für Mundartforschung*, Beiheft N. F. 6

SED = Orton *et al.* 1962–71

Shaw, F. 1966. *Lern yerself Scouse.* Edited with notes by Fritz Spiegl. Liverpool: Scouse Press

Sivertsen, E. 1960. *Cockney phonology.* Oslo University Press

SPE = Chomsky & Halle 1968

Speitel, H. -H. 1968. Some studies in the dialect of Midlothian. PhD thesis, University of Edinburgh

Speitel, H. -H. & Mather, J. Y. 1968. Schottische Dialektologie. In Schmitt 1968: 520–41

Spencer, J. 1957. Received Pronunciation: some problems of interpretation. *Lingua* 7.1

Stevens, M. 1973. *The Walsh language today.* Llandysul: Gomer

Taniguchi, J. 1972. *A grammatical analysis of artistic representation of Irish English, with a brief discussion of sounds and spelling.* Tokyo: Shinozaki Shorin

Taylor, M. V. 1974. The great Southern Scots conspiracy: patterns in the development of Northern English. In Anderson & Jones 1974: 2.403–26

Thomas, A. R. 1958. Astudiaeth seinegol o Gymraeg llafar Dyffryn Wysg. Dissertation, University of Wales

Thomas, A. R. 1967. Generative phonology in dialectology. *Transactions of the Philological Society* 179–203

Thomas, A. R. 1973. *The linguistic geography of Wales.* Cardiff: University of Wales Press

Thomas, C. 1967. Welsh intonation – a preliminary study. *Studia Celtica* 2.8–28

Trim, J. L. M. 1961. English Standard Pronunciation. *English Language Teaching* 16.1.28–37

Trudgill, P. J. 1972. Sex, covert prestige and linguistic change in the urban British English of Norwich. *Language in Society* 1.179–95

Trudgill, P. J. 1973. Phonological rules and sociolinguistic variation in Norwich English. In *New ways of analyzing variation in English*, ed. C. J. Bailey & R. W. Shuy (1973, Georgetown University Press)

Trudgill, P. J. 1974. *The social differentiation of English in Norwich.* Cambridge University Press

Trudgill, P. (ed.) 1978. *Sociolinguistic patterns in British English.* London: Edward Arnold

Trudgill, P. J. & Foxcroft, T. 1978. On the sociolinguistics of vocalic merger: transfer and approximation in East Anglia. In Trudgill 1978: 69–79

Truninger, A. 1976. *Paddy and the paycock.* Bern: Francke

Viereck, W. 1966. *Phonematische Analyse des Dialekts von Gateshead-upon-Tyne/Co. Durham.* Hamburg: Cram, de Gruyter & Co

Wagner, H., 1958. *A linguistic atlas and survey of Irish dialects. Lochlann* 1.9–48 (= supplement 5 of *Norsk Tidskrift for Sprogvidenskap*)

References

Wakelin, M. F. 1972a. *English dialects: an introduction.* London:
   Athlone Press
Wakelin, M. F. (ed.) 1972b. *Patterns in the folk speech of the British Isles.*
   London: Athlone Press
Wakelin, M. F. 1975. *Language and history in Cornwall.* Leicester
   University Press
Wakelin, M. F. & Barry, M. V. 1969. The voicing of initial fricative
   consonants in present-day dialectal English. In Ellis 1969: 47–64
Ward, I. 1948. *The phonetics of English.* Fourth edn, reprinted with
   minor corrections. Cambridge: Heffer (First edn 1929)
Warrack, A. 1911. *A Scots dialect dictionary.* London: Chambers
Watkins, T. A. 1962. Background to the Welsh Dialect Survey.
   Lochlann 2.38–49
Waugh, L. R. & van Schooneveld, C. H. (eds) 1980. *The melody of
   language.* Baltimore: University Park Press
Weissmann, E. 1970. Phonematische Analyse des Stadtdialektes von
   Bristol. *Phonetica* 21.151–81, 211–40
Wells, J. C. 1970. Local accents in England and Wales. *Journal of
   Linguistics* 6.231–52
Wells, J. C. & Colson, G. 1971. *Practical phonetics.* London: Pitman
Wilson, D. 1970. The phonology and accidence of the dialect of the
   North Staffs Potteries. MA diss., University of Birmingham
Wilson, J. 1915. *Lowland Scotch.* London: Oxford University Press
Wilson, J. 1923. *The dialect of Robert Burns as spoken in central Ayrshire.*
   London: Oxford University Press
Wilson, J. 1926. *The dialects of central Scotland.* London: Oxford
   University Press
Windsor Lewis, J. 1964. Specimen of Cardiff English. *Maître Phonétique*
   121.6–7
Windsor Lewis, J. 1969. *A guide to English pronunciation.* Oslo:
   Scandinavian Universities Press
Windsor Lewis, J. 1972. *A concise pronouncing dictionary of British and
   American English.* London: Oxford University Press
Windsor Lewis, J. n.d. British non-dialectal accents. Mimeo
Winston, M. 1970. Some aspects of the pronunciation of educated Scots.
   MLitt thesis, University of Edinburgh
Wise, C. M. 1957. *Applied phonetics.* Englewood Cliffs, NJ: Prentice-
   Hall
Wölck, W. 1965. *Phonematische Analyse der Sprache von Buchan.*
   Heidelberg: Carl Winter Universitätsverlag
Wood, R. E. 1979. Scotland: the unfinished quest for linguistic identity.
   Word 30.1–2.186–202
Woolley, J. S. 1954. *Bibliography for Scottish linguistic studies.*
   Edinburgh: James Thin
Wright, J. 1905. *The English dialect grammar.* Oxford: Henry Frowde
Wyld, H. C. 1936. *A history of modern colloquial English.* Oxford:
   Blackwell (First edn 1920)

Index

Index

NURSE–SQUARE Merger 372, 421, 444

one 362
Orkney 398–9
Oxford English 280

palatalization 433–4, 446
Pembroke, Dyfed 377–8
Peterborough, Cambs. 349
Peterhead, Grampian 398
Plymouth, Devon 341, 345
Potteries *see* Stoke-on-Trent
pre-aspiration 409
Pre-R Breaking 407
Pre-Schwa Laxing 407
Preston, Lancs. 368
PRICE–MOUTH Crossover 310
prosodic characteristics: Cockney 331–2; East Anglia 341; Wales 391–2; Scotland 414–15; Ireland 436, 447–8

quasi-RP 285

/r/: intrusive 284–5; tapped 282, 372; sandhi 284–5; uvular 368–70, 374, 390, 411, 432
[ɾ] 389
Reading, Berks. 341
'refayned' speech 302
Rhondda, Mid Glam. 384, 390, 392
rhotic accents, rhoticity: west of England 341–3; north of England 367–8; Wales 378–80; Scotland 407, 410–11; Ireland 418, 432, 437–8
rhythm 341, 400
Rochdale, Greater Manchester 368
Roscommon 426
RP 279–301 *et passim*; adoptive 279, 283–5; advanced 280; conservative 279; a fiction? 301; general 279; mainstream 279, 285–97; upper-crust 279–83; variability 285–97

Schwa Absorption 434–5
Schwa Deletion 321
Schwa Epenthesis 320
Scotch-Irish 417, 437, 440–2, 448–9
Scotland 393–417
Scots 393–9, 406, 417; in Ireland 436–8, 448–9
Scouse 361, 366, 371–3
Scunthorpe, Humberside 362
Shaw, G. B. 306, 332–4
Sheffield, S. Yorks. 350, 359, 365

Shetland 398–9
sibilants 413, 419–20, 433–4
Sligo 430
Smoothing: RP 286, 288, 292–3; Norwich 339; Bristol 349
Southampton, Hants. 341, 345–6
Southern British Standard 301
Staffordshire 357; *see also* Stoke-on-Trent, Cannock
Stoke-on-Trent 350, 360–1, 364–5
Strathclyde 397; *see also* Glasgow
STRUT–Schwa Merger 380–1
Suffolk 337; *see also* East Anglia
Swansea, W. Glam. 378, 384–5
Syllabic Consonant Formation 286, 320–1, 435

T Glottalling: RP? 299, 300; London 323–6; East Anglia 341; west of England 344; north of England 367, 374; Scotland 409, 416; Ireland 430
T Opening 429–30
T Voicing 324–6, 344, 445
TH Fronting 328–30
TH Stopping 329–30, 428
THOUGHT Split 310–11
Tipperary 432
TRAP in RP 281, 291–2
TRAP–PALM Merger 400, 403, 440
T-to-R Rule 370, 374
Tyneside 350, 360, 374–6

Uist, Western Isles 413; *see also* Hebrides
Ulster 402, 429, 436–50; Lengthening 439
U-RP 279–83
uvular /k/ 371
uvular /r/: England 368–70, 374; Wales 390; Scotland 411; Ireland 432

voice quality 283, 373

Wales 377–93
weak forms 376, 414, 428
Welsh (language) 377–93 *passim*
Wessex 335, 346–7
west country 335, 341–9
West Midlands 350, 356; *see also* Birmingham
west of England 335, 341–9
west of Ireland 420, 423, 433
Wigan, Greater Manchester 361, 368, 372
[ʍ] 408

CPSIA information can be obtained at www.ICGtesting.com
Printed in the USA
LVOW10s1202110815

449604LV00001B/61/P